CONVIVIUMPRESS

José A. Pagola

The Way Opened Up by Jesus: a Commentary on the Gospel of Matthew

Translated by Margaret Wilde

CONVIVIUMPRESS

SERIES KYRIOS

2012

The Way Opened Up by Jesus: a Commentary on the Gospel of Matthew

http://www.conviviumpress.com
sales@conviviumpress.com
ventas@conviviumpress.com
convivium@conviviumpress.com

7661 NW 68th St, Suite 108,
Miami, Florida 33166. USA.
Phone: +1 (305) 8890489
Fax: +1 (305) 8875463

Edited *by* Rafael Luciani
Translated *by* Margaret Wilde
Designed *by* Eduardo Chumaceiro d'E
Series: *Kyrios*

ISBN: 978-1-934996-28-7

Printed in Colombia
Impreso en Colombia
D'VINNI, S.A.

Convivium Press
Miami, 2012

The Way Opened Up by Jesus: a Commentary on the Gospel of Matthew

Contents

7

Blessed are Those

8

You are the Salt of the Earth

9

Love of Enemy

16

Liberating Life PAGE 113

17

The Father is Revealed to the Simple Folk PAGE 119

18

Sowing the Gospel PAGE 124

25

Taking Up the Cross PAGE 160

26

The Transfiguration of Jesus PAGE 165

27

Gathered in the Name of Jesus PAGE 170

31

The Danger of Defrauding God

32

An Invitation from God

33

To God the Things that are God's

Preface

The first Christian communities thought of themselves, above all, as followers of Jesus. For them, believing in Jesus meant walking in his «way» by following his footsteps. One ancient writing, known as the letter to the Hebrews, calls it a «new and living way». It is not the path trodden in the past by the people of Israel, but a way «that he opened for us» (Hebrews 10:20).

This Christian way is a journey we follow, step by step, throughout our lives. Sometimes it seems simple and plain, sometimes hard and steep. There are moments of certainty and joy along the way, and hours of weariness and discouragement. To follow in Jesus' footsteps means taking steps, making decisions, overcoming obstacles, turning away from wrong paths, discovering new horizons… It's all part of the way. The first Christians tried to follow it by «looking to Jesus, the pioneer and perfecter of our faith» (Hebrews 12:2).

Unfortunately, Christianity as most people live it today does not raise up «followers» of Jesus, but «adherents» to a religion. It does not make disciples identified with Jesus' vision, committed to opening ways to the reign of God, but members of an institution who more or less fulfill their religious obligations. The danger is that many of them will never have the most original and inspiring experience of the Christian life: walking in the way that Jesus opened up.

The renewal of the Church today requires us to be transformed from communities made up mostly of «adherents» into communities of «disciples» and «followers» of Jesus. That is the only way to live as people more identified with his vision, less enslaved by a past that was not always faithful to the gospel, and more free from the fears and enslavements that can keep us from hearing his call to conversion.

Right now, the Church does not have the spiritual energy it needs to confront the challenges of the present moment. This spiritual mediocrity may be caused by many factors, inside and outside the Church, but probably the most important cause is the lack of a living commitment to Jesus Christ. Many Christians have never felt the dynamic energy that his disciples receive from living with and following Jesus directly. Many Christian communities cannot imagine the transformation that would occur today, if the real-life person of Jesus and his gospel were to become the center of their life.

Now is the time to take action. We must make the effort to place the Jesus story in the heart of believers and at the center of our Christian communities. We need to look closely at his face, put ourselves in tune with his real life, embrace the Spirit that enlivens him, follow the path of commitment to the reign of

God that he followed unto death, and let ourselves be transformed by his resurrection. The best way to do that is to dig deeply into the story told in the gospels.

For followers of Jesus, the four gospels are a unique and irreplaceable resource. They are not textbooks, expounding an academic doctrine of Jesus. They are not detailed biographies, tracing his life in history. These stories bring us close to Jesus as the first generations of Christians remembered him, with faith and love. On the one hand, they show us the great impact Jesus caused in the people who first were attracted to him and followed him. On the other, they were written to inspire new disciples to do the same.

Thus the gospels invite us into a process of change, a process of following Jesus and identifying with his vision. They are narratives of conversion, and that is how they must be read, preached, meditated on, and kept in the heart of every believer and every Christian community. In this way the experience of listening to the gospels together becomes the most powerful force of transformation that a community can call on. This living contact with the story of Jesus gives us as believers the light and power to live as he lived, and to open new ways into the vision of God's reign.

These four volumes, together titled *The Way Opened Up by Jesus*, are devoted in turn to the gospels of Matthew, Mark, Luke, and John. They are written to help us walk in his way, centering our faith on following him in person. Each volume offers an approach to the story of Jesus as it was compiled and presented by one of the gospel writers.

The commentary on each gospel follows the plan laid out by the gospel writer, focusing on the passages that the Church recommends for proclamation when the community gathers for the Sunday eucharist. For each passage we shall examine the gospel text and make five brief comments, with suggestions for deepening our understanding of the Jesus narrative.

As the reader will see, the comments are selected on the basis of certain criteria: they emphasize the Good News of God proclaimed by Jesus, an inexhaustible source of life and compassion for all; they suggest ways of following him, re-enacting his way of living and his attitudes in today's world; they suggest ways of fostering the renewal of Christian communities by embracing his Spirit; they remind us of his call to real-life commitment to the vision of the reign of God in today's society; and they invite us to live these times of crisis and uncertainty with a deeply rooted hope in the risen Christ[1].

1 See my book *Jesus, An Historical Approximation.* Convivium Press, 2009.

In writing these pages I am thinking especially about today's Christian communities, so much in need of encouragement and new spiritual energy; I have in mind so many believers, in whom Jesus can light the fire of a new faith. But I also want to offer the gospel of Jesus to those who have not found ways to God, who are lost in the labyrinth of a disjointed life, or sinking into an existence out of sight of the ultimate mystery of life. I know that Jesus may be the best news for them.

This book is inspired by my wish to recover the Good News of Jesus for the men and women of our time. I did not receive the vocation of an evangelist in order to condemn, but to liberate. I do not feel called by Jesus to judge the world, but to awaken hope. He has not sent me to quench a flickering flame, but to light a candle of faith that is trying to ignite.

San Sebastián, July 31, 2010
Feast of St. Ignatius of Loyola

Introduction

Matthew has been the most widely read and cited of the four gospels ever since the first centuries. It always commanded special prestige and appeared first on lists of the gospels. It has been called «the great gospel», because its twenty-eight chapters expound the teachings of Jesus more extensively than any other.

We don't know exactly when or where it was composed. It was probably written in Antioch of Syria between 80 and 90 A.D., certainly after the destruction of Jerusalem in 70 A.D. It was written for Christians of Jewish origin, who consider themselves «sons of Abraham» and have been instructed in the law of Moses.

This gospel was written at a critical moment. After the destruction of the temple in 70 A.D., the pharisaic rabbis were trying to rebuild Judaism around the law of Moses as it was proclaimed in the synagogues. At about the same time, the followers of Jesus were establishing Christian communities among the Jews of the diaspora. There were often tensions and conflicts between the «world of the synagogue» led by the Pharisees, and the «Jesus movement» started by his disciples and followers.

At this crucial moment, Matthew proclaims that Jesus is not a false prophet put to death on the cross, but the true «Messiah», raised by God, in whom the history of Israel is reaching its climax. He is not a failed teacher, but the «new Moses», bringer of a new law of life. From this Jesus, the Christ, a «new Israel» is being born as the Church called together by the Risen One. After the destruction of the temple, Jesus, «God's beloved son», is the new presence of God in the world. Here I shall briefly list some key themes to help us understand the story of Jesus according to Matthew's gospel.

- Although he was rejected by his own people, Jesus is the fulfillment of God's promises to Israel. Matthew emphasizes this throughout his gospel. For us today, the history of Israel is the prototype of a humanity that seeks the fulfillment of its deepest desires, but which resists the «newness» of Christ and closes itself off to the salvation God offers through him. Resisting this newness and salvation is also a temptation in Christian communities. The gospel of Matthew will help us to discover the newness of Christ and embrace it with a renewed faith.
- Jesus is the presence of God among us. We are told from the beginning that Jesus is the «Emmanuel» promised by Isaiah: «God with us». As we read this gospel, Matthew wants us to see God's presence among us in everything Jesus says and does: to hear the Word of God in his words, to experience God's saving love in his actions. At the climax of the story, the Risen One makes this unfor-

gettable promise to his disciples: «I am with you always, to the end of the age» (Matthew 28:20). We are not alone in these hard times. God is walking with us in Jesus. We can find him in the community of followers, because where two or three are gathered in his name, he is there. And we must embrace him in the little people, because what we do to them we are doing to him.

• Jesus is the Prophet of the new Law. Matthew structures his writing around five great discourses, which form the pillars of his gospel. We see the fundamental teachings of Jesus in the discourse of the mountain (chapters 5-7); the discourse on mission (chapter 10); the discourse of the parables of the reign of God (chapter 13); the discourse on the Church (chapter 18); and the discourse on waiting for the last Day (chapters 24-25). We can say that the gospel of Matthew is a great invitation to embrace Jesus as the only Teacher of life. On this journey we will learn the essential elements of his message, and we shall work toward becoming his disciples and followers.

• Jesus is the Messiah, the Son of God, who calls together the new Israel. The gospel writer's word for the new Israel is «the Church». This Church is the community formed by those who hear Jesus' call to follow him. It is not a new rabbinical school; it is not the religion of a people, or of a chosen race. It is a community open to a universal mission. This is Christ's Church. He builds it on the «rock», who is Peter. In the Church we are all «disciples», because Christ is the one Teacher from whom we must all learn. We are all «brothers and sisters», because we are sons and daughters of the one Father in heaven. In the Church the «little ones» must be cared for. The Church must practice loving correction and unconditional forgiveness. In the gospel of Matthew we will keep discovering challenges, standards, and attitudes that can move us to renew our Christian communities.

• The discourse on the mountain shows us one of the most important keys to understanding the newness of our faith. We are no longer to live by the law of Moses but by the gospel of Jesus, proclaimed on a mountain which represents the new Mount Sinai. On our journey we will stop to look closely at the beatitudes, which are the real lesson plan for a disciple of Jesus; we will engrave in our hearts his command to love our enemies, which is the most enigmatic and scandalous declaration in the gospel; we will be challenged by his warning, «You cannot serve God and wealth»; we will hear his call to be the «salt» that gives new flavor to existence, and the «light» that can illuminate the way for all humankind, even today.

• The discourse of the parables of the reign of God will awaken in us the desire to discover and live that great vision, which Jesus carried in his heart. The parables of the hidden treasure and the precious pearl call us to be always open to unexpected encounters with God. The one about yeast invites us to bring the transforming power of fermentation to our life in society. The story of the sower teaches us to plant the gospel as Jesus did. The parable of the wheat and the weeds will ask us to learn to live without condemning others.

• By meditating on Jesus' actions and hearing his words, we will learn about other things that shape the life of those who walk in the way opened by Jesus. We must be willing to carry the cross on that way, expelling fear from our lives; and we must walk it with the heart of the simple ones —those who receive the revelation of the Father— forgiving seventy-seven times, comforting those who suffer, finding our rest in Jesus when we are weary.

• On our journey through the gospel of Matthew we will also find parables in which Jesus asks us to stay awake and watch for his definitive coming with our lamps lit in the darkness, investing our talents without being overcautious, and preparing to be judged by our compassion or indifference toward the people in need whom we find along the way.

The Gospel of Matthew

1

The Name of Jesus

Now the birth of Jesus the Messiah took place in this way. When his mother Mary had been engaged to Joseph, but before they lived together, she was found to be with child from the Holy Spirit. Her husband Joseph, being a righteous man and unwilling to expose her to public disgrace, planned to dismiss her quietly. But just when he had resolved to do this, an angel of the Lord appeared to him and said, «Joseph, son of David, do not be afraid to take Mary as your wife, for the child conceived in her is from the Holy Spirit. She will bear a son, and you are to name him Jesus, for he will save his people from their sins». All this took place to fulfill what had been spoken by the Lord through the prophet:

> *«Look, the virgin shall conceive and bear a son,*
> *and they will call him Emmanuel»,*
> *which means, «God is with us».*

When Joseph awoke from sleep, he did as the angel of the Lord commanded him; he took her as his wife (Matthew 1:18-24).

1. YOU SHALL NAME HIM JESUS

The Hebrew people did not arbitrarily give names to their newborn children. For them, as in most ancient cultures, a name represented the person's being, his or her true identity, what he or she would become.

That is why Matthew is so interested in telling his readers from the beginning, the deep significance of the name of the protagonist of this story. Even before he is born this is named Jesus, which means «God saves». He is called that because «he will save his people from their sins».

In the year 70 A.D., Vespasian —who was appointed the new Roman emperor while he was putting down the Jewish rebellion— marched back to Rome, where he was acclaimed with two names: «Savior» and «Benefactor». Matthew wants to make it clear: the «savior» the world needs is not Vespasian but Jesus.

Salvation will not come from any emperor, or from any victory by one nation over another. Humanity needs to be saved from evil, injustice and violence;

it needs to be forgiven, and reoriented toward a life more worthy of human beings. This is the salvation we receive through Jesus.

Matthew also gives him another name: «Emmanuel». He knows no one has ever been called that. It is a shocking name, absolutely new; it means «God is with us». It is given to Jesus by those who believe that God accompanies us, blesses us, and saves us, in and through Jesus.

Jesus' name was etched in the hearts of the first generations of Christians. They repeated it over and over. They were baptized in his name; they gathered for prayer in his name. For Matthew, the name of Jesus is a synthesis of their faith. For the apostle Paul it was above every other name. In one of the first Christian hymns, every knee would bend at the name of Jesus (Philippians 2:10).

Twenty centuries later, Christians must learn to pronounce Jesus' name in a new way: affectionately and lovingly, with renewed faith, and with an attitude of conversion. We can live and die in hope, with his name on our lips and in our heart.

2. GOD IS WITH US

The Christmas season has been so disfigured that today it seems almost impossible to help people understand the mystery it conveys. There may be a way, but we all have to find it for ourselves. It is not about understanding great theological explanations, but about living a humble, inward experience before God.

The great experiences of life are a gift, but in most cases they can only lived by people who are ready to receive them. In order to experience the Son of God made man, we have to prepare ourselves inwardly. Matthew is saying that Jesus, the child born in Bethlehem, is the only one we can truly call «Emmanuel», which means «God with us». But what does that mean? How can you «know» that God is with you?

Don't be afraid to be alone. Look for a quiet, restful place. Listen to yourself. Move quietly into the most intimate part of your being. You may very well feel a sense of awe: how alone you are in life, how far from the people around you, even those you love. They love you deeply, but they are not a part of you.

Remain quiet. Perhaps you have a strange feeling: you live because your roots go down in an immense, unknown reality. Where does your life come from? What is there in the depth of your being? If you can withstand the silence a little longer, you will probably begin to feel a sense of fear, and at the same time, peace. You are looking at the ultimate mystery of your being. Believers call this God.

Entrust yourself to this mystery. God seems immense and far away from you. But if you open up to God, you will feel him near. God is inside you, upholding you in your fragility and giving you life. God is not like the people who love you from the outside. God is in your very being.

According to Karl Rahner, «this experience of the heart is the only one that can help us understand the Christmas message of faith: God became man». Now you will never be alone. No one is alone. God is with us. Now you know something about Christmas. You can celebrate it, enjoy it, and wish Christmas joy to others. You can share the joy with your loved ones, and be more generous toward those who live in suffering and sadness. God is with you.

3. DON'T WE NEED GOD AMONG US?

One question nags at me every year, when Christmas preparations begin to appear in the streets: Is there any truth left in these celebrations, so riddled with consumerist self-interest and with our own mediocrity?

It's not just me. I often hear people talk about the superficiality of Christmas, its loss of connection with home and family, the shameful manipulation of its religious symbols, all the excesses and distortions that make a mockery of Christmas today.

But I believe the problem goes deeper than that. How can the mystery of «God made man» be celebrated by a society that has practically turned its back on God, and destroyed human dignity in so many ways?

How can «God's birthday» be celebrated in a society so indifferent to God that the famous professor G. Lipovetsky could say: «God is dead; the things worth living for are being snuffed out, but nobody cares; is that the good news?»

A lot of people don't seem to care whether they believe or not, whether «God is dead» or «God is born». For them, life goes on as always. They don't feel any need for God.

But history today is forcing us to take the question seriously. Not long ago, people talked about «the death of God»; now we talk about «the death of humanity». We used to talk about «the disappearance of God»; now we talk about «the disappearance of humanity». Could it be that the death of God leads inevitably to the death of humanity?

With God expelled from our lives, leaving us trapped in a world that we have created in the image of our own contradictions and suffering, can anyone tell us who we are and what we really want?

We don't have to look very far to find God. We only need to look quietly into ourselves. We only need to dig down into our deepest questions and desires.

This is the message of Christmas: God is very near to you, right where you are, if you will only open yourself up to God's Mystery. The inaccessible God has become a man, and his mysterious presence is all around us. God can be born in each of us.

4. EMBRACING GOD IN A LITTLE CHILD

Christmas is much more than the superficial, manipulative atmosphere that fills our streets during this season. It is a celebration, deeper and more joyful than all the gadgetry of our consumer society. As believers we need to reawaken that spirit of celebration and discover, behind all the superficiality and dizziness, the mystery that brings us so much joy.

We cannot understand Christmas until we let our hearts be still, until we open our souls to the mystery of a God who comes to us, until we embrace the life he holds out to us and celebrate the arrival of God our Friend.

In the midst of our day to day life—so often boring, sad and dismal—comes the invitation to rejoice. «There can be no sadness when life is being born» (St. Leo the Great). This is not the empty, superficial kind of happiness that people feel without knowing why they're happy. «There's a reason for our radiant joy, for rejoicing and solemn celebration: God has become man and come to live among us» (Leonardo Boff).

There is a kind of joy that only comes when we open ourselves up to the nearness of God, and let ourselves be drawn into his tenderness. A joy that frees us from fear and nervousness in the presence of God. How can we be afraid of a God who comes to us as a child? How can we flee from one who shows himself as a fragile, defenseless baby? God has not come in power to impose himself on humankind. He comes with the tenderness of a little child, who responds to us with laughter or tears.

God is not the omnipotent, powerful Being we sometimes imagine, enveloped in the seriousness and mystery of his inaccessible world. God is that little child, tenderly placed in our care, who catches our eye in order to cheer us with his smile. The fact that God became a child tells us more than all our abstract speculations about his mystery.

If we could only stand in silence before this Child, if we could embrace God's nearness and tenderness from the depth of our being, perhaps we would understand why believers are so full of a different kind of joy: simply because God is with us.

5. MARY, THE MOTHER OF JESUS

Marian devotion has receded in recent years, partly because of abuses and distortions in its practice, but today's Christians are rediscovering Mary's rightful place in Christian experience.

It's not about looking to Mary for «apocalyptic messages» that threaten terrible punishments for a world engulfed in profanity and disbelief, while offering motherly protection to those who do the right penance or recite the right prayers.

It's not about fostering the piety of infantile dependency and projection on an idealized mother image. Psychologists have long warned us about the risks of a devotion that holds up Mary as «Virgin and Mother», while vilifying «the woman» as man's eternal temptress.

We can recognize «Christian truth» in Marian devotion by asking whether it encourages self-centeredness in believers or opens them up to God's plan; whether it pulls them into an infantile relationship with an «imaginary mother», or pushes them to live their faith in a mature, responsible following of Jesus Christ.

Contemporary mariology at its best offers Christians an image of Mary as the Mother of Jesus Christ, her Son's first disciple, and a model of authentically Christian life.

More specifically, for us today Mary is a model of faithful acceptance of God in obedient faith; an exemplary attitude of service to her Son and solidary concern for all who suffer; a woman committed to the «reign of God» that is preached and promoted by her Son.

In these days of weary and pessimistic skepticism, Mary's radical obedience to God and her confident hope can lead us toward a deeper, more faithful Christian life.

Thus devotion to Mary is not a secondary element, added to encourage the religiosity of «simple people» with their «folkloric» practices and rites. Rather, turning to Mary helps us to discover and embrace the mystery of Christ. Matthew the evangelist gives us the memory of Mary as the mother of «Emmanuel», that is, the woman who can bring us to Jesus, «God with us».

2

The Adoration of the Wise Men

In the time of King Herod, after Jesus was born in Bethlehem of Judea, wise men from the East came to Jerusalem, asking, «Where is the child who has been born king of the Jews? For we observed his star at its rising, and have come to pay him homage». When King Herod heard this, he was frightened, and all Jerusalem with him; and calling together all the chief priests and scribes of the people, he inquired of them where the Messiah was to be born. They told him, «In Bethlehem of Judea; for so it has been written by the prophet:

"And you, Bethlehem, in the land of Judah,
are by no means least among the rulers of Judah;
for from you shall come a ruler who is to shepherd my people Israel"».

Then Herod secretly called for the wise men and learned from them the exact time when the star had appeared. Then he sent them to Bethlehem, saying, «Go and search diligently for the child; and when you have found him, bring me word so that I may also go and pay him homage». When they had heard the king, they set out; and there, ahead of them, went the star that they had seen at its rising, until it stopped over the place where the child was. When they saw that the star had stopped, they were overwhelmed with joy. On entering the house, they saw the child with Mary his mother; and they knelt down and paid him homage. Then, opening their treasure chests, they offered him gifts of gold, frankincense, and myrrh. And having been warned in a dream not to return to Herod, they left for their own country by another road (Matthew 2:1-12).

1. WHOM DO WE WORSHIP?

The wise men come from «the East», which the Jews thought of as the center of astrology and other strange sciences. The wise men are pagans. They don't know the sacred Scriptures of Israel, but rather the language of the stars. They seek truth and set out to find it. They let the mystery guide them, because they feel a need to «adore»; they need to worship.

Their presence causes a shock in all Jerusalem. The wise men have seen a new star rising, which leads them to think that «the king of the Jews» has been born;

they have come «to worship him». The new king is not Augustus Caesar. It isn't Herod. Where is he? they want to know.

Herod is shocked. This is not good news to him. He has been appointed by Rome as «king of the Jews». This newborn babe has got to be eliminated; where is he? The «high priests and learned men» know the sacred Scriptures, and they know he is supposed to be born in Bethlehem, but they have no interest in the child and no intention of worshiping him.

This is what Jesus will face throughout his life: hostility and rejection from the wielders of political power, indifference and resistance from the religious leaders. He will only be welcomed by those who seek the reign of God and his justice.

The wise men continue their search. Sometimes the star they are following disappears, leaving them in their uncertainty. Then sometimes it shines brightly, filling them with «overwhelming joy». Finally they see the Child, and «they kneel down and pay him homage». Then they place before him the wealth and treasure they have brought. This Child can count on them, because they recognize him as their King and Lord.

With all its apparent naivete, this story raises important questions for us. To whom do we bow down? Who is the «god» we adore from the depth of our being? We call ourselves Christians, but do we worship the Child of Bethlehem with our lives? Do we lay our wealth and our well-being at his feet? Are we ready to hear his call, to enter into the reign of God and his justice? In every life there is a star that leads to Bethlehem.

2. TO KILL OR TO WORSHIP

Herod and his court represent the world of the powerful. Anything goes in that world—deviousness, manipulation, mendacity— as long as it strengthens our own power. Even cruelty, terror, indifference to human life and the death of the innocent. This world appears to be great and powerful; it presents itself as the defense of order and justice, but it is weak and selfish; it is always looking for the child to kill him.

In Matthew's narrative, some wise men from the East come into this world of darkness. Some modern interpreters retell this gospel legend in the language of depth psychology. The wise men represent those who listen to the noblest desires of the human heart; their guiding star is a nostalgic longing for the divine; the path they follow is desire. In order to discover the divine in the human, to worship the child instead of seeking his death, to recognize human dignity instead of destroying it, we have to move in the opposite direction from Herod's path.

This is not an easy path to follow. It is not enough to listen to the heart's call; we have to move toward it, stick our neck out, take risks. The wise men end up doing something wonderful. They do not kill the child; they worship him. They kneel down respectfully before his dignity; they discover the divinity in his humanity. This is the meaning of their adoration of the Son of God incarnate in the child of Bethlehem.

We can also discern the symbolic meaning of the gifts they offer him. The gift of gold recognizes the dignity and inestimable value of the human being. Everything is set aside in favor of his happiness; a child deserves to have all the world's riches placed at his or her feet. The gift of incense represents a wish that the child's life will unfold and his dignity will rise up to heaven: every human being is called to participate in God's own life. The gift of myrrh is a medical potion to cure disease and relieve suffering: human beings need care and comfort, not violence and aggression.

Later, by caring for the weak and showing tenderness to the humiliated, this Child born in Bethlehem will bring into the world the magic of love, the one force of salvation that is already striking fear into the powerful Herod.

3. OUR INABILITY TO WORSHIP

Humanity today has lost much of its ability to discover God. It's not that we've become atheists; we have a «God deficiency». When people seek or find love only in decadent forms, when their lives are motivated only by selfish interest in benefit or profit, then their hearts begin to dry up.

Many people today live a life style that wears them out and impoverishes them. Aging prematurely, hardening from within, unable to open any part of themselves to God, they go through life with no inward companionship at all.

Theologian Alfred Delp, who was executed by the Nazis, saw this «inner hardening» as the greatest danger for modern humanity: «Man ceases to lift up the hands of his being to the stars. Modern man's inability to worship, to love, to venerate, is the result of his endless ambition and the hardening of his existence».

This inability to worship God also afflicts many believers, who are only looking for a «useful God». All they want is a God who will help them accomplish their individual projects. God thus becomes a «consumer item» to be used at our convenience, for our own purposes. But God is something else. God is infinite Love, incarnate in our own existence. We stand before that God in a position of adoration, rejoicing, thanksgiving.

If we forget that, Christianity runs the risk of becoming a gigantic project of human development; the institutional Church is always tense, always worn out, its moral struggles and goals always frustrated.

But more than anything else, Christian faith is the discovery of God's goodness, the grateful experience of God's salvation. The wise men's adoration of the Child of Bethlehem expresses the immediate reaction of all believers toward God made man.

God exists. God is there, at the deepest level of our life. We are accepted by God. We are not lost in the midst of the universe. We can live with confidence. Standing before a God whom we know as Love, there is no room for anything but joy, worship, and thanksgiving. For that reason, «when Christians think they can't even pray, at least they should feel joy» (Ladislao Boros).

4. LEARNING TO WORSHIP GOD

There's a lot of talk today about a crisis of faith, but we don't talk much about a crisis of religious feeling. Yet as some theologians point out, the dilemma of humanity today is not our inability to believe; it is our inability to feel God as God. Even people who call themselves believers seem to be losing the ability to relate to God in religious ways.

One clear example is our inability to worship him. Not so long ago, people felt reverence and awe in the presence of the immensity and the unfathomable mystery of God. It is harder today to worship one whom we have reduced to a strange, awkward, superfluous outsider.

The way to worship God is to feel like children, infinitely small before him, but infinitely loved by him; to admire his immeasurable greatness, and taste his near and loving presence that envelops our whole being. Adoration is admiration. It is love and surrender. It means surrendering our whole being to God, and standing in grateful and joyful silence before him, looking up to his mystery from our smallness.

There are different reasons for our inability to worship. When we are inwardly confused by all kinds of noise and a thousand fleeting images spin around us, when we can never stop to look at the essential, it is hard to see the «adorable face» of God.

Another reason is that to worship God we need to stand before the mystery of the world, and learn to look at it with love. If we can look lovingly into the depth of life, before we know it we are seeing traces of God's presence.

Only God is worthy of adoration. Nothing and no one —not the most valued possessions, the most beloved people— deserves to be worshiped as God does. We can only truly worship God when we are inwardly free.

Worshiping God does not relieve us of other commitments. Those who worship God must struggle against everything that destroys human beings, God's «sacred image». Those who worship God must respect and defend God's creation. Adoration is directly related to solidarity, and to ecology. The great scientist and mystic, Teilhard de Chardin, was right: «The more human a man becomes, the more he will feel the need to worship».

The story of the wise men offers us a model of authentic worship. They are wise enough to look deeply into the cosmos, to read the signs, to approach the Mystery and offer humble homage to God, incarnate in our existence.

5. FOLLOWING THE STAR

We are so familiar with the story of the wise men that we no longer take it seriously. We don't stop to look at length into the stars. It's probably not just for lack of time. Our generation sees the dark of night more easily than we see the points of light that shine in the midst of the darkness.

But we are moved by the gospel writer telling the story of the wise men; he imagines them in the middle of the night, following the tiny light of one star. The story breathes with the deep trust of the first believers after the resurrection. Jesus has fulfilled the words of the prophet Isaiah: «The people who walked in darkness have seen a great light; those who lived in a land of deep darkness—on them light has shined» (Isaiah 9:2).

The age we live in is not uniquely dark, tragic, or anguished. Don't we see the same darkness, frustration and helplessness at almost every stage of the human journey through the centuries?

We need only skim through the pages of history to see it. Certainly there are moments of light that promise great liberations, new worlds, more humane horizons. But then what? Revolutions can lead to new forms of enslavement, solutions that create new problems, ideals that end up as «band-aid remedies», noble struggles that end in weak truces. Back to the darkness.

There is some truth in the saying that «to be human is often a frustrating experience». But it's not the whole truth. In spite of all the failures and frustrations, human beings collect themselves, begin to hope again, make a new start. There is something in human beings that calls them back to life and hope, again and again. There is always a star that starts to glow again.

For believers, that star always leads to Jesus. Christians don't believe in just any messianic movement. That is why they are not easily disillusioned. The world is not a «lost cause». It is not plunged into utter darkness. The world is oriented toward salvation. One day, God will be the end of our exile and darkness. Absolute light. Today we can see it only in a humble star, leading us to Bethlehem.

3

Prepare the Way of the Lord

In those days John the Baptist appeared in the wilderness of Judea, proclaiming, «Repent, for the kingdom of heaven has come near». This is the one of whom the prophet Isaiah spoke when he said,

«The voice of one crying out in the wilderness:
Prepare the way of the Lord, make his paths straight».

Now John wore clothing of camel's hair with a leather belt around his waist, and his food was locusts and wild honey. Then the people of Jerusalem and all Judea were going out to him, and all the region along the Jordan, and they were baptized by him in the river Jordan, confessing their sins.

But when he saw many Pharisees and Sadducees coming for baptism, he said to them, «You brood of vipers! Who warned you to flee from the wrath to come? Bear fruit worthy of repentance. Do not presume to say to yourselves, "We have Abraham as our ancestor"; for I tell you, God is able from these stones to raise up children to Abraham. Even now the ax is lying at the root of the trees; every tree therefore that does not bear good fruit is cut down and thrown into the fire».

«I baptize you with water for repentance, but one who is more powerful than I is coming after me; I am not worthy to carry his sandals. He will baptize you with the Holy Spirit and fire. His winnowing fork is in his hand, and he will clear his threshing floor and will gather his wheat into the granary; but the chaff he will burn with unquenchable fire» (Matthew 3:1-12).

1. THE CALL TO CONVERSION

Between the fall of the year 27 A.D. and the spring of 28, a strange and independent prophet appears on the religious horizon of Palestine, provoking a strong impact on the people. His name is John. The first generations of Christians consistently saw him as the man who prepared the way for Jesus.

There is something new and surprising about this prophet. He doesn't preach in Jerusalem, as Isaiah and other prophets did; he stays away from the religious elite in the temple. He isn't a court prophet; he stays away from the palace of

Herod Antipas. They call him «a voice crying out in the wilderness», in the desert, beyond the control of any power.

Decrees from Rome and orders from Antipas' palace don't get to the desert. The hubbub of the temple can't be heard there. No one listens to the debates of the teachers of the law. But one can listen to God in the silence and solitude of the desert. It is the best place to start a conversion to God by preparing the way for Jesus.

That's just what John is talking about: repentance, conversion. «Prepare the way of the Lord, make his paths straight». He's not talking about the Roman highways where Tiberius' legions march. He's not talking about the roads that lead to the temple. John is calling the people to open a new way for the God who is coming in Jesus.

That's also what we need today: to repent and be converted to God, to return to Jesus, to open up his way in the world and in the Church. This is not just an *aggiornamento* or an updating for the present time. It's much more than that. It means bringing the whole Church to a state of repentance and conversion.

This is not an easy task. It will probably take a long time to set compassion at the center of Christian life. It will be hard to change from a «religion of authority» to a «religious calling». Years may go by before the Christian communities learn to live for the reign of God and his justice. It will take a profound change to make the poor the center of our religion.

It doesn't matter how long it takes. To follow Jesus we must first repent and be converted. We have to begin that conversion ourselves, now, and pass it on as orientation and nourishment for future generations. We will need to nourish and sustain it together, among ourselves. Only a repentant, converted church is worthy of Jesus.

2. MOVED BY THE SPIRIT OF JESUS

The Baptist speaks very clearly: «I baptize you with water for repentance», but water is not enough. We must reach out to «one who is more powerful», filled with God's Spirit: «He will baptize you with the Holy Spirit and fire».

Many «Christians» have never gone beyond the religion of the Baptist. They have been baptized with water, but they have not known the baptism of the Spirit. Perhaps the first thing we all need is to be transformed by the Spirit that brought about the change in Jesus. How does Jesus live, filled with God's Spirit, after he comes up out of the river Jordan?

Jesus moves away from the Baptist and begins living in a new context. We no longer need to prepare for the imminent judgment of God. This is the time to embrace the Father God who seeks to turn humanity into a more just family of brothers and sisters. We have to live in that context, in order to learn what it means to be Christian.

Moved by that conviction, Jesus leaves the wilderness and returns to Galilee, to live in the midst of the people's problems and sufferings. It is there, in the midst of life, that we have to feel the goodness of God: a Father who calls everyone together, to work together for a more human life. Until we know God that way, we cannot understand how Jesus lived.

Jesus also leaves behind the Baptist's threatening language, and begins to tell the kind of parables that would never have occurred to John. He wants the world to know how good God is: so good that he seeks out and embraces his lost children, because he wants to save them, not condemn them. Unless we speak as Jesus does, we are not proclaiming his good news.

Jesus leaves behind the austere life of the desert and does what the Baptist never did: «good deeds». He heals the sick, defends the poor, touches the lepers, invites sinners and prostitutes to his table, embraces the children of the streets. People need to feel God's goodness in their own flesh. To talk about a good God without doing good, will only discredit Jesus' message.

3. LOSING OUR WAY TO GOD

Many people are neither believers nor nonbelievers. They have simply adopted a way of life that never asks about the ultimate meaning of existence. In these cases the problem is less a matter of unbelief than a lack of the necessary conditions for choosing between belief and unbelief.

These are men and women without an «inner infrastructure». Their way of life prevents them from getting in touch with themselves. They never come close to the depth of their being. They cannot hear the questions that come from within them.

But one cannot relate to the mystery of life in a responsible way without first digging down into one's inner depth, opening oneself to life sincerely and honestly, right to the end.

People often go through a religious crisis, and find an earlier crisis hidden within it. When people seem to have turned away from God, could it be because they have turned away from themselves and moved to a level of existence where they can't hear God's voice?

When people are made happy by things, when their hearts are filled with material concerns, how can they think clearly about God?

When we are always looking for immediate satisfaction, for pleasure at any price, how can we look deeply into the ultimate mystery of existence?

When we lose our inner life, and think only about looking good to other people, how can we think sincerely about the ultimate meaning of our life?

When people are turned inside out, and lose themselves in the many kinds of escapism and entertainment this society offers, how can they really find themselves and think about their ultimate destiny?

«Prepare the way of the Lord». The cry of John the Baptist has not lost its meaning for our time. Whether or not we are aware of it, God is always coming to us. We can always meet him again. Faith can be born again in our hearts. But first we need to find ourselves, more deeply and sincerely.

4. FINDING OUR WAY AGAIN

It's easy to go through life with «no way» to God. We don't have to be atheists. We don't have to reject God consciously. All we need is to go with the flow of today's world, and adopt an attitude of religious indifference. Little by little, God disappears from the horizon. We lose interest in God. Is it too late to find our way again?

Perhaps we can begin by rediscovering «the humanity of religion». We can turn off from the false roads that lead to a self-interested, controlling God who cares only about his own glory and power, and open ourselves to the God who seeks and desires what is best for us, now and always. God is not a Supreme Being who tramples us and humiliates us, but a God of Love who invites us in and gives us life. People today are not pushed toward God out of fear, but drawn toward him by his love.

At the same time we need to broaden the horizon of our own life. We are filling up our existence with things, and are left with an inner emptiness. We have lots of information, but we no longer know which way to point our life. We see ourselves as the most intelligent and forward-looking generation in history, but we can't find adoration or thanksgiving in our hearts. We could get closer to God by clearing out new space in our lives.

It is also important to lay a «solid foundation» for living. What can sustain us in the midst of such great fear and uncertainty? Life is like a house: we need to maintain the walls and roof, but it is more important to build it on a strong foundation. In the end we all need to place ultimate trust in something or someone. Does that mean we need God?

To find our way back to God, we need to learn to be still. What can we lean on in the midst of fear and uncertainty? We can't go back to the heart of our existence when we are stressed and fearful, but only when we are quiet. If we back off and stand in silence before God, sooner or later our hearts will begin to open up.

We can live closed in on ourselves, with no way to move toward anything new and creative. Or we can prepare new ways to God, as the Baptist is asking us to do.

5. SUGGESTIONS

More and more people have been living far from any religious experience for years, and are now feeling the need to believe in a living God. How can they find him? Here are some suggestions.

First you need to honor your own desire for God. Even when you feel powerless, unable to transform that desire into immediate reality, God knows your heart and your weakness. God is very near, and God understands. Don't compare yourself with other people. You have to follow your own path. Your past doesn't matter. What matters now is to trust God and yourself.

Think about what is good in your life. What sustains you and helps you live in the midst of all the problems and crises: the love of your spouse, your joy in your children, your friends, your happy experiences, the things that make you feel alive and strong. The God you're looking for is there.

Look inside your heart for the good that is within you. Don't get caught up in endless psychological self-analysis. This inner journey doesn't take a long time. Think about your good feelings, your noble and generous acts, your desire to live more authentically. In spite of your feelings of mediocrity, you can hear God calling you from within.

Then you can take another step. Look back on some religious experience that once left its mark on your heart. Some important moment in your life when you were truly calling on God, some gospel verse that you learned long ago, some encounter with a person of faith that made a difference for you.

If you're ready to pray, try to do so. Perhaps nothing will come at first. Praying may seem strange and artificial at first. You don't need many words. You might tell God: «I want to believe; help me in my weakness». Charles de Foucauld used to say: «My God, if you exist, help me to know you».

Then what? No one knows what will happen. Will your faith be reawakened? Will your life change? Will everything stay the same? What's important is the sincerity of your search for God.

In any case, remember that even if you go back to your everyday, mediocre life, God will be there to uphold you with his love. Even if you can't hear him calling, even if your faith keeps flickering out, God will not leave you. This is the Great News of Jesus: God doesn't leave us even when we sin against him. Even when you sin, he forgives you; if you don't feel his forgiveness, it's only because you aren't open to it.

Remember the words of John the Baptist: «Prepare the way of the Lord, make his paths straight». You can open yourself more to God. Some day, you don't know when, you may encounter the living God of Jesus Christ. You'll know him by the peace you feel within you.

4

The Baptism of Jesus

Then Jesus came from Galilee to John at the Jordan, to be baptized by him. John would have prevented him, saying, «I need to be baptized by you, and do you come to me?» But Jesus answered him, «Let it be so now, for it is proper for us in this way to fulfill all righteousness». Then he consented. And when Jesus had been baptized, just as he came up from the water, suddenly the heavens were opened to him and he saw the Spirit of God descending like a dove and alighting on him. And a voice from heaven said, «This is my Son, the Beloved, with whom I am well pleased» (Matthew 3:13-17).

1. FEELING GOD AS A FATHER

Hanna Wolf, a German theologian and psychotherapist, has called Jesus the first person in history to live and communicate a healthy experience of God, without projecting human fears, fantasies and ambitions onto the concept of divinity.

Some Christian sources tell of an early experience in which Jesus heard these words from heaven: «You are my beloved son». The story was a later elaboration, but it conveys a reality that can readily be documented.

Jesus lives and feels God as a Father. This is something that surprises the biblical scholars. Although Jesus constantly speaks of the «reign of God» as the central symbol of his message, he never describes God as a king or lord, but as a «father» (*abba*). There is no doubt about this. Jesus does not relate to God as a servant relates to the emperor Tiberius, or a Galilean to the court of Herod Antipas. He entrusts himself to the mystery of God as a beloved son. This is the first Christian attitude toward God.

His experience of God as a beloved father does not enclose Jesus in an individualistic, exclusive piety. The Father is the God of all peoples, the loving Father of all his children. Jesus calls him «Father in heaven», because God is not tied down to one sacred place, does not belong to one specific people or race. He does not fit into any religion. He is the God of all, even those who forget about him. «He makes his sun rise on the evil and on the good» (Matthew 5:45). Jesus lives God within this universal horizon.

Neither is Jesus enclosed in a self-centered experience of God. He doesn't look for God to free him from his fears, to fill up his emptiness, or to live out his religious fantasies. All he wants is for the justice, mercy and goodness of this

Father to spread to everyone, and for all humanity to live with the dignity that befits the sons and daughters of God.

Another thing. The God we see in Jesus is not mainly interested in how we think of him or how we feel him, but rather in how we relate to the people who suffer. We are truly living as sons and daughters of God when we respond as brothers and sisters to those who cannot live such a life of dignity.

2. GOD S GOOD SPIRIT

Jesus is not inwardly shallow or fragmented. As he goes about Galilee he does not act arbitrarily, or out of self-interest. The gospels show clearly from the beginning that Jesus lives and acts in response to «the Spirit of God».

The writers don't want us to confuse him with a «teacher of the law», concerned with imposing more order on the behavior of Israel. They don't want him to be seen as a false prophet, trying to strike a balance between the religion of the temple and the power of Rome.

The gospel writers also don't want anyone to compare Jesus with John the Baptist. They don't want him seen simply as a disciple and collaborator of that great prophet of the desert. Jesus is the «beloved Son» of God. The Spirit of God «descends» on him. Only he can «baptize» with the Holy Spirit.

Throughout the biblical tradition, the «Spirit of God» is the power of God, who creates and sustains all of life. It is the force by which God renews and transforms the living. It is the loving energy with which God always seeks the best for his sons and daughters.

That is why Jesus feels called not to punish, destroy, or condemn, but to heal, build, and bless. The Spirit of God leads him to empower and improve life. Filled with the good Spirit of God, he sets out to liberate people from «evil spirits» that only harm, enslave, and dehumanize.

The first generations of Christians knew very clearly who Jesus was. This is how they described the memory that he imprinted on his followers: «how God anointed Jesus of Nazareth with the Holy Spirit and with power, how he went about doing good and healing all who were oppressed by the devil, for God was with him» (Acts of the Apostles 10:38).

What «spirit» moves us, Jesus' followers, today? What «passion» moves his Church? What «mystique» gives life and purpose to our communities? What are we doing in the world? If the Spirit of Jesus is within us, we will go about «healing» those who are oppressed, depressed, and repressed by evil.

His encounter with John the Baptist is the experience that turns Jesus' life around. After his baptism in the Jordan, Jesus doesn't go back to his old job in Nazareth; nor does he join the Baptist's movement. His life revolves around a single purpose: to cry out the Good News of a God who seeks to save humanity.

What turns Jesus' life around is not the words he hears from the Baptist, nor the purifying rite of baptism. Jesus is living something deeper than that. He feels overwhelmed by the Father's Spirit. He recognizes himself as the Son of God. From now on his life will be devoted to radiating and spreading the unfathomable love of a Father God.

Jesus' experience has meaning for us as well. Faith is a personal journey that we all must make for ourselves. What we have learned as children from our parents and teachers is important, of course. What we hear from priests and preachers is important. But in the end we all have to ask ourselves one question: in whom do I believe? Do I believe in God, or in the people who tell me about him?

We mustn't forget that faith is always a personal experience; it cannot be replaced by blind obedience to what others tell us. They can stand outside us and turn us toward the faith, but we are the only ones who can open ourselves trustfully to God.

For the same reason, faith is not a matter of simply accepting a given set of formulas. To be a believer does not depend mainly on the doctrinal content of a catechism. Of course all that helps to shape our Christian vision of life. But prior to that, giving it meaning, is the inner dynamic that leads us always to love, trust, and hope in the God revealed in Jesus Christ.

Neither is faith a legacy that we inherit through baptism, that we can invest as we choose. It is not something we own forever. To be a believer means to be always listening for the voice of God incarnate in Jesus, learning to live more fully and freely every day.

This faith is not made up only of certainties. Believers often live a part of their life in darkness. In the words of the great theologian Romano Guardini, «faith means having enough light to endure the dark places». More than anything, faith is made up of faithfulness. True believers know how to believe in the dark moments what they have seen in the moments of light. They always go on looking for the God who is beyond all our formulas, clear or confusing. Cardinal de Lubac once wrote that «our ideas of God are like waves on the ocean; they support the swimmer so he can move beyond them». What matters is faithfulness to the God who reveals himself in his Son Jesus Christ.

4. THE RENEWAL OF BAPTISM

Jesus' baptism in the waters of Jordan is one of the best documented events in the gospel record. Jesus has expressed solidarity with the Baptist's conversion movement, by receiving baptism from his hands. Then on coming out of the river, he has an experience that leads him to return to Galilee and begin his own mission.

The first Christian communities spoke of the «baptism of water» practiced by John, and the «baptism of the Spirit» introduced by Jesus. They were baptized, not in order to become disciples of John the Baptist but to symbolize their commitment to the gospel, their openness to the Spirit of Jesus, and their entrance into the community of believers.

For them baptism was the natural culmination of a whole process of conversion; it was a vivid expression of their conscious and responsible acceptance of the Christian faith.

It is different for us today. We are baptized soon after we are born, with no opportunity to make it a personal expression of our own decision. The practice of infant baptism was introduced very early in the Christian communities, and it is certainly a meaningful way for believing families to integrate their children into the Christian community.

But although it is a legitimate intergenerational custom, the practice entails grave risks if we do not take our responsibility seriously. Infant baptism should not be understood as the culmination of a process of conversion. It is meaningful only if we think of it as the beginning of a lifetime process that needs to be ratified later on.

The baptism we receive as children requires us, as adults, to confirm and personally ratify our faith. Unless we do, our baptism will be incomplete; it becomes an empty sign without responsible content, like a call without a true response.

5. LISTENING FOR OUR OWN CALLING

The gospel narratives do not stop to describe the baptism of Jesus. They place more importance on the experience he lived at that moment, which was decisive for his future action.

Jesus does not return to his home in Nazareth. Neither does he stay on as a disciple of the Baptist. Moved by the Spirit, he starts a new life, totally committed to his evangelizing mission.

We might say that his baptism was the privileged moment in which he experienced his prophetic calling; it was when he became aware that his life was possessed by the Father's Spirit, and heard the call to proclaim a message of salvation to God's sons and daughters.

Hearing one's own calling is not just the task of a group of men and women called to a special mission. Sooner or later we all have to ask about the ultimate reason for our daily life; we have to ask why a new day begins for us every morning. It's not about making great discoveries. It is simply knowing that our small life has meaning for other people, that by living we can give life to someone.

Neither is it about hearing a definitive calling every day. We discover the meaning of life little by little, morning after morning. There is something uncertain in every calling. We are always asked to keep looking, to be ready, to be open.

Only by responding faithfully to our mission can we gradually discover, precisely by the way we respond, the broad horizon of demands and promises that is contained in our everyday life.

We often live our life in a rhythm of wearisome, distracting, and dehumanizing tasks. We do many things every day, but do we know what we are doing and why? We are constantly going here and there, but do we know where to go? We hear a lot of voices, slogans, and calls, but can we hear the voice of the Spirit who invites us to live our daily mission with faithfulness?

5

The Temptations of Jesus

Then Jesus was led up by the Spirit into the wilderness to be tempted by the devil. He fasted forty days and forty nights, and afterwards he was famished. The tempter came and said to him,

«If you are the Son of God, command these stones to become loaves of bread».

But he answered,
«It is written,
"One does not live by bread alone,
but by every word that comes
from the mouth of God"».

Then the devil took him to the holy city and placed him on the pinnacle of the temple, saying to him,

«If you are the Son of God, throw yourself down; for it is written,
"He will command his angels concerning you",
and "On their hands they will bear you up,
so that you will not dash your foot against a stone"».

Jesus said to him,
«Again it is written, "Do not put the Lord your God to the test"».

Again, the devil took him to a very high mountain and showed him all the kingdoms of the world and their splendor, and he said to him,

«All these I will give you, if you will fall down and worship me».

Jesus said to him,
«Away with you, Satan! for it is written,
"Worship the Lord your God,
and serve only him"».

Then the devil left him, and suddenly angels came and waited on him
(Matthew 4:1-11).

1. FAITHFUL TO JESUS IN THE MIDST OF TEMPTATIONS

The first generation of Christians soon became interested in the «temptations» of Jesus. They didn't want to forget the kind of conflicts and struggles he had to overcome in order to stay faithful to God. That helped them keep their eyes on their one task: building a more human world by following in Jesus' footsteps.

It's a moving story. In the wilderness, or desert, one can hear the voice of God, but one can also feel the attraction of the dark forces that pull us away from him. The «devil» tempts Jesus by using the Word of God, especially the psalms that were prayed in Israel. The temptation to turn away from God is hidden even in the heart of religion.

In the first temptation, Jesus refuses to use God to turn stones into bread. What a hungry person needs most is to eat, but «one does not live by bread alone». The hunger to be human is not satisfied by feeding the body. We need much more than that.

Precisely in order to liberate the people who don't have bread from their misery, hunger, and death, we need to awaken a hunger for justice and love in the dehumanized world of the well-fed.

In the second temptation, on the pinnacle of the temple, the devil suggests looking to God for security. He will be safe, held up on angels' hands, and can walk without the risk of stumbling. Jesus replies: «Do not put the Lord your God to the test».

It is demonic to organize religion as a system of beliefs and practices that ensure our security. We cannot build a more human world by taking shelter in our own private religion. Sometimes we have to take risks, trusting in God as Jesus did.

The last scene is impressive. Jesus is looking down on the world from a high mountain. Below him lie «all the kingdoms» with their conflicts, wars, and atrocities. This world is where Jesus wants to introduce God's reign of peace and justice; the devil offers him power and glory if he will worship him instead.

Jesus' reaction is immediate: «You shall worship the Lord your God». The world cannot be humanized by force. It is impossible to wield power over others, without serving the devil. Those who follow Jesus in search of power and glory, end up kneeling down before the devil. They are not worshiping the true God.

2. THE TEMPTATIONS OF THE CHURCH TODAY

The first temptation takes place in the wilderness, or desert. After fasting for a long time, struggling to find God, Jesus is hungry. That is when the tempter suggests thinking about himself instead of the Father's project: «If you are the Son of God, command these stones to become loaves of bread». Weak from hunger but filled with God's Spirit, Jesus responds: «One does not live by bread alone, but by every word that comes from the mouth of God». He will not live by seeking his own self-interest. He will not be a selfish Messiah. When he sees people hungry, he will multiply the loaves. He will feed on the living Word of God.

Whenever the Church seeks its own self-interest, neglecting the project of the reign of God, it is turning away from Jesus. Whenever we Christians put our own welfare ahead of the needs of the poor, we are turning away from Jesus.

The second temptation takes place at the «temple». The tempter proposes to Jesus a triumphal entry into the holy city, descending from the heights as a glorious Messiah. Jesus is assured of God's protection. God's angels will «take care» of him. Jesus immediately responds: «Do not put the Lord your God to the test». He will not be a triumphalistic Messiah. He will not use God for his own glory. He will not call down «signs from heaven»; only signs to heal the sick.

Whenever the Church uses God for its own glory, and «descends from the heights» to show its own power, it turns away from Jesus. When followers of Jesus would rather «look good» than «do good», we turn away from him.

The third temptation takes place on a «very high mountain». There he can see all the kingdoms of the world. They are all in the power of the devil, who makes Jesus an amazing offer: he will give him all the power in the world. On one condition: «if you will fall down and worship me». Jesus responds sharply: «Away with you, Satan!» «Worship the Lord your God, and serve only him». God has not called him to control the world as the Roman emperor does, but to serve those who are oppressed by the empire. He will not be a controlling Messiah, but a servant. The reign of God is not imposed by force, but offered with love.

The Church today must chase away all the temptations of power, glory, or domination, crying out with Jesus: «Away with you, Satan!» Worldly power is a demonic offer. When Christians seek it, we are turning away from Jesus.

3. OUR MISTAKES

Anyone who does not want to live in alienation will have to be alert and watchful toward the mistakes we can make in life. One of the most important things Jesus does is to offer, to those who know and follow him, the possibility of becoming more human every day. In Jesus we hear the cry of alarm against the grave mistakes we can fall into throughout our life.

The first mistake is to make the satisfaction of our material needs the absolute objective of our life; to think that the greatest happiness of being human lies in the possession and enjoyment of material goods.

Jesus tells us that the satisfaction of material needs is important, but not sufficient. Human beings become more human when we learn to hear the Word of the Father, who calls us to live as brothers and sisters. Then we discover that to be human is to share, not to possess; to give, not to monopolize; to create life, not to exploit a brother or sister.

The second mistake is to seek personal power, success, or triumph ahead of everything else and at any price. To do that is to be unfaithful to our own mission, to become a slave of the most ridiculous idolatries.

Jesus tells us that we do right, not when we seek status and power in competition and rivalry with others, but when we are able to live in generous and unselfish service to others.

The third mistake is to try to solve the ultimate problems of life without risks, struggles, or hard work, by selfishly using God in magical ways.

Jesus tells us that to use religion in this way is to destroy it. True faith does not lead to passivity, evasion, or neglect in the face of problems. On the contrary, if we have any understanding of what it means to be faithful to a God who is Father of all, we will take greater risks every day in order to make life more abundant and just for everyone.

4. LOST IN ABUNDANCE

One of the characteristics of a modern society is its excess, its lack of proportion, its profusion of choices, its multiple possibilities. We can have everything, we can try everything. It's not easy to live that way. With a thousand things calling for our attention, we may end up confused and unable to take care of the important things.

Shopping malls and supermarkets lay out an incredible array of products. Restaurant menus offer all kinds of combination meals. The number of television channels increases every day. Travel agencies offer all kinds of experiences. The Internet opens up a limitless world of images, impressions, and networking contacts.

Information has never been so invasive. We are overwhelmed with data, statistics, and warnings. Rapid-fire news bulletins make calm reflection and meditation impossible. Oversaturated with information, our consciousness is hijacked by everything and by nothing. It is easier every day to slip into indifference and passivity.

This way of living has consequences. Many people focus intensely on artificial needs, and neglect the important things. They live outwardly, obsessed with external novelties, and almost completely ignore their inner world. The excess of information and the pressure of consumerism exhaust the strength of their convictions. Many are distracted by anecdotal campaigns, without any goals or ideals. Little by little their selves become fragile and inconsistent. Everything is a problem, even the most everyday things: sleeping, going on vacation, getting fat, getting old.

Many people —sometimes vaguely and diffusely, sometimes more clearly and precisely— are disappointed and disillusioned to find themselves depersonalized, inwardly empty, incapacitated for any kind of healthy growth. This dissatisfaction can be the beginning of salvation, for it can help us to hear the words of Jesus: «One does not live by bread alone, but by every word that comes from the mouth of God». These words are a call to respond. We cannot be satisfied by distraction, function without a soul, live by bread alone. We need the life-giving Word that comes from God. Can we hear it?

5. DO WE WANT TO GO ON LIKE THIS?

The problem with our «consumer society» is that we not only consume what we need to live, but we consume mostly superfluous things. This is the decisive reality behind political and economic life. It's all about «increased growth» and «raising the standard of living». That is what every citizen wants.

Everything turns on this consumption of superfluous goods. People have learned to measure success, personality, even their personal identity by the car model they drive or the label on the clothes they wear. It is the way to live. We «live, move, and have our being» by consuming.

But do we know what we are doing? Do we want to go on consuming this way? Is this the best life style for a progressive society? Don't we need to change, to humanize our life a little more?

Perhaps we need above all to realize what we are doing. That is the first, but very important step. Why do I buy so many things? Is it to keep up with my friends and acquaintances? To prove to myself and others that I am «somebody»? So everyone will know that I won?

We can also ask whether we are free or enslaved. Do I make my own decisions, or do I shop for what the commercials tell me to? Do I buy what I need to live well and happily, or am I filling my life with useless things? Do I know enough to boycott the advertisements that try to manipulate me in degrading ways? Am I one of those «happy slaves» who can't live without a particular name brand?

Above all we should ask whether this irresponsible consumerism is fair to others. Nothing is enough for a good life any more. We keep inventing new needs, and none of them satisfy us. Meanwhile millions of human beings don't have enough for survival. How should we think about that? Isn't it unjust and stupid? Isn't it cruel?

«One does not live by bread alone». Jesus' words are not just a pious exhortation to believers. They convey a truth that we all need to hear.

6

The Call to Conversion

Now when Jesus heard that John had been arrested, he withdrew to Galilee. He left Nazareth and made his home in Capernaum by the sea, in the territory of Zebulun and Naphtali, so that what had been spoken through the prophet Isaiah might be fulfilled:

«Land of Zebulun, land of Naphtali,
on the road by the sea, across the Jordan, Galilee of the Gentiles
the people who walked in darkness have seen a great light,
and for those who sat in the region and shadow of death
light has dawned».

From that time Jesus began to proclaim, «Repent, for the kingdom of heaven has come near».

As he walked by the Sea of Galilee, he saw two brothers, Simon, who is called Peter, and Andrew his brother, casting a net into the sea —for they were fishermen. And he said to them, «Follow me, and I will make you fish for people». Immediately they left their nets and followed him. As he went from there, he saw two other brothers, James, son of Zebedee and his brother John, in the boat with their father Zebedee, mending their nets, and he called them. Immediately they left the boat and their father, and followed him.

Jesus went throughout Galilee, teaching in their synagogues and proclaiming the good news of the kingdom and curing every disease and every sickness among the people (Matthew 4:12-23).

1. JESUS' FIRST WORD

Matthew the evangelist carefully sets the stage for Jesus' first public appearance. The Baptist's voice is muted, and we hear the new voice of Jesus. The dry desert scene is replaced by the verdant beauty of Galilee. Jesus leaves Nazareth and settles in Capernaum, on the lakeshore. Everything hints at the appearance of a new life.

Matthew reminds us that we are in «Galilee of the Gentiles». He knows well that Jesus preached in the Jewish synagogues of those towns, and did not go among pagans. But Galilee is a crossroads; Capernaum is a city open to the sea. This is where salvation will come to all peoples.

For now the situation is tragic. «The people sat in darkness», Matthew says in words from the prophet Isaiah. «The shadow of death» was upon the earth. Injustice and evil prevail. Life cannot flourish. Things are not as God wants them to be. This is not the reign of the Father.

But in the midst of the darkness, the people will start to see «a great light». A light will shine among the shadows. Jesus is always like that: a great light shining in the world.

According to Matthew, Jesus begins his preaching with a shout: «Repent». That is his first word. It is a time for conversion. We must open up to the reign of God. It's not a time to «sit in darkness», but to walk in the light.

There is a «great light» in the Church. It is revealing God. We must not hide it with our quarreling. We must not set it aside for anything. We must not turn it into theoretical doctrines, cold theology, or boring words. If the light of Jesus is dimmed, we Christians will become what Jesus so feared: «the blind leading the blind».

That is also his first word to us today: «Repent, be converted»; reclaim your Christian identity; return to your roots; help the Church to move into a new stage of Christianity, more faithful to Jesus; become more aware of following him; place yourself at the service of the reign of God.

2. HOW MUST WE CHANGE?

It's not hard to summarize Jesus' message: God is not a distant, uncaring being who moves in his own world, interested only in his own honor and his own rights. He wants the best for everyone. His saving power is working in the deepest part of life. He only wants his creatures to collaborate with him in moving the world toward fullness: «The kingdom of heaven is at hand. Change».

But what does it mean to collaborate in God's project? How must we change? Jesus' call is not addressed only to «sinners», to change their behavior and become more like those who are already living by God's law. That's not what concerns him. Jesus is addressing everyone, because everyone needs to learn a different way of acting. His goal is not for Israel to live by a religion more faithful to God, but for his followers to introduce a new dynamic into the world, one that responds to God's project. Here are its main points:

First, compassion must always be the guiding principle of action. We must bring compassion for those who suffer into the world: «Be compassionate, as your Father is». We have heard more than enough great words about justice, equality, or democracy. They are meaningless without compassion toward the last and the least. There can be no human progress without practical assistance for the wretched of the earth.

Second, the first goal must be the dignity of the last and the least; «the last will be first». We have to turn history in a new direction. We have to turn culture, the economy, democracy, and our Churches toward those who cannot live with dignity.

Third, we must initiate a healing process that liberates humanity from everything that destroys and degrades it: «Go and heal». Jesus had no better way to say it. What is important is to heal, relieve suffering, make life more healthy, build a life together that moves toward health, dignity, and happiness for all.

This is what we have inherited from Jesus. We can never build a life according to God's will, except by liberating the last and the least from their humiliation and suffering. No religion will ever be blessed by God, unless it seeks justice for them.

3. IT'S NEVER TOO LATE

We don't like talking about conversion. It makes us think almost instinctively of something sad, painful, something like repentance, mortification and asceticism. It takes more effort than we are willing or able to summon.

But if we stop and listen to Jesus' message, the first thing we hear will be words of encouragement to change our hearts and learn to live a more human life, because God is near and wants to heal our life.

Jesus is not talking about a forced conversion. It is a change that grows within us, as we discover that God is someone who wants to make our life more human and happier.

Because conversion isn't mainly about trying to do everything better; it's about letting ourselves be found by this God who wants us to be better and more human. It's not just about «becoming a good person», but about returning to the One who is good to us.

So conversion is not something sad, but the discovery of true joy. It doesn't mean we stop living; we become more alive than ever. We discover the direction our lives should take. We start to understand what it means to live.

Conversion is something joyful. It is cleansing our mind of selfish interests that diminish our daily life. Freeing our heart from the anguish and complications caused by our struggle for power and possessions. Freeing ourselves from things we don't need, and living for people who need us.

Conversion begins when we discover that the important thing is not figuring out how to earn more money, but how to be more human. Not how to get something, but how to become ourselves.

When we hear Jesus calling: «Repent, for the kingdom of heaven has come near», it reminds us that it's never too late to be converted; it's never too late to love; it's never to late to be happy; it's never too late to let ourselves be forgiven and renewed by God.

4. LOST IN A RELIGIOUS CRISIS

We live in times of religious crisis. In many people's lives it seems as if faith is being smothered, repressed by modern culture and by today's life style. But at the same time we see in many lives a new search for meaning, a yearning for a different kind of life, a need for God as a Friend.

It's true that many of us are skeptical of great projects and beautiful words. No one listens any more to religious speeches offering «salvation» or «redemption». Hope is fading, almost disappearing, that we will ever really hear some Good News for humankind.

At the same time many people are beginning to suspect that we have lost our sense of direction. Something is sinking beneath our feet. We are losing our goals, and our landmarks. We know we can solve «problems», but we are less and less able to solve «the problem» of life. Don't we need salvation now more than ever?

We also live in times of «fragmentation». Life has become splintered. We all live in our own compartments. We have gotten far away from the kind of humanism that looked for truth and a sense of wholeness. We no longer listen to people who know about life; we listen to specialists who know a lot about one small piece of it, but nothing about the meaning of existence.

At the same time, many people are growing weary of this dizzying world of data, information, and statistics. We can't get away from the eternal human questions: Where did we come from? Where are we going? Where can we look for an ultimate meaning of life?

These are also times of scientific pragmatism. Modern men and women have decided (no one knows why) that nothing exists beyond what science can prove. That's all there is. What science can't explain, simply doesn't exist. Of course there's no room for God in this simple but unscientific assertion, and religious faith is seen as belonging to the out-of-sync world of the conservatives.

But many people are realizing that this assertion doesn't make sense, doesn't reflect reality. Human beings are not «small cogs» in a «big machine» that science can take apart. The intuition of mystery is all around us: inside each one of us, in the immense cosmos, in human history.

So we come back to the suspicion: aren't the questions the scientists refuse to talk about, precisely the questions that give meaning to life? Wouldn't it be a big mistake to overlook the answer to the mystery of life? Isn't it tragic that we so naively decide to do without God? Meanwhile we can still hear Jesus' words: «Repent, for the kingdom of heaven has come near».

5. FOLLOWING JESUS

If we ask Christians what they mean by faith, we find that for many of them it simply means belonging to the Church, reciting the creed, abiding by Catholic morality and fulfilling the prescribed rituals.

People in the first Christian communities would have answered that being Christian means «following» Jesus. That is the almost technical term that the first believers used. Christians are people who try to build their lives around walking in Jesus' footsteps. That is what those Galilean fishermen did when they answered his call.

Perhaps now, twenty centuries later, we Christians need to be reminded that the first and essential element of Christian faith consists of following Jesus Christ.

But we need to understand what following means. It's not about childish imitation, without creative spirit. Rather, following Jesus means being inspired by him to continue in our own time, responsibly, the passionate work that he and the people around him began. It means taking on the great attitudes that gave meaning to their life, and living them creatively today, in our own historical context.

If we see it that way, Christian faith takes on a completely different dynamic and vitality. To be Christian is to discover little by little the salvific meaning of Jesus, to become identified with the fundamental attitudes that gave meaning to his existence, to learn to live in his «life style».

Following Jesus means believing what he believed, giving importance to what he considered important, taking interest in what interested him, defending the cause he defended, seeing people as he saw them, getting close as he did to people in need, loving people as he loved them, trusting the Father as he did, facing life with hope as he did. The first believers saw the Christian life as a perpetual adventure of renewal, a process of becoming «new men» and «new women».

If faith means following Jesus, then we all have to ask ourselves who we are following in our lives, what messages we hear, who are our leaders, what causes we defend, what interests we serve. Can we go on doing those things and still be Christians, that is, followers of Jesus Christ?

7

Blessed are Those

When Jesus saw the crowds, he went up the mountain; and after he sat down, his disciples came to him. Then he began to speak, and taught them, saying:

«Blessed are the poor in spirit, for theirs is the kingdom of heaven.
Blessed are those who mourn, for they will be comforted.
Blessed are the meek, for they will inherit the earth.
Blessed are those who hunger and thirst for righteousness, for they will be filled.
Blessed are the merciful, for they will receive mercy.
Blessed are the pure in heart, for they will see God.
Blessed are the peacemakers, for they will be called children of God.
Blessed are those who are persecuted for righteousness' sake, for theirs is the kingdom of heaven.

Blessed are you when people revile you and persecute you and utter all kinds of evil against you falsely on my account. Rejoice and be glad, for your reward is great in heaven» (Matthew 5:1-12a).

1. JESUS' HAPPINESS

Jesus called his listeners «blessed», meaning «happy», and the people of his time knew what that meant. A happy person would be a healthy, adult male, married to an honest and fertile woman, a father of sons and owner of productive land, a religious leader, respected by his neighbors. What more could anyone want?

Of course that wasn't the happiness Jesus wanted for himself. With no wife or children, no land or possessions, living the life of a drifter around Galilee, he wasn't happy in any conventional sense. He was a kind of gadfly. If he was happy, it was the countercultural happiness of flouting the established rules.

In fact, he wasn't thinking much about his own happiness. His life revolved around a project that gave him energy and intensity. He called it «the reign of God». He seemed to be happiest when he could make others happy. He felt good when he was restoring people's health, and the dignity that had been unfairly taken from them.

He never sought his own self-interest. He lived to create a new kind of happiness for everyone. He could never be happy alone, without sharing his happiness with others. He offered everyone a new, more radical and liberating set of criteria for a world of dignity and happiness.

He believed in a «happy God», the creator God who looks on all his creatures with compassionate love, the God of life and not of death, who cared more about the people's suffering than about their sins.

Out of faith in that God he broke all the normal religious and social molds. He did not preach, «Blessed are the righteous and devout, because they will be rewarded by God». He did not say, «Blessed are the poor, because God will be their happiness».

Instead he challenges us: «Don't look for happiness in the satisfaction of your own interests, or in selfish devotion to your religion. Find happiness in faithfully and patiently working toward a world of happiness for everyone».

2. HEARING THE BLESSINGS FROM UP CLOSE

When Jesus went up the mountain and sat down to pronounce his blessings, he was surrounded by a crowd, but only his disciples came closer to hear his message. What do Jesus' disciples hear today, if we come up close?

Blessed are «the poor in spirit», those who know how to live with less, trusting God to meet their needs. Blessed is a Church that lives with a spirit of poverty; it will have fewer problems, be more attentive to people in need, and be more free to live the gospel. The kingdom of heaven belongs to such a Church.

Blessed are «the meek», those with kind and merciful hearts. Blessed is a Church full of humility. Such a Church is a gift to this world of violence; it will inherit the promised land.

Blessed are «those who mourn» because of their unjust suffering and marginalization; together with them we can create a better world, a world of dignity. Blessed is a Church that suffers for its faithfulness to Jesus; it will receive God's comfort.

Blessed are «those who hunger and thirst for righteousness», who have not lost their desire to be more just and to make a more just world. Blessed is the Church that passionately seeks the kingdom of God and its justice, which nourishes the best of the human spirit. One day that yearning will be fulfilled.

Blessed are «the merciful» who live, work, and act out of compassion. Of all the people in the world, they are most like the heavenly Father. Blessed is the Church when God takes away its heart of stone, and gives it a human heart; such a Church will receive mercy.

Blessed are the «peacemakers», who patiently and faithfully seek good for everyone. Blessed is the Church that brings peace rather than hostility into the world, reconciliation rather than confrontation. Such a Church will be called the child of God.

Blessed are those who, «persecuted for righteousness' sake», respond to injustice and insults with humility. They help us to overcome evil with good. Blessed is the Church that is persecuted for following Jesus; the kingdom of heaven belongs to such a Church.

3. INEXHAUSTIBLE CONTENT

If we keep coming back to Jesus' words of blessing, we find them always full of new meaning. They always shine a new and different light on the moment we are living now. Today as always, I hear new «resonance» in the words of Jesus.

Blessed are the poor in spirit, those who know how to live with less. They will have fewer problems, be more attentive to people in need, live in greater freedom. When we are able to understand that, we will become more human.

Blessed are the meek, those who empty their hearts of violence and aggressiveness. They are a gift to our violent world. When we can all do that, we will be able to live together in true peace.

Blessed are those who weep over the suffering of others. They are good people; they can help to build a world of brotherhood and solidarity.

Blessed are those who hunger and thirst for justice, who have not lost the desire to be more just and to make a society with dignity for all. They nourish the best that the human spirit has to offer.

Blessed are the merciful, those who know how to forgive from the bottom of their heart. Only God understands their inner struggle and their greatness. They are the people best able to bring us reconciliation.

Blessed are those who purify their hearts of hatred, deception, and mixed motives. We can trust them to build a new future.

Blessed are those who work for peace with patience and faith; who are never discouraged by obstacles and difficulties; who are always seeking the best for everyone. We need them to restore our life together.

Blessed are those who are persecuted for acting justly, and who respond with meekness to injustice and insults. They help us to overcome evil with good.

Blessed are those who suffer insults, persecution, and calumny for faithfully following the way opened up by Jesus. Their suffering will not be wasted.

One thing stands out in all these blessings; to read them without noticing it would distort the meaning of the blessings themselves. With these beautiful words Jesus calls our attention to God as the ultimate guarantor of human happiness. Those who live for the project described here will one day be comforted, will be filled, will receive mercy, will see God—and will live forever in the reign of God.

4. THE GOD OF THOSE WHO SUFFER

What is especially clear in the blessings is that God is the God of the poor, the oppressed, those who mourn and suffer. God is not immune to suffering. He is not impassive or apathetic. God «suffers wherever love suffers» (Jürgen Moltmann). Therefore the future that God wills belongs to those who suffer, because there is not enough room for them in today's society or in the human heart.

Many thinkers believe that apathy is spreading in modern society. We seem to be losing the ability to recognize other people's suffering. This is the blindness of those who can no longer see pain; the numbness of those who cannot feel suffering.

We are learning a thousand ways to avoid relationships and contact with people who suffer. We build walls to keep out other people's suffering. We focus on our own problems and live in our own private, hermetically sealed world, after putting up a sign: «Do not disturb».

The compartmentalization of modern life also helps to cover up people's suffering and loneliness. We seldom experience other people's anguish directly, or see the lostness in their faces. We don't touch our neighbor's loneliness and desperation.

We have reduced human problems to data and statistics. We look at human suffering indirectly, on the television screen. Then we hurry back to our own tasks; we don't have time to look into a suffering face.

This social apathy gives special significance to Christian faith in a God who is «friend of the suffering», a crucified God who came to suffer with those whom the world has abandoned: the God of the blessings.

Dorothee Sölle once said: «We can change the social conditions in which people suffer… We can even reduce or eliminate suffering, which is profitable for some people. But all those paths end at boundaries we cannot cross. Not only death… but also inhumanity and insensitivity. We can only cross those boundaries by sharing people's suffering, by not leaving them alone, by echoing their cries of pain».

People often think that faith has to do with a person's eternal salvation, but not with everyday happiness, which is what we care about right now. Some people even suspect that they would be happier without God and without religion. So it is worth while to recall some Christian convictions that may have been forgotten or hidden because of a misleading or inadequate presentation of the faith. Here are a few:

We were created by God only out of love, not for God's benefit or self-interest but for our own happiness. God's only concern is our well-being.

God wants us to be happy not only after we die, in what we call «eternal life», but here and now, in this life. He is present in our lives to enable us to flourish, not to restrict or harm us.

God respects both the laws of nature and the freedom of human beings. He does not forcibly restrict either human freedom or the created order. God is with us, supporting our struggle for a more human life and drawing our freedom toward the good. Thus at every moment we rely on God's grace for our greatest possible happiness.

Morality does not consist of obedience to laws arbitrarily imposed by God. God wants us to hear the moral requirements that we carry in our hearts, because obeying them is good for us. God does not prohibit what is good for human beings, nor does he require what might harm us. God only seeks our well-being.

To be converted to God does not mean choosing an unhappier or more bothersome way of life, but orienting our own freedom toward a more human, more healthier, and happier life, even when it requires sacrifice and renunciation. Happiness always comes with responsibilities.

To be Christian is to learn to «live well» by following the way Jesus opened up for us. Jesus' blessings are the most meaningful and «scandalous» markers along that way. One walks toward happiness with a pure and transparent heart, hungering and thirsting for justice, working for peace out of heartfelt mercy, bearing the burden of the journey with humility. The way laid out in these blessings helps us to experience, here and now in this earthly life, the same happiness Jesus felt.

8

You are the Salt of the Earth

Jesus told his disciples:

«You are the salt of the earth; but if salt has lost its taste, how can its saltiness be restored? It is no longer good for anything, but is thrown out and trampled under foot».

«You are the light of the world. A city built on a hill cannot be hid. No one after lighting a lamp puts it under the bushel basket, but on the lampstand, and it gives light to all in the house. In the same way, let your light shine before others, so that they may see your good works and give glory to your Father in heaven» (Matthew 5:13-16).

1. IF THE SALT HAS LOST ITS TASTE...

Few writings today have moved believers' hearts as powerfully as a small book by Paul Evdokimov, *The Crazy Love of God.* With burning faith and words of fire, this theologian from St. Petersburg unmasks our routine, self-satisfied brand of Christianity.

He says of the present time: «Christians have done all they can to sterilize the gospel; we might say they have plunged it into a neutralizing solution. Everything that stands out, everything that challenges us or turns our expectations upside down, is turned to mush. By turning it into an inoffensive, smoothed-out, prudent and reasonable religion, they make us want to vomit it up». Where did we get this bland, useless Christianity?

This Russian Orthodox theologian is not criticizing secondary details, but focusing on essentials. The Church does not look to him like «a living organism of the real presence of Christ», but like a static organization and a «self-feeding station». Christians have no sense of mission, and the Christian faith «has strangely lost its fermenting character». The gospel lived by today's Christians «meets nothing but total indifference».

According to Evdokimov, Christians have lost contact with the living God of Jesus Christ and wandered into doctrinal blind alleys. God's truth is confused with dogmatic formulas, which in reality are only «icons» that invite us to open ourselves up to the holy Mystery of God. Christianity is displaced toward the external and the marginal, when God lives in the depths.

So people look for a diminished, comfortable Christianity. In the words of Marcel More, «Christians have found a way, no one knows how, to sit comfortably on the cross». We forget that Christianity «is not a doctrine but a life, an incarnation». And when the life of Jesus no longer shines in the Church, there is no visible difference between the Church and the world. The Church «becomes an exact mirror for the world», which it recognizes as «flesh of its flesh».

People will surely react by softening or deflecting such a strong denunciation, but it is hard to discredit the underlying truth that Evdokimov is pointing to: the Church has lost its holiness, its living faith, its contact with God. It needs saints who are scandalized because they are living «the crazy love of God»; it needs living witnesses to the gospel of Jesus Christ.

The burning pages of the Russian theologian remind us of Jesus' words: «You are the salt of the earth; but if salt has lost its taste, how can its saltiness be restored? It is no longer good for anything, but is thrown out and trampled under foot».

2. WHERE IS THE SALT?

We Christians probably don't notice the touch of wry humor in Jesus' description of his followers. He sees his disciples as men and women who are called to be «the salt of the earth». People who make life salty. «You are the salt of the earth; but if the salt has lost its taste, how can its saltiness be restored?»

Biblical scholars have explored the religious symbolism of salt in the ancient world. It meant something that purifies, adds flavor, preserves and gives life to people's food. The simple folk who listened to Jesus probably grasped the symbolism of salt in all its freshness, and understood that the gospel can add unexpected humor to human life.

The North American theologian Harvey Cox once said that people in the West «have gained the world and lost their soul. They have bought prosperity at the cost of a dizzying impoverishment of its vital elements». Many of us seem threatened by the tedium, the boredom, the meaninglessness of life.

The roots of this phenomenon are complex. It seems that industrial society has made us more productive, methodical, and organized, but also less festive, less in touch with each other, less imaginative. Social analysts say that the traits of festivity, tenderness, fantasy, creativity and sharing «are in a terrible state».

We often search obsessively for ways to have a good time, but we cannot find in ourselves a true source of life. Perhaps we are suffering an «anemia of the inner life», which keeps us from feeling and living day-to-day life intensely, joyfully, and fruitfully.

Where is the believers' salt? Where are the believers who can spread their enthusiasm to everyone else? Hasn't our faith lost its saltiness? We need to rediscover the salty faith that can make everything new: life together and loneliness, joy and sadness, work and play.

3. PUTTING MORE FLAVOR INTO LIFE

One of the Church's most urgent tasks, today and always, is to bring faith to people as «good news».

We tend to see evangelization almost exclusively as a doctrinal task. To evangelize means bringing the doctrine of Jesus Christ to those who don't know about it, or don't know it well enough.

As a result we are concerned with strengthening religious education and the propagation of the faith in comparison with other ideologies and ways of thinking. We want well-prepared men and women, who understand the Christian message perfectly and can transmit it correctly. We work to improve our pastoral skills and organization.

Of course those things are important, because evangelization means proclaiming the message of Jesus Christ. But they are not the only or the most important things. Evangelization means not only proclaiming a doctrine in words, but making present in people's lives the humanizing, liberating, and salvific power that comes from the event and the person of Jesus Christ.

If we see evangelization in this way, what is important is not developing powerful and efficient methods of religious propaganda, but knowing how to act in the liberating style of Jesus.

What counts is not having men and women well-versed in doctrine, but having living witnesses to the gospel. Believers whose lives reveal the humanizing and salvific power that comes from the gospel when it is embraced firmly and responsibly.

We often confuse evangelization with the desire to make «our Christianity» socially acceptable. Jesus' words, calling us to be «the salt of the earth» and «the light of the world» force us to ask some very serious questions.

Are we Christians «good news» for anyone? Is the way we live in our Christian communities, the way believers act, «good news» for people today?

Do we Christians add anything to modern society that gives taste to life, anything that purifies, heals, and liberates it from spiritual decline and from cruel self-centeredness? Do we bring light to people in these days of uncertainty? Do we offer any hope or new horizons to people who are looking for salvation?

4. THE LIGHT OF GOOD WORKS

We humans want to appear more intelligent, more good, more noble than we really are. We spend our lives trying to fool ourselves and everyone else into thinking we are perfect.

Psychologists say that this comes from the desire to affirm ourselves, in our own and other people's eyes, in order to protect ourselves from their possible superiority.

We don't understand the meaning of «good works», so we fill our lives with long-winded debates. We can't set a worthy example for our children, so we spend our days insisting that they do what we don't do.

Our life is not coherent with our Christian faith, so we justify ourselves by criticizing people who have stopped practicing religion. We don't witness to the gospel, so we focus on preaching it to others.

Perhaps we should begin by patiently acknowledging our lack of coherence, and letting others see the truth of our lives. If we have the courage to accept our mediocrity, we will be more open to God's action that can still transform our lives.

Jesus warns us that salt can lose its taste. St. John of the Cross says something similar: «May God protect you from salt that goes stale, that seems to do something on the outside but has no substance; good works can only be done in virtue of God».

To be «salt of the earth», what we need is not activism, agitation, superficial busyness, but «the good works» that are born of love and of the Spirit's action in us.

We need to listen carefully to St. John of the Cross again: «Watch out, therefore, for people who are very active and think they can encompass the world with their preaching and outer works; they would bring much more benefit to the Church and would please God much more... if they spent even half as much time with God in prayer».

Otherwise, said the mystical doctor, «it is all hammering that does very little, or sometimes nothing, and sometimes even causes harm». In the midst of all that activity and agitation, where are our «good works»? Jesus said to his disciples: «let your light shine before others, so that they may see your good works and give glory to your Father».

5. AGAINST CORRUPTION

Day after day the news media are filled with new and scandalous cases of corruption and fraud. These events haven't just suddenly sprung up in our midst; they are the sad result of a contradiction that has accompanied modern democratic society from its beginning.

On the one hand, democratic philosophy proclaims and demands freedom and equality for everyone. But on the other a savage economic pragmatism, seeking to maximize profit, leads to inequality and the exploitation of the weak at the heart of democratic society itself.

This is the primary breeding ground for the corruption we see today. In the words of the Italian writer Claudio Magris, «we live a life of plunder». We still defend the democratic values of freedom, equality, and solidarity for everyone, but the important thing is to make money however we can. The attitude that «anything goes» as long as it's profitable is corrupting people's behavior, undermining institutions, and rendering our solemn proclamations meaningless.

We have confused progress with increasing prosperity for the wealthy. Economic activity, driven by a savage spirit of profit, ends up forgetting that its purpose is to raise the standard of human life for all citizens. Everything is sacrificed to the «god» of economic self-interest: people's right to work and a life of dignity, transparency and honesty in public office, truth and cultural or educational value in television programming.

Is there any «salt» that can preserve us against all that corruption? We ask for investigations and a strict application of justice. We consider new social and political measures. But we can't find people who can heal the society by bringing honesty into it. Men and women who refuse to be corrupted by economic ambition or by the desire for easy success.

«You are the salt of the earth». These words of Jesus have a very specific meaning for his believers today. They are a call to stay free in the face of the idolatry of money, and in the face of material well-being that enslaves, corrupts, and marginalizes people. A call to responsible solidarity in the face of corporate self-interest. An invitation to bring compassion into a heartless society that seems determined to suppress «the civilization of the heart».

9

Love of Enemy

Jesus told his disciples:

«You have heard that it was said, "An eye for an eye and a tooth for a tooth". But I say to you, Do not resist an evildoer. But if anyone strikes you on the right cheek, turn the other also; and if anyone wants to sue you and take your coat, give your cloak as well; and if anyone forces you to go one mile, go also the second mile. Give to everyone who begs from you, and do not refuse anyone who wants to borrow from you».

«You have heard that it was said, "You shall love your neighbor and hate your enemy". But I say to you, Love your enemies and pray for those who persecute you, so that you may be children of your Father in heaven; for he makes his sun rise on the evil and on the good, and sends rain on the righteous and on the unrighteous. For if you love those who love you, what reward do you have? Do not even the tax collectors do the same? And if you greet only your brothers and sisters, what more are you doing than others? Do not even the Gentiles do the same? Be perfect, therefore, as your heavenly Father is perfect» (Matthew 5:38-48).

1. LOVING THE ENEMY

«Love your enemies and pray for those who persecute you». How can today's believers respond to these words of Jesus? Cross them out of the gospel? Erase them from the depths of our conscience? Set them aside until things get better?

The basic human attitude toward «the enemy», that is, the people we expect to harm or threaten us, doesn't change much from one culture to another.

Lysias the Athenian (fifth century B.C.) expressed the prevailing view of the ancient Greeks with a formula that would meet approval in our time: «I consider it an established norm that one must try to harm one's enemies and place oneself at the service of one's friends».

So we must take note of the revolutionary significance of the evangelical mandate to love one's enemy, which biblical scholars consider the most important aspect of the Christian message.

When Jesus speaks of the love of enemies, he is not thinking about affectionate and tender feelings, nor about passionate love, but about a radically human relationship of positive concern for the enemy as a person.

In Jesus' way of thinking, we are human when love is the basis of all our actions. That is true even of our relationship with an enemy. The ultimate sign of our humanity is our recognition and respect for the human dignity of the enemy, no matter how disfigured it appears to us. We do not exclude and condemn our enemies, but take a positive attitude of real concern for their welfare.

This kind of universal love —which is extended to all and truly seeks the welfare of all, without excluding anyone— is the most positive, human contribution that Christians can make in the violent society of our time.

Love of enemy seems almost impossible in situations that call forth righteous indignation in everyone around us. Sometimes even hearing the gospel words can be annoying. But we must hear them if we want to be free of the dehumanization caused by hatred and vindictiveness.

We Christians can and must remember two things in this environment, even if it causes us to be rejected. Loving the unjust and violent wrongdoer does not at all mean condoning his or her unjust and violent behavior. On the other hand, firmly condemning the injustice and cruelty of violence does not necessarily mean hating those who perpetrate it.

2. EVEN THE ENEMY

We are undeniably living in a paradoxical situation. As the Fathers Provincial of the Company of Jesus said in the final document of their General Assembly a few years ago: «The more sensitive we become to trampled rights or violent injustice, the more we feel we have to resort to brutal or heartless violence in order to bring about the deep changes we yearn for».

Resorting to violence seems to be the only way to solve problems. It is not surprising that Jesus' words sound like a naïve and discordant cry in our society: «Love your enemies, pray for those who persecute you».

Yet this is perhaps the word we most need to hear at a time when, in our deep perplexity, we don't know what specific actions will help to eliminate violence from the world.

Someone has said that «if a problem can only be solved by violence, it needs to be looked at in a new way» (F. Hacker). This is precisely where the gospel of Jesus comes in, not to offer a technical solution to the conflict, but to help us find a better way of looking at it.

Jesus is expressing a deep conviction. Evil cannot be overcome by hatred and violence. Evil can only be overcome by good. As Martin Luther King said, «the great defect of violence is that it causes a vicious circle that destroys everything it creates. Instead of reducing evil, it increases it».

Jesus does not say whether violence might be a legitimate response to some specific situations. Rather he invites us to work and struggle to make it unnecessary. For that reason we must always look for paths that lead to brotherhood and not to fratricide.

Love of enemies does not mean tolerating injustice and comfortably withdrawing from the struggle against evil. What Jesus saw clearly is that we cannot struggle against evil by destroying persons. We have to combat evil without seeking the destruction of the adversary.

We must also remember that this call to renounce violence is not only addressed to the weak, who have no access to the power of destructive violence; it is especially for those who have the power, money, or arms to violently oppress the weak and defenseless.

3. NONVIOLENCE

We Christians do not always recognize what Gandhi so joyfully discovered from reading the gospel: Jesus' deep conviction that only nonviolence can save humanity. After meeting Jesus in the gospel, Gandhi wrote: «Reading the whole story of this life… it seems to me that Christianity has yet to be made real… Until we have uprooted the violence of civilization, Christ has not yet been born».

Jesus' whole life was a call to resolve the problems of humanity through nonviolent means. Violence is always destructive; it seeks to solve the problems of life together by wiping out the one we see as an enemy, but instead it only sets off a chain reaction that never ends.

Jesus calls us «to do violence to violence». The real enemy that we should be fighting is not the other person but our own selfish «ego», the one that seeks to destroy whoever opposes it.

It is a mistake to believe that evil can put an end to evil, or injustice to injustice. Total respect for the human being, as Jesus sees it, requires a constant effort to suppress mutual violence; it requires us to promote dialogue and the search for a more just and brotherly life together.

We Christians must ask ourselves why we have not drawn from the gospel all the lessons of Jesus' «nonviolence», and why we have not given it the central place it deserves in the life and preaching of the Church.

It's not enough to denounce terrorism. It's not enough to show our horror and repulsion at every attack on human life. We have to work day by day to build a different society, uprooting «an eye for an eye and a tooth for a tooth» , and cultivating an attitude of reconciliation that is difficult but not impossible to achieve. Jesus' words challenge us and uphold us: «Love your enemies and pray for those who persecute you».

4. WE ARE NOT INNOCENT

«What do you know of salvation, you who have never sinned?» The French writer George Bernanos addressed this challenge to certain Catholics of his time, condemning their pharisaical belief that they were clean and immaculate, with no need for repentance and conversion.

Since the brutal attacks in Madrid we have heard vehement condemnations of terrorism, but almost total silence about our possible role in that event. Apparently what happens in the world is «a tale of good guys and bad guys». We are the good guys, of course. We Christians are more human than the Muslims; the developed countries are more just than the countries that live in misery. It's not true.

Terrorism is certainly a horrible, unjustifiable crime. But it is also a symptom. It isn't the result of a demonic hatred that suddenly takes control of bad people. It is born of despair and fanaticism, of fear and hatred toward the powers that be, of helplessness in the face of those who want to rule over them. All this comes together in irrational ways. But we are not innocent either.

We have turned the world into a «global holocaust». Many millions of people die of hunger every year, and we don't want to be bothered. We are determined to protect our supremacy and power in order to secure our own well-being, and expect there to be peace in the world. We don't need to commit «terrorist acts» to spread hunger and death in other countries. We do it through unjust, self-interested policies.

The tragedy of 3/11 (the Madrid train bombings on March 11, 2004) led to a magnificent cry of solidarity: «We are all *madrileños*», «we were all riding on that train». But the cry needs to be broadened further: «We are all Iraquis, Palestinians, or Rwandans», «we were all floating on that raft».

We would see things differently if we lived as sons and daughters of a good Father who «makes his sun rise on the evil and on the good, and sends rain on the righteous and on the unrighteous».

The best way to show Christian love is not by the outward expression of feelings, but by acts of concern for the other person's well-being. In general, humble service to people in need is a better way to express love than many words of sympathy.

But sometimes we insist so much on charity as a deliberate effort, that we forget that it is also an expression of love. Christian love comes from deep inside a person, but it also inspires feelings and is expressed in cordial affection.

Matthew 5:38-48

To love one's neighbors means doing good to them, but it also means accepting, respecting, valuing what is lovable in them, letting them feel our acceptance and love. Christian charity leads to a friendly attitude of sympathy, solicitousness and affection, which can overcome hostility, indifference or rejection.

Of course everyone's personal way of loving is conditioned by his or her individual sensitivity, tenderness, or ability to communicate. But Christian love does encourage cordiality, sincere affection, and friendship toward other people.

This friendliness is not just the outer courtesy of good manners, or the spontaneous good feelings that come from contact with likable people, but the sincere attitude of people enlivened by Christian love.

Perhaps we don't give enough importance today to cultivating this friendliness in our family, our workplace, and all our relationships. Friendliness helps people to feel better, eases tensions and conflicts, brings opposing positions together, strengthens friendship, increases brotherly and sisterly relations.

Friendliness helps to free us from feelings of indifference and rejection, because it works directly against our tendency to dominate, manipulate, or hurt our neighbor. By communicating good feelings in a healthy, generous way, we can make the world around us more human and hospitable.

Jesus insists on spreading friendliness not only to our friends and other likable people, but also to those who reject us. We recall the words that reveal his way: «If you greet only your brothers and sisters, what more are you doing than others?»

10

God or Wealth

Jesus said to his disciples:

«No one can serve two masters; for a slave will either hate the one and love the other, or be devoted to the one and despise the other. You cannot serve God and wealth».

«Therefore I tell you, do not worry about your life, what you will eat or what you will drink, or about your body, what you will wear. Is not life more than food, and the body more than clothing? Look at the birds of the air; they neither sow nor reap nor gather into barns, and yet your heavenly Father feeds them. Are you not of more value than they? And can any of you by worrying add a single hour to your span of life? And why do you worry about clothing? Consider the lilies of the field, how they grow; they neither toil nor spin, yet I tell you, even Solomon in all his glory was not clothed like one of these. But if God so clothes the grass of the field, which is alive today and tomorrow is thrown into the oven, will he not much more clothe you —you of little faith? Therefore do not worry, saying, "What will we eat?" or "What will we drink?" or "What will we wear?" For it is the Gentiles who strive for all these things; and indeed your heavenly Father knows that you need all these things. But strive first for the kingdom of God and his righteousness, and all these things will be given to you as well».

«So do not worry about tomorrow, for tomorrow will bring worries of its own. Today's trouble is enough for today» (Matthew 6:24-34).

1. GOD OR WEALTH

One of Jesus' strongest and most scandalous warnings is quoted by Matthew in these words: «You cannot serve God and wealth».

There is a devastating logic in Jesus' thinking. God cannot reign among us except by being concerned with everyone, and doing justice to the people who never receive justice from anyone else. In other words, we can only serve God by promoting solidarity and brotherhood.

That means that the rich and privileged are called to share their goods with people in need. The Father, who loves all his sons and daughters, cannot be served by people who serve wealth and forget about their brothers and sisters.

That is precisely why throughout his life, Jesus sharply condemns those who collect and possess more than they need in order to live, without being concerned about the people in need around them. As long as there are poor and needy people, all the wealth that people needlessly collect for themselves is «unjust», because they are keeping it away from others who need it.

In the last analysis, the wealth of a few can only be maintained and increased at the cost of poverty for others. Thus everyone who focuses on increasing their own capital without concern for people in need, is preventing the birth of the brotherly society that God wills. Either we serve the God who wants all his children to be brothers and sisters, or we are serving our own economic interests.

It does no good to say that we are spiritually detached from the goods we so comfortably enjoy without caring about other people. People who are truly «poor in spirit» and inwardly detached, will seek ways to share what they have in order to liberate the needy from their dehumanizing poverty.

It also does no good to think of everyone else as «the rich». Many of us are relatively rich; the rich are those who have more than they need, while others do not have the basic necessities of life.

Something is missing in our Christian life when we can go on thoughtlessly enjoying our material goods, without ever feeling challenged by Jesus' words and by the needs of the poor.

2. THE GOLDEN CALF

We who live in the so-called «free nations» of the West are more enslaved than ever by a «heartless capitalism», which seeks to protect the relative well-being of one billion people but unhesitatingly condemns to misery the other six billion inhabitants of the earth.

The statistics show that in the rich countries, the economic «pie» is gradually but inexorably being divided among fewer people. The Europe that a few years ago «graciously welcomed» foreign workers for jobs that no one else wanted, today is passing «immigration laws» that raise insuperable barriers for the people whose hunger we have helped to create in the world.

Does it matter to anyone in Europe that two continents —Africa and Latin America— now have a lower standard of living than they had ten years ago? Does anyone in Europe—where racist exclusion is increasing, sometimes overtly but usually under a thousand different disguises— care about the fourteen million who die of hunger every year?

We're getting used to watching, from the comfort of our sofas, the expulsion of those sick, hungry and desperate Albanians who arrive in the ports of Italy.

No one is particularly concerned by the spectacle of the Africans who attempt the «impossible crossing» by raft but end up sinking in the ocean.

The Church cannot proclaim the gospel in Europe today without unmasking all that inhumanity, and without raising the questions that no onewants to hear.

Why are so many people dying of hunger, if God put in our hands an earth with enough resources for everyone?

Why do we have to be competitive rather than human? Why are relations among people and nations governed by competitiveness, rather than solidarity?

Why do we accept as logical and inevitable, an economic system that claims to improve the well-being of all by plunging so many victims into poverty and marginalization?

Why do we give credence to consumerism as a «philosophy of life», when it creates a vicious circle of artificial needs that empties our life of spirit and humanitarian sensitivity?

Why do we go on worshiping wealth as the only god that can give us security, power and happiness? Can this be the «new religion» that will lead today's people toward higher levels of humanity?

These are not questions for other people to answer. Each of us must hear them in our conscience, echoing the words of Jesus: «You cannot serve God and Wealth».

3. MAKING MONEY

Few of us are aware of the human damage caused by some of the principles and standards that are considered «indisputable values» in today's economy. Luis González-Carvajal calls them «the demons of the economy» that are on the loose among us.

Perhaps the first is *productivity*. For many years, human beings had enough common sense to work only as much as they needed in order to live a satisfying life. Modern capitalism, in contrast, has raised labor to the status of «the meaning of life». Benjamin Franklin is said to have coined the phrase, «time is money». If we don't use our time profitably, we are wasting our life.

This drive for productivity has certainly contributed to material progress for human beings, but an increasing number of them are being harmed by overwork. More wealth is created, but are we any happier? Meanwhile we no longer enjoy activities that are not counted as productive. What do we gain by contemplating beauty? What good does it do to cultivate friendship, or poetry? What usefulness is there in prayer?

The second demon would be the *obsessive accumulation of wealth.* We all know that money started out as an intelligent way to measure value and thus to facilitate the exchange of goods. But today, «making money» has become a duty. It is hard to «be somebody» unless we have economic power.

Competition is closely related to accumulation. Getting ahead of everyone else is the decisive issue for many people. Certainly a «healthy dose» of competitiveness can be beneficial, but when a society is motivated almost entirely by rivalry, its members risk becoming dehumanized; life becomes a race where the important thing is to be more successful than anyone else.

Some years ago the philosopher Emmanuel Mounier described the Western bourgeoisie this way: «A kind of person totally devoid of mystery, devoid of the meaning of existence and the meaning of love, devoid of suffering and joy, devoted to happiness and security; with a veneer of courtesy, good humor and human virtue; underneath, squeezed in between a lethargic reading of the newspaper, the defense of their career or the boredom of Sundays, and an obsession with arithmetic». To Jesus, life was more than that. His words invite us to live in a different horizon: «You cannot serve God and wealth... Do not worry about your life, what you will eat, or for the body, what you will wear... Strive first for the kingdom of God and his righteousness, and all these things will be given to you as well».

4. A «NEW RELIGION»

Consumerism penetrates our lives in subtle ways. No one chooses this way of life as the result of a reflection process. We sink into it slowly, victims of an almost unconscious seduction. Clever advertising and attractive styles softly capture our will. In the end it seems impossible to live any other way.

We know what is right without thinking very much about it. Most people have a simple goal for their lives: to work for the money we need in order to enjoy times of leisure (a weekend, a vacation), in which we spend what we have earned and renew our strength to go back to work.

But consumerism has become the «new religion» of modern men and women. Now our ultimate goal (the dogma of the new religion) is possession and enjoyment. To that end we have to work and earn money (its ethics and virtues). We faithfully attend to the weekend ritual of shopping. Our devotion becomes especially intense around the great feasts of Christmas, Three Kings Day, holidays, weddings, Mother's Day, Father's Day, etc.

It is hard to free ourselves from the slavery of consumerism. As Erich Fromm said, «men and women don't need chains to be slaves». Consumerism simply trades our outer chains for inner chains. Inwardly we are chained to endless whims and false illusions. These inner chains are stronger than the outwardly visible ones. How can we free ourselves from that slavery if we think we are already free?

Our life doesn't make sense. The common afflictions of obesity and anorexia offer a graphic image of our growing spiritual lethargy and loss of vitality. We have everything but inner peace and joy. We want to succeed in life, but we are the accomplices of other people's misery and hunger.

Surrounded by a culture of the good life, we worry about choosing the restaurant where we will eat, the quality of the wine we will drink, or the label on our clothes. Jesus had his own view on that. What you will eat, what you will drink, what you will wear are important, he said. But don't let them become an obsession: «strive first for the kingdom of God and his righteousness, and all these things will be given to you as well».

5. NOT ONLY IN EUROPE

People in extreme suffering often lose their voice. Oppression leaves them without words. They lose the ability to cry out in protest, or to speak in their own defense. Their cries become wails. That is the case today, around the world, with millions of exploited child laborers, and women whose dignity is abused and humiliated in a thousand ways. It is the case of the countries consumed by hunger and misery.

We don't hear their voice on the radio or television. We don't see them in advertisements. They aren't interviewed in the fashion magazines, or invited to speak at international conferences. The wail of the last and the least can only be heard in the depth of our conscience.

It's not easy to hear them. First we must want to hear them: we must notice their suffering and powerlessness, become aware of the injustice and abuse that prevail in the world. We must also stop listening to those other voices that invite us to think only of our own well-being; we must stop paying attention to the voices telling us to close ourselves off in our own little world, indifferent to their pain and destruction.

But above all we must take the risk of hearing them. If we really hear the voice of the suffering, we won't be able to live any way we want. We'll have to do something. We'll have to think about how «the rich» can share more of what we have, more effectively; we'll have to participate in development projects, support campaigns on behalf of earth's poorest peoples.

Our Church must not let the intensity of the current economic crisis stop us from building solidarity with the peoples whose poverty we ourselves have created. We must not look only at Europe. The Spirit of Christ is challenging us in the voice of the poor and hungry around the world.

Nothing is more important in the life of a true disciple, or in the mission of a Church faithful to its Lord, than striving for dignity and happiness for everyone. As Jesus said: «strive first for the kingdom of God and his righteousness, and all these things will be given to you as well».

11

Building on Rock

Jesus said to his disciples:

«Not everyone who says to me, "Lord, Lord", will enter the kingdom of heaven, but only the one who does the will of my Father in heaven. On that day many will say to me, "Lord, Lord, did we not prophesy in your name, and cast out demons in your name, and do many deeds of power in your name?" Then I will declare to them, "I never knew you; go away from me, you evildoers"».

«Everyone then who hears these words of mine and acts on them will be like a wise man who built his house on rock. The rain fell, the floods came, and the winds blew and beat on that house, but it did not fall, because it had been founded on rock. And everyone who hears these words of mine and does not act on them will be like a foolish man who built his house on sand. The rain fell, and the floods came, and the winds blew and beat against that house, and it fell —and great was its fall!» (Matthew 7:21-27)

1. HOW ARE WE BUILDING?

The first Christians attributed transcendental importance to Jesus' «words». Heaven and earth would pass away; the words of Jesus never would. The Galileans had seen how powerfully a word from him could free them from illness, suffering, sin, or fear. Later the Christian communities saw it bringing truth into their lives, «resurrecting them» from within, and filling them with life and peace.

That is why Matthew gives us this parable, which emphasizes something important for Christians to remember: to be Christian means putting Jesus' words into «practice», «making real» his gospel. If we don't, our Christianity is «foolish». It doesn't make sense.

The parable is short, symmetrical, and rhythmical. It was probably written down in that form for use in catechetical instruction. Everyone needs to learn that this is the first concern of the Christian community: to «hear» and «act on» the words spoken by Jesus. That is the only way to build a Church of Jesus' followers, and to build a better world.

The wise man doesn't build his house any old way. The important thing is to build on a layer of firm rock. The foolish man doesn't think about what he is doing: he builds on sand, down in the valley. When the rainy season brings floods and rain, the house built on rock stands firm; but «great is the fall» of the one built on sand.

The parable is a sharp warning. It forces Christians to ask whether we are building the Church of Jesus on rock, hearing and acting on his words —or building on shifting sands that have neither the solidity nor the assurance of the gospel.

The current crisis is uncovering the truth or falsehood of our Christian life. Here we need more than sociological analyses. Hasn't the time come to undertake an examination of conscience, at every level of our communities and the Church, to challenge false certainties and face up to our lack of evangelical vigor? It's not enough confess Jesus, saying «Lord, Lord», if we are not doing the Father's will.

2. CHECKING THE FOUNDATIONS OF THE CHURCH

Perhaps now is the right time to listen to this parable with which Jesus ends the Sermon on the Mount.

Two men are building their houses. They both seem to be doing the same thing. Both are committed to a beautiful and lasting project: building a house. But they're not doing it in the same way. When the storm comes, we see that one has built on a layer of rock, while the other was building on sand.

Jesus' teaching is clear. We cannot build something lasting, just any old way. Only those who hear Jesus' words and act on them are building on rock.

The crisis that Christians are now experiencing has deep sociological and cultural roots, but it requires us to check our foundations and ask on what basis we are building our Christian life.

Perhaps our Christianity is not built on the solid foundation of the gospel, but on customs, styles and traditions that do not always fit with the spirit of Jesus.

We have tried to support our religion with secure formulas and strict discipline, but perhaps we have not taken the trouble to dig into the truth of the gospel.

We have sometimes paid too much attention to codes of behavior, rubrics, norms, and slogans, and have not learned to shoulder our own responsibility and the risks of Christian freedom.

We are used to receiving the sacraments as a sure and simple way to obtain grace and salvation. Although we have fulfilled our «religious obligations», perhaps we have not been sufficiently concerned with making the sacrament a real expression of sincere repentance and conversion.

This time of crisis may also be a moment of grace and conversion, «the moment of fundamental testing» (P. A. Liege). The point is not to reduce Christianity to the «necessary minimum» to maintain our existence, but to reawaken our faith with the gospel spirit.

In the midst of so much uncertainty, debate and division, today as always we need to bring ourselves back to the truth of the gospel. The time has come to ask ourselves, realistically and honestly, on what foundations we are building the life of our Christian communities. It's not enough to go on saying to Jesus, «Lord, Lord». We need to listen together to his Word, and encourage one another to put it in practice.

3. ACTING ON THE GOSPEL TODAY

There are many ways to live in the present moment. Some of us focus on condemning the public corruption that seems to go on and on. Others are constantly wailing over an economic crisis that seems to have no easy solutions. Most people just want to enjoy life as long as we can. But there are healthier ways to respond. Where should we look for them?

One way is the defense of persons, against a pragmatism that reduces everything to self-interested calculations. The human person is more important than anything else, and should never be sacrificed to anything or anyone.

Another way is solidarity and concern for the victims, against an exaggerated individualism that goes by the rule «everyone for himself». Nobody should be left to their own fate, excluded from our solidary concern.

Dialogue and reconciliation must be upheld in the face of violence and destructive confrontation. We cannot build the future together except by means of mutual respect, tolerance, and a search for common ground.

Compassion must be fostered instead of the apathy and social insensitivity that turn our attention away from the victims of economic development. We are only truly human when we can see life from the viewpoint of those who have been excluded from well-being.

Tenderness and mercy must take the place of a social system that is based on efficiency and productivity, with no thought for the needs of the human heart. There are more and more persons who need affection, tenderness, and accompaniment in order not to fall into despair.

We need to stay alert, in the face of a naïve permissiveness that proclaims «freedom» and then falls into the new slavery of wealth, sex, or fashion. Only those who live out of inner freedom and generous love, can enjoy life with a liberated heart.

We need faith in a God who is the Friend of human beings, to protect us from disillusionment and the loss of hope. Without God, human life becomes a question with no answers, an impossible goal, a road to nowhere. We need a more positive, confident way of seeing things. It does us good to believe in the «God of hope».

These are clear ways to hear Jesus' call to us today, to build our life on the «rock» of the gospel.

4. THE GOSPELS OF JESUS

When the first Christians discovered that God had raised up Jesus —thus overruling the people who condemned him— they realized that God was confirming something unique in Jesus' life and message.

What happened next was also unique in world literature. The disciples began to collect the words they had heard Jesus speak in his earthly life, not in the way people collect the works of a dead teacher, but as the words of someone who is alive and still speaking to those who believe in him. That was the beginning of a new literary genre: the gospels.

The gospels were read in the early Christian communities, not as words Jesus had spoken in the past, but as words that the risen Lord is speaking to his followers in every age. Christians hear them as words of «spirit and life», words that make us truly alive, «words of eternal life».

For this reason, Christians can never confuse the gospel with any other written work. When we read Jesus' words, we aren't just reading a book but listening to Jesus, who speaks to our hearts. The Second Vatican Council was trying to reawaken this faith of the first Christians, when it solemnly proclaimed that «Christ is present in the Word, because it is he who speaks when it is read in the Sacred Scriptures».

When believers open the gospels, we are not reading the biography of a dead person. We don't come to Jesus as someone from the past. His life did not end with his death. His words were not forever silenced. Jesus lives. Those who read the gospel with faith, hear him in the depth of their hearts. They will never be alone.

It is the same Jesus who invites us to build our life on his words: «Everyone who hears these words of mine and acts on them will be like a wise man who built his house on rock».

5. HEARING THE WORD OF GOD

Many people have a copy of the Bible in their homes, but few open and read it on a regular basis. We have different reasons: We don't have time. We haven't learned to read it the right way. We don't know where to start. That's not where we go to nourish our Christian life.

But reading the Bible in person is one of the best ways to «hear Jesus' words and act on them». Vatican II invites us to read it regularly, by quoting the words of St. Jerome: «Not to know the Scriptures is not to know Christ».

What can a Christian do, who hasn't learned the right way but still wants to read the Bible? How do we learn to hear God in the Scriptures? Here are some practical guidelines. We can:

Set aside fifteen minutes every day for reading and reflecting on the Bible, calmly and with tranquility.

Begin with a period of silence, to move away from today's distractions and worries, and think about what we are doing: «I'm not going to read just any book; I'm going to listen to God, who is trying to tell me something».

Before we start reading a passage, it helps to know which book of the Bible we are going to read; who wrote it, and for what purpose. Most Bibles have a brief but informative introduction at the beginning of each book.

While we are reading, it is good to look at the footnotes at the bottom of the page; they can sometimes explain words and phrases that are new to us.

We must read slowly, much more slowly than usual, in order to grasp the meaning of the words. We shouldn't be in any hurry to finish a passage or a chapter.

We can pass over confusing or hard to interpret phrases, and spend time on what we do understand. One day we will understand the hard parts more clearly.

It is good to follow a plan for reading the Bible. The best way is to start with the gospels in this order: Luke, Mark, Matthew, and John; then the Acts of the Apostles, the letters of John, the shorter letters of the apostle Paul. Another good way is to read during the week, the passages that will be read at the eucharistic service the next Sunday.

After reading a short passage we can ask ourselves: What is God showing me in these words? What aspect of my life do they shed light on? What is God inviting me to do in this passage? What commitment does it require? How is God awakening trust in me through this passage? What hope do I find in it?

12

A Friend of Sinners

As Jesus was walking along, he saw a man called Matthew sitting at the tax booth; and he said to him, «Follow me». And he got up and followed him.

And as he sat at dinner in the house, many tax collectors and sinners came and were sitting with him and the disciples. When the Pharisees saw them, they said to his disciples, «Why does your teacher eat with tax collectors and sinners?» But when he heard this, he said, «Those who are well have no need of a physician, but those who are sick. Go and learn what this means, "I desire mercy, not sacrifice". For I have come to call not the righteous but sinners» (Matthew 9:9-13).

1. MERCY ABOVE ALL

It is an unusual scene. To the most religious sectors of Israel, it is a scandal. Jesus is at Matthew's house, sitting around the table with his friends. But they are not alone. «Many tax collectors and sinners» have come to the banquet and are «sitting with him and the disciples». The story says there are many of them. They are all sitting at the table, mixed in with his disciples.

The most religious sectors immediately start pointing fingers. Why is Jesus acting so scandalously? They look down on the «sinners» as undesirables, the cause of the chosen people's suffering. Everyone who does not live according to the Covenant should be kept out. How can a man of God receive them in such a friendly way?

Jesus pays no attention to their criticism. They are all invited to his table, because God is the God of them all, including those who have been kept out by religion. These meals symbolize the great plan of a God who offers salvation to everyone: the Father's mercy cannot be meted out or explained away by the men of religion.

Jesus replies to the accusations by showing the deep roots of his action. In the first place he has a different way of seeing those who, for different reasons, do not live by the high moral standards of those who follow the prescribed rules. He sees them as «sick». They are victims rather than culprits, more in need of help than of condemnation. That is how Jesus sees them.

In the second place, he has a different way of relating to them. «Those who are well have no need of a physician, but those who are sick». What they need most is not a teacher of the law who will judge them, but a doctor and friend who will help them be healed. That is how Jesus sees himself: not as a judge handing down a sentence, but as a doctor who comes to seek and to save those who are «lost».

This is not just the cheerful behavior of a good prophet. Here Jesus is revealing who God is. This is why he says, stop the accusations and «learn» from my example the meaning of Hosea's words: God wants mercy rather than cultic sacrifice.

Unless we learn from Jesus that mercy is always God's first concern, then we are missing something essential for discipleship. A Church without mercy is a Church that is not following in Jesus' footsteps.

2. WILL WE EVER BE CALLED FRIENDS OF SINNERS?

There is no doubt about it. Jesus' most scandalous behavior was his friendship with sinners and undesirables. Nothing like this had ever happened in Israel. What Jesus did was unheard of. No one had ever seen a prophet living with sinners in that kind of intimacy and friendship.

How can a man of God accept them as friends? How dare he eat with them, instead of keeping them at a proper distance? One doesn't eat with just anyone. We eat with our own kind. We have to protect our identity and holiness by not mixing with sinners. This was the accepted norm in any pious group that considered itself holy.

Jesus, in contrast, is sitting down to eat with just anyone. That is his identity: he doesn't exclude anyone. His table is open to all. You don't have to be holy. You don't have to be an honest woman to sit beside him. You don't have to show proof of repentance. Jesus doesn't care about having a holy table, just a welcoming one.

He is guided by his experience of God. No one can tell him otherwise: God does not discriminate against anyone. They called him «a friend of sinners», and he never denied it, because God also is a friend of sinners and undesirables. For him these meals are like a healing process: «Those who are well have no need of a physician, but those who are sick».

It is true. Those tax collectors and prostitutes don't see him as a teacher of morality; they feel him as a friend who is healing them inside. For the first time they are sitting beside a man of God. Jesus breaks down all the discrimination. Little by little, dignity grows inside them, and with it a new trust in God. Next to Jesus, anything is possible. They can even begin to change.

Where is anything like that happening in our Church? We say over and over that the Church is holy, as if we were afraid no one would notice. Will they ever call us «friends of sinners»? Separated couples who cannot be faithful to each other, youth destroyed by drugs, criminals whom everyone hates, slaves of prostitution—will they see us as a welcoming Church?

3. WHAT WOULD THE CHURCH BE WITHOUT COMPASSION?

God aches with human suffering. That is why his first reaction to human beings is compassion. God doesn't want to see anyone suffer. Neither does Jesus. His first concern is to eliminate or alleviate suffering. If he grieves over sin it is because sin causes suffering, or allows the suffering to continue.

That is why compassion is not just another virtue. It is the only way to become like God, the only way to be and act like Jesus. The first thing Jesus asks of his followers is: «Be compassionate, as your Father is compassionate».

Compassion, therefore, should be the attitude that most inspires and shapes the action of the Church. If what we do as Church is not born of compassionate love, it will almost always be irrelevant or even dangerous, because it disfigures the very face of God.

It is not always easy for the Church, or any institution, to respond with compassion. It is even harder to maintain the primacy of compassion. It takes real effort to stand in the place of real people who suffer. It is hard for the so-called «institutional» church, and also for the so-called «progressive» Church.

But what is a Church without compassion? Who would listen to it? How can its message find an echo in anyone's heart? Certainly our society needs moral guidelines and orienting principles, but real people need to be understood with all their problems, suffering, and contradictions. Words without compassion are hard for anyone to accept.

It's not just about Christians doing «works of mercy», but about the whole Church becoming a sign of God's compassionate mercy and love for today's men and women. This «sick» society urgently needs a word of criticism and encouragement. That is what the Church can communicate in the gospel. But such a word must come from a Church that is accessible and compassionate—never permissive; a Church that visibly suffers with people's physical, moral and spiritual injuries. As Jesus said: «Those who are well have no need of a physician, but those who are sick».

4. GOD IS FOR SINNERS

Many people don't like to hear talk about God. They can't think about God without feeling their own unworthiness and sin. For these people God is the demanding one, who constantly and implacably rebukes us for the way we live. A God who reminds us of our insignificance and mediocrity. Someone who is always waiting for our confession of guilt. We cannot get close to such a God without first feeling ashamed.

Naturally we want to stay away from this God, because we want to protect ourselves from such an uncomfortable experience. No one wants to be humiliated, always accused of something. Better to keep that God out of sight and out of mind.

Those people don't know that this is not the God revealed in Jesus Christ, but a false projection of the «superego» that Sigmund Freud made famous, the «eye forever open inside us» that unblinkingly monitors all our acts, reminds us of what we should be, and reproves our transgressions.

Psychoanalysis has taught us a lot about guilt. Guilty feelings can contribute to growth and maturity, but they can also be repressive and destructive. To acknowledge our guilt and be transformed is a sign of maturity; to close ourselves off in remorse and unforgiving self-condemnation is destructive. Religion can either help people cope with guilt in healthy and liberating ways, or reinforce its pathological deviations.

It's not enough to believe in God. The important thing is to know which God we believe in. God should not be confused with the unblinking eye of conscience. The God incarnate in Jesus is radically merciful. We don't have to feel ashamed in order to meet that God.

Today we know that feelings of guilt often come from a deep fear of being abandoned or rejected by the person we need most in order to live. We can accept our guilt with confidence in the presence of the God of Love. When believers commit themselves to that bottomless love, our feelings of sinfulness do not move us away from but closer to God.

Before God we should not feel accused, but restored to peace and invited into transformation. Remember the words of Jesus: «Those who are well have no need of a physician, but those who are sick... I have come to call not the righteous but sinners».

Many people today «pass by» God and take a position of total indifference to any religious calling. They closed their ears long ago against any invitation to grace.

Some men and women have kept alive the memory of God. A forgotten God perhaps, stuck off in a corner somewhere, but not completely absent from their conscience.

Many, however, are not at peace with that memory. God immediately reminds them of their dark lives, impoverished by selfishness, mediocrity, and the superficial search for pleasure. They are believers who feel a need for God, but who are afraid to come near him with their sinful conscience.

We are all tempted to think of sin as something that keeps God away from us. Very few believe in a God who comes near precisely when he sees us lost and in need of peace and forgiveness. We believe in a God who looks favorably on those who live faithful lives, but whose face grows dark in the presence of sinners.

We often turn God into a caricature of ourselves. We imagine him as petty and mean, just like us. Someone who only loves those who love him, and rejects those who go against him. It's hard to believe in a God who is big enough to love us unconditionally, not because we deserve it but because we need it.

We need to be constantly reminded of Jesus' words and actions: «Those who are well have no need of a physician, but those who are sick. I have come to call not the righteous but sinners». It is a terrible mistake to feel we have to hide our sin, calm our conscience, or justify our life, in order to come before God with a sense of dignity.

As grave as our sin may be, it can never block us from humbly approaching God. On the contrary, we are almost never so close to God as when we recognize our sin and thankfully accept God's forgiveness and renewing power.

Precisely in our sin we can always come close to the God of Jesus Christ who forgives us, calls us, and invites us to a better, more worthy, and happier life.

13

A Healing Mission

When he saw the crowds, he had compassion for them, because they were harassed and helpless, like sheep without a shepherd. Then he said to his disciples, «The harvest is plentiful, but the laborers are few; therefore ask the Lord of the harvest to send out laborers into his harvest».

Then Jesus summoned his twelve disciples and gave them authority over unclean spirits, to cast them out, and to cure every disease and every sickness. These are the names of the twelve apostles: first, Simon, also known as Peter, and his brother Andrew; James son of Zebedee, and his brother John; Philip and Bartholomew; Thomas and Matthew the tax collector; James son of Alphaeus, and Thaddaeus; Simon the Cananaean, and Judas Iscariot, the one who betrayed him.

These twelve Jesus sent out with the following instructions: «Go nowhere among the Gentiles, and enter no town of the Samaritans, but go rather to the lost sheep of the house of Israel. As you go, proclaim the good news, "The kingdom of heaven has come near". Cure the sick, raise the dead, cleanse the lepers, cast out demons. You received without payment; give without payment» (Matthew 9:36-10:8).

1. AUTHORITY TO HEAL LIFE

Jesus is always aware of the people in need around him. He looks at the paralyzed man in Capernaum, the two blind men in Jericho, or the woman bent over by disease, and his heart is moved. He cannot pass by without doing something to alleviate their suffering.

The gospels also show his response to «the crowds». He saw people hungry, or afflicted by all kinds of illness and pain, and the same thing always happened: he felt compassion.

One thing caused him a special kind of pain. According to Matthew, «when he saw the crowds, he had compassion for them, because they were harassed and helpless, like sheep without a shepherd». Neither the representatives of the Roman empire nor the religious leaders of Jerusalem cared about the people of the villages.

Jesus' compassion is not a momentary feeling. It is his way of looking at people, and his way of caring for them. It is his way of incarnating God's mercy. His decision to call the «twelve apostles» and send them out to the «lost sheep of Israel» is born of that compassion.

Jesus himself gives them «authority», but that is not a sacred power to be used as they please. It is not the kind of authority that the Romans have, to «rule the nations with their power». It is the authority to do good, «casting out demons» and «curing every disease and every sickness».

The Church's authority stems from and is based on Jesus' compassion for the people. It is focused on healing, alleviating suffering, and doing good. It is a gift of Jesus. Those who wield authority must do these things «without payment», because the Church is Jesus' gift to the people.

The disciples are instructed to preach what Jesus preached, and nothing else: «The kingdom of heaven has come near». He wants people to hear that news and enter into God's plan. But they must deliver the message by bringing health, life, and freedom from evil. Jesus' four instructions make that clear: «Cure the sick, raise the dead, cleanse the lepers, cast out demons».

2. BRINGING LIFE INTO TODAY'S WORLD

The reign of God is not only a salvation that begins after death. It is a welling-up of grace and life in our present existence. And it is more than that. The current of life that is already flowing on earth is the clearest sign that the kingdom is near. «As you go, proclaim the good news, 'The kingdom of heaven has come near.' Cure the sick, raise the dead, cleanse the lepers, cast out demons». Today more than ever, believers need to hear Jesus' invitation to bring new life into today's world.

A troubling gap is opening up today between our increasing technical progress and our spiritual development. We might say that people lack the spiritual energy to enliven and give meaning to this endless progress. The results are obvious. Many people are impoverished by their wealth and by the things they believe they possess. World-weariness and boredom are taking over our lives. An «inner contamination» is polluting the best in many people's lives. Many men and women are lost, unable to find meaning in their lives. Some are always running around, flooded by an intense, nervous activity, but inwardly empty, not knowing exactly what they want.

Are these men and women not «sick» and in need of curing, «dead» and in need of resurrection, «possessed» and in need of liberation from all the demons that keep them from living as human beings? There are people who in the last analysis, want to come back to life. They want to be cured and resurrected. They want to laugh and enjoy life again, to wake up every day with joy.

There is only one way: to learn to love. To relearn the things that love requires, which are not in fashion today: simplicity, acceptance, friendship, solidarity, generous attentiveness to others, faithfulness. There is still not enough love in our world. We need someone to awaken it. Men and women today will not find salvation or comfort in electronic appliances, but in love. If we have the ability to love, we need to spread it around. It was given to us as a free gift, and we must pass it on as a free gift to everyone we meet along the way.

3. A LIBERATING PROGRAM

Many people think they are responsibly living their faith by fulfilling certain religious practices, and by trying to adjust their behavior to certain moral laws and ecclesiastical norms.

In the same way, many Christian communities think they are faithfully carrying out their mission by zealously offering catechesis and religious education, and by celebrating Christian worship in the proper way.

Is this all that Jesus wanted to set in motion when he sent his disciples out into the world? Is this the life that he hoped to infuse in the heart of human history?

We need to hear Jesus' words again, in order to rediscover the real mission of believers in this world. Matthew summarized it this way: «As you go, proclaim the good news, "The kingdom of heaven has come near". Cure the sick, raise the dead, cleanse the lepers, cast out demons. You received without payment; give without payment».

Today as always, our first task is to proclaim that God is near, working tirelessly to save human beings for happiness. But we cannot proclaim God's salvation simply through speeches and appealing words. Catechesis and religious education classes are not enough. Jesus reminds us of his way of proclaiming God: by working without payment to bring new life to women and men.

«Cure the sick»: liberate people from everything that diminishes their life and causes them suffering. Heal the body and soul of those who feel destroyed by pain and torn apart by the terrible hardships of everyday life.

«Raise the dead»: liberate people from whatever obstructs their life and kills their hope. Reawaken the love for life, the trust in God, the will to struggle and the desire for freedom in all the men and women in whom life is dying out, little by little.

«Cleanse the lepers»: cleanse our society of lies, hypocrisy, and conformism. Help people to live with greater truth, simplicity, and integrity.

«Cast out demons»: liberate people from the idols that enslave us, possess us, and pervert our life together. Wherever people are being liberated, God is being proclaimed.

4. SEEING PEOPLE AS JESUS SAW THEM

How we look at people was very important to Jesus. That is what shapes the way we act. Matthew has preserved this saying from Jesus: «The eye is the lamp of the body. So, if your eye is healthy, your whole body will be full of light; but if your eye is unhealthy, your whole body will be full of darkness» (Matthew 6:22-23). Seeing clearly lets the light come inside us, and enables us to act intelligently.

How did Jesus look at people? The gospel writers tell us again and again that he had a different way of seeing. He didn't look at people as the radical Pharisees did, seeing only impiety, ignorance of the law, and religious indifference. Neither did he look at them as John the Baptist did, seeing only sin, corruption, and ignorance of the imminent arrival of God.

Jesus saw people with eyes of tenderness, respect, and love. «When he saw the crowds, he had compassion for them, because they were harassed and helpless, like sheep without a shepherd». It hurt him to see them lost and leaderless. It caused him pain to see so many people abandoned, lonely, weary, and abused by life.

These people were victims more than sinners. They didn't need more condemnation; they needed a healthier life. So he started a new and unique movement. He called his disciples and gave them authority, not to condemn but to «cure every disease and every sickness».

The Church will change when we begin to look at people as Jesus did. When we see them more as victims than as sinners, when we look more closely at their suffering than at their sin, when we see them with eyes of mercy rather than fear.

Jesus did not «authorize» us to condemn people, but to cure them. He does not call us to judge the world, but to heal life. He never intended to start a movement to combat, condemn, and defeat his enemies. He wanted his disciples to look at the world with tenderness. He wanted to see them committed to alleviating suffering and bringing hope. That is his gift to us.

5. REMEMBERING THOSE WHO SUFFER

A few years ago I spent Christmas in Rwanda. As I flew from Kigali to Brussels on the way home, my mind was filled with one thought. Behind me were all the horror, misery, and death I'd seen in the people of the Great Lakes region of

Africa. Ahead, in Europe, was a society obsessed with its own well-being. What a difference a few hours in the airplane makes, from those people who are dying while we live in detachment from everything but our own self-interest! How can we go on living in a world that «works» that way? I can only think of one reason: our incredible lack of awareness.

After that I reread some pages from Johann-Baptist Metz, the great theologian who has been saying for years that only «the memory of the suffering of innocents» can make us human. Where can we begin thinking differently? How can we humanize history? «In reality», says Metz, «I only know of one truly universal category; it is called *memoria passionis*».

According to the theologian from Münster, the suffering of innocents challenges every theological anthropology —every philosophy, political position, or religion— that fails to take it seriously. It is inhuman to advocate any cause if our advocacy trivializes the suffering of the victims. The only authority by which we are all judged is «the authority of those who suffer».

That is why it is important to listen, not only to people who think and people who pray, but especially to those who suffer. When we forget the suffering of real persons, humanity is in danger. When politicians use human suffering as a strategy, they diminish their own cause. When religion turns its back on those who suffer, religion itself is dehumanized. When the Church does not come near to them, it turns away from the Crucified One.

Metz insists on the need to develop a culture with «the memory of suffering» at its heart. We have to struggle against amnesia; we have to rebel against our easy forgetfulness of those who suffer hunger, kidnapping, torture or death. Our defense of humanity is proven only by our concern for those who suffer. We only become human ourselves, by making their cause our own.

The gospel reminds us that Jesus spent his time and energy, not only preaching in the synagogues, but liberating from suffering and sickness the people who were crushed by evil. So when Jesus entrusted the evangelizing task to his disciples, he sent them not only to preach but to put an end to suffering. «As you go, proclaim the good news, "The kingdom of heaven has come near". Cure the sick, raise the dead, cleanse the lepers, cast out demons. You received without payment; give without payment».

14

Do Not Be Afraid

Jesus said to his apostles:

«So have no fear of them; for nothing is covered up that will not be uncovered, and nothing secret that will not become known. What I say to you in the dark, tell in the light; and what you hear whispered, proclaim from the housetops. Do not fear those who kill the body but cannot kill the soul; rather fear him who can destroy both soul and body in hell. Are not two sparrows sold for a penny? Yet not one of them will fall to the ground apart from your Father. And even the hairs of your head are all counted. So do not be afraid; you are of more value than many sparrows».

«Everyone therefore who acknowledges me before others, I also will acknowledge before my Father in heaven; but whoever denies me before others, I also will deny before my Father in heaven» (Matthew 10:26-33).

1. FOLLOWING JESUS WITHOUT FEAR

When Matthew was writing, the memory of Jesus' execution was still very recent. Different versions of the story of his suffering were circulating in the Christian communities. Everyone knew it was dangerous to follow someone who had ended up so horribly. They remembered something Jesus had said: «A disciple is not above the teacher». If people had called him Beelzebul, what would they say of his followers?

Jesus didn't want his disciples to have any illusions. No one could follow him without sharing his fate in some way. At some point someone would reject them, abuse them, insult or condemn them. What should they do?

The answer comes from Jesus' heart: «Have no fear of them». Fear is bad. It must never paralyze his disciples. They must never stop speaking out. They must not stop proclaiming his message for any reason.

Jesus tells them how to stand in the face of persecution. The revelation of God's Good News has begun with him. They must trust him. What is still «covered up» and «secret» for many, will one day become known: everybody will know the Mystery of God, his love for human beings, and his plan for a happier life for everyone.

Jesus' followers are called to take part in that process of revelation: «What I say to you in the dark, tell in the light». What he said at night, before going to bed, they were to pass on fearlessly in the daylight. «What you hear whispered, proclaim from the housetops». What he whispers in their ear so it will penetrate their hearts, they must say publicly.

Jesus insists on not being afraid. Those who acknowledge him, those who take his side, have nothing to fear; for them the last judgment will be a joyful surprise. The judge will be «my Father in heaven», who loves them unconditionally. The defender will be Jesus himself, who will take their side. Who can give us more hope in the midst of our trials?

Jesus sees his followers as a group of believers who can fearlessly take his side. Why are we so reluctant to open new ways, more faithful to Jesus? Why are we afraid to proclaim the essence of the gospel in simple, clear, and concrete ways?

2. LIBERATING OUR COMMUNITIES FROM FEAR

The gospel writers describe Jesus as dedicated to liberating the people from fear. It made him sad to see people living in terror of the power of Rome, intimidated by threats from the teachers of the law, separated from God by fear of his anger, condemned for their lack of faithfulness to the law. A single desire welled up in his heart, filled with God: «Have no fear of them». These words of Jesus are repeated over and over in the gospels. We ought to repeat them today as well, in the Church.

Fear takes control of us when distrust, insecurity, or a lack of inner freedom grows in our hearts. This fear is the central problem of human beings, and we can only be free of it when our lives are rooted in a God who only seeks our good.

That is how Jesus saw it. For that reason he devoted himself above all to inspiring trust in human hearts. His deep and simple faith was contagious: if God so tenderly cares for the sparrows of the field, the smallest birds in Galilee, how can he care less for you? You are more important and beloved than all the birds in the sky. A first-generation Christian put it this way: «Lay all your burdens on God, for he only cares for your good».

Jesus spoke forcefully to each sick person: Have faith. God has not forgotten you. He joyfully took leave of them when he saw them cured: Go in peace. Live well. That was his great wish. He wanted people to live in peace, without fear or anxiety: Don't judge one another, don't condemn one another, don't hurt one another. Live as friends.

Many fears cause people to suffer in secret. Fear is very, very harmful. Where fear grows, God is lost from sight; the goodness in human hearts is suffocated. Life is extinguished, joy disappears.

A community of Jesus' followers must be, more than almost anything else, a place where people are liberated from fear and learn to live by trusting God. A community that lives by spreading peace and heartfelt friendship, which enable us to hear Jesus' call today: «Do not be afraid».

3. LEARNING TO TRUST GOD

I am convinced that the experience of God, as Jesus offers and conveys it, will always bring peace to hearts filled with uncertainty, fear, and insecurity. This peace is almost always the best sign that we have heard his call from the depth of our being: «Do not be afraid, you are of more value than many sparrows». How can we get close to that God?

Perhaps the first step is to stop and experience God as love. Everything that comes from him is love. God only gives us life, peace, and well-being. I can turn away from him and forget about his love, but God does not change. The only change is in me. God never stops loving me.

Here is something even more surprising. God loves me unconditionally, just as I am. I don't have to earn his love. I don't have to win his heart. I don't have to change or improve myself to make him love me. On the contrary, knowing that God loves me in this way, I can change, grow, and become good.

Now I can think about my life: What does God ask of me? What is God's hope for me? He only asks me to learn to love. I don't know what will happen in my life or what choices I will have to make, but God only asks me to love people and seek their good; to love myself and treat myself well; to love life and work to make it happier and more human for everyone. He asks me to be more aware of love.

There is one thing I must not forget. I will never be alone. We all «live, move, and have our being» in God. He will always be the understanding, challenging presence that I need, the strong hand that upholds me in my weakness, the light that guides me on his way. God will always invite me to say «yes» to life. One day, when my journey through this world is finished, with God I will come to know peace and rest, life and freedom.

4. FACING THE FUTURE WITH CONFIDENCE

In every age there have been «prophets of doom» who proclaim all sorts of evil for the future. Today too, there are unbalanced people who prophesy catastrophes and misfortunes, perhaps because they live their own lives as a failure and have projected on the world their own wishes for destruction.

These false prophets can destroy the fragile souls of some people, but there are people even more dangerous than they. More harm is done by those who constantly spread pessimism, poisoning daily life with their dark vision and pessimistic predictions.

Believing the gospel does not mean clinging to illusions about the world situation. Believers are not fooled by naïve «solutions» to the problems. They know the power of evil, but their faith in God helps them remember that the world has not been left to its misfortune. Beyond the headlines and statistical data, believers are aware of the ultimate reality, which is the salvation that comes from God.

This is the fundamental trust that Jesus conveys to his disciples: «Do not fear those who kill the body but cannot kill the soul». It is true that life is full of bad experiences, and that faith does not offer any magic prescriptions for our problems. But human existence is in God's hands. Our salvation from death and ultimate failure is in God.

This robust faith in God does not lead to evasiveness or passivity. On the contrary, it gives us the courage to make decisions and take responsibility. It leads us to accept risks and sacrifices in order to be faithful to ourselves and our own dignity. Believing the gospel does not lead to cowardice and resignation, but to audacity and creativity.

Another consequence of trust in God is patience, the art of resisting the power of evil without being diminished or destroyed by it. In the ancient Greek of the early Christian communities, the word we translate as «patience» meant «standing firm», bearing up under everyday evil. This is the secret attitude of people who place their ultimate trust in God.

5. SAYING NO TO FEAR

It is not overly dramatic to say that social fear and insecurity are growing in our midst. Life gets harder and harder; at least that is the perception of people who feel threatened in many ways and cannot see their future clearly.

This social fear is vague, but real. It is the subtle feeling that the existing social, political and economic institutions are incapable of resolving today's problems.

This fear manifests itself in different ways, and affects people differently. Some feel a need to consume more in order to feel more secure, and seek a life of entertainment in order to forget their everyday problems.

Some slip into passivity, resignation and disillusionment, because they are overwhelmed by feelings of powerlessness; they see little opportunity to play an active role in a society so complex, so dominated by the interests of the powerful.

Some are fearful of the risks that come with greater social freedom; they want to go back to a strong State that defends a rigid, secure order, even if it means building a less free, less human society.

Overcoming fear is not only or primarily a question of good will. Human beings need a clear hope, and a power that gives meaning to their daily struggle. They need to have a reason for living, and trust for dying.

Perhaps more than anything else, faith is the power we have over fear, the courage to go on believing in the future of humanity, based on humble commitment and unconditional trust in the Father of all. That is Jesus' call to us: «Do not be afraid».

15
How to Follow Jesus

Jesus said to his apostles:

«Whoever loves father or mother more than me is not worthy of me; and whoever loves son or daughter more than me is not worthy of me; and whoever does not take up the cross and follow me is not worthy of me. Those who find their life will lose it, and those who lose their life for my sake will find it».

«Whoever welcomes you welcomes me, and whoever welcomes me welcomes the one who sent me. Whoever welcomes a prophet in the name of a prophet will receive a prophet's reward; and whoever welcomes a righteous person in the name of a righteous person will receive the reward of the righteous; and whoever gives even a cup of cold water to one of these little ones in the name of a disciple—truly I tell you, none of these will lose their reward» (Matthew 10:37-42).

1. PREPARED FOR SUFFERING

Jesus didn't want to see anyone suffer. Suffering is evil. Jesus never sought it for himself or for others. On the contrary he spent his life struggling against suffering and evil, which are so harmful to persons.

The gospel sources show him always combating the suffering that comes with sickness, injustice, loneliness, despair, or guilt. That's who Jesus was: a man dedicated to eliminating suffering, ending injustice, and spreading the strength to live.

But seeking the good and happiness of everyone causes problems. Jesus knew that from experience. One cannot be with those who suffer, and do good for the last and the least, without provoking rejection and hostility from those who want nothing to change. We cannot be with the crucified ones, without eventually being «crucified» ourselves.

Jesus never tried to hide that from his followers. He sometimes used a disturbing metaphor that Matthew expresses this way: «whoever does not take up the cross and follow me is not worthy of me». He couldn't have said it more graphically than that. Everyone had seen the terrible sight: a naked and defenseless convict forced to carry the horizontal bar of a cross on his shoulders, to the place of execution where it would be attached to the vertical bar already standing there.

«Carrying the cross» was part of the ritual of crucifixion. The purpose was to parade the condemned man before society as a criminal, unworthy of living among his people. Everyone would imagine him dead when they went to sleep that night.

The disciples tried to understand him. Jesus was telling them: «If you follow me, you must be prepared for rejection. What happens to me will happen to you. You will be seen as a criminal. You will be condemned. They will try to get rid of you. You will have to carry your cross. Then you will be more like me. You will be worthy of following me. You will share the fate of the crucified. One day you will enter the reign of God with them».

To carry the cross doesn't mean seeking out «crosses to carry», but accepting the «crucifixion» that will come to everyone who follows in Jesus' footsteps. It was that clear.

2. THE DANGER OF A CROSSLESS CHRISTIANITY

One of the greatest risks of today's Christianity is gradually changing from a «religion of the cross» to a «religion of well-being». A few years ago I read some thought-provoking words by Reinhold Niebuhr. The North American theologian was talking about a «religion without a stinger», which would end up preaching «a God without anger who leads men without sin to a kingdom without judgment through a Christ without a cross». That is a real danger, and we must avoid it.

To insist on the unconditional love of God as Friend must never mean inventing a convenient God, a permissive God who legitimizes a «bourgeois religion» (Johann Baptist Metz). To be Christian doesn't mean looking for a God who fits my interests and says «yes» to everything, but to stand before the God who —precisely because he is a Friend— awakens my responsibility and by doing so, often makes me suffer, cry out, or fall silent.

To discover the gospel as a source of life and healthy growth doesn't mean becoming «immune» to suffering. The gospel is not a sedative, enabling us to enjoy a life centered on our own fantasies of pleasure and well-being. Christ makes us rejoice and makes us suffer, comforts us and afflicts us, supports us and contradicts us. That is what makes him the way, the truth, and the life.

To believe in God the Savior, who seeks to liberate us —now, in this life— from everything that harms us, should not lead us to see the Christian faith as a religion for our own private use, to deal with our own problems and suffering.

The God of Jesus Christ is always turning our attention to those who suffer. The gospel does not help people focus on their own suffering, but on that of others. That is the only way to live faith as an experience of salvation.

In faith as in love, everything is mixed together: trusting submission and possessiveness, generosity and selfishness. So we cannot afford to strike out of the gospel these hard words of Jesus, which force us to confront the truth of our faith: «whoever does not take up the cross and follow me is not worthy of me. Those who find their life will lose it, and those who lose their life for my sake will find it».

3. LEARNING TO GIVE

Sometimes it isn't so easy to answer a simple question. We often hear that loving means giving. But what does giving mean? Many people think of giving as depriving oneself, renouncing something, «sacrificing ourselves» by giving something up. We are so conditioned by our society of well-being, so inclined toward possessing, accumulating, and earning, that «giving» seems like an unproductive thing to do. A material loss that we are not prepared to accept. In our society, a person who gives without receiving is impractical, unrealistic, not very smart.

But giving is something very different. An act of giving is the richest expression of vitality, richness, and creative power. When we really give, we feel ourselves full of life, overflowing, able to enrich others at least in some modest way. «Only love makes life worth living. Only helping others brings us the great joy of living» (Karl Tillmann).

Giving means being alive, and being rich. People who have much but cannot give, are not rich. No matter how much they have, they are small, powerless, and poor. People are only rich when they can give something of themselves to others.

We all need to listen more deeply and attentively to Jesus' words. Even a cup of cold water given to a thirsty person will not go unrewarded. We must learn to give what is alive in us and can help others; to give our joy, understanding, encouragement, hope, acceptance, or presence.

Often it isn't about great or spectacular gifts. Just «a cup of cold water»: a smile of acceptance, an unhurried ear to listen, a hand to lift up fallen spirits, a gesture of solidarity, a visit, a sign of support and friendship. Never forget that. There is always someone in our life who blesses, accepts, and rewards every loving gesture, no matter how small it seems to us. That someone is God, our Father.

4. ANONYMOUS ARTISTS

We never see their faces on television. No one gossips about them on the radio or in the press. But they are great men and women, because their life is a blessing in this society. They make up the peaceful army of volunteers who work quietly, without payment, simply because their heart brings them to the side of those who suffer.

Young people who spend the weekend with a disabled person who needs friendship and company. Women who take care of elderly people who has no one to help them. Married couples who bring a drug addict into their home, and accompany him or her in rehabilitation.

I have seen these artists serving the hungry in the «Aterpe» meal kitchen or in homeless shelters. I have seen them listening on the hot line to people suffering from depression or anguish. I know how they visit the jail, Sunday after Sunday, to share a few hours with the inmates.

The volunteers are not unusually gifted people. They are simply human beings. They have eyes to see people's needs, ears to hear their suffering, feet to walk with the lonely, hands held out to the helpless, and above all, a great heart open to everyone with a disability.

That is the most important thing: these volunteers bring real love into our present society. They help us to see that love is not to be confused with sentimentality or almsgiving. That solidarity is built out of deeds, not words. That loving the neighbor means loving real people, not only proclaiming high ideals.

The volunteers are not paid in money, but they receive their reward. They are rewarded by the smiles of the sick, the affection of the prisoners, the grateful tears of the elderly. They are rewarded, above all, by the pleasure of alleviating human suffering.

With a poet's tenderness, Gloria Fuentes says that the volunteer's reward is to become an artist. «The volunteers have not painted a picture, have not carved a statue, have not composed a song, have not written a poem, but they have turned their free time into a work of art».

Jesus is thinking of an even greater reward for them: «whoever gives even a cup of cold water to one of these little ones… truly I tell you, none of these will lose their reward».

5. AN ADMIRABLE VOCATION

One of the most positive and hopeful things about our society is the growth of social volunteerism. More and more people are devoting their free time to unpaid activities and services. How do we awaken this admirable vocation of service to others?

The first step is to open our eyes and realize that not everyone's hopes for well-being are fulfilled. The future volunteer takes a long look at the suffering, marginalization, and problems of so many people in need of support and companionship. The wish to «do something» to relieve their suffering is awakened in their hearts.

But good wishes are not enough. Volunteers have to make a decision: a commitment to serve people in need, in specific ways. Not because everybody's doing it, or out of silly sentimentality, but because their human convictions or Christian faith require it. This commitment is not a kind of entertainment or hobby. It is a specific way of living, which over time becomes a part of them.

Volunteers do not give things; they give themselves. They offer their person, their qualities, their free time. There is time in their lives for other people. Time given freely to those who suffer and need some kind of help. This is their way of living solidarity, of living Christian love.

Volunteers do not look for repayment. They are moved to act by unselfish love. Their life challenges us: money is not everything. While others are mainly concerned with their own well-being, volunteers dedicate themselves to bring love, companionship, and help to lives that seem to be made up only of suffering, marginalization, and misfortune.

Volunteers usually do not work alone, or when they feel like it. They know that their service is more effective when it is part of a specific association or institution. In particular, Christian volunteers nourish and sustain their commitment in the life of a Christian community.

Good will is not enough. Volunteers need technical training as well as practical experience. By seeking out the training they need, they show the seriousness of their commitment to effective service.

But technical and professional service by itself does not relieve human pain. Think of all the lonely elderly, the sick in need of care, the physically and psychologically handicapped who have no family, the men and women alone with chronic depression. Their need for accompaniment, a helping hand, and constant care requires more than the technical service of a professional. Jesus says that nothing will go unrewarded. Not even the «cup of cold water» that we give to «one of these little ones».

When John heard in prison what the Messiah was doing, he sent word by his disciples and said to him, «Are you the one who is to come, or are we to wait for another?» Jesus answered them, «Go and tell John what you hear and see: the blind receive their sight, the lame walk, the lepers are cleansed, the deaf hear, the dead are raised, and the poor have good news brought to them. And blessed is anyone who takes no offense at me».

As they went away, Jesus began to speak to the crowds about John: «What did you go out into the wilderness to look at? A reed shaken by the wind? What then did you go out to see? Someone dressed in soft robes? Look, those who wear soft robes are in royal palaces. What then did you go out to see? A prophet?» Yes, I tell you, and more than a prophet. This is the one about whom it is written,

«See, I am sending my messenger ahead of you,
who will prepare your way before you».

«Truly I tell you, among those born of women no one has arisen greater than John the Baptist; yet the least in the kingdom of heaven is greater than he» (Matthew 11:2-11).

1. THE IDENTITY OF JESUS

John the Baptist is in prison at Machaerus, where he was sent by Herod Antipas, when he hears about Jesus. What he hears is disconcerting. It is not what he expected. He is waiting for a Messiah who will bring down God's judgment with terrible power, saving those who accept his baptism and condemning those who reject it. Who is this Jesus?

To resolve his doubts, John sends two disciples to ask Jesus about his true identity: «Are you the one who is to come, or are we to wait for another?» This was a decisive question in the first days of Christianity.

Jesus' answer is not theoretical, but very clear and precise: «Go and tell John what you hear and see». They have asked about his identity, and he answers with his healing acts in the service of the sick, the poor and unfortunate ones he meets in the Galilean villages, people without resources and without hope for a better life. «The blind receive their sight, the lame walk, the lepers are cleansed, the deaf hear, the dead are raised, and the poor have good news brought to them».

The best way to know Jesus is to see the people he goes to and the things he does. His identity is not explained by confessing him theoretically as the Messiah, the Son of God. We need to be attuned to his way of being the Messiah, which is precisely that: to alleviate suffering, heal life, and open up a horizon of hope to the poor.

Jesus knows that his answer will disappoint anyone who has been dreaming of a powerful Messiah. So he adds: «Blessed is anyone who takes no offense at me». They shouldn't expect a different Messiah, doing a different kind of «works»; they shouldn't invent another Christ, more to their liking, because the Son has been sent to give life with more dignity and happiness to everyone, until it reaches its fullness in the final feast of the Father.

What kind of Messiah are Christians following today? Are we doing the «works» that Jesus did? If not, what are we doing in this world? What do people «see and hear» in Jesus' Church today? What do they see in our lives? What do they hear in our words?

2. ACTS OF LIBERATION

Jesus did not perform acts of power and oppression. The «acts» he describes to the Baptist's disciples are not deeds of judgment, but liberating service to those who need to live.

The act that best describes his true identity is his work in curing, healing, and liberating life. We can paraphrase his answer to John this way: «I am: the blind see and the lame walk; the lepers are cleansed and the deaf hear; the dead are raised, and the poor have good news brought to them».

Jesus lives the life of someone close to people in need. A prophet totally committed to liberating men and women from everything that blocks the growth of life and keeps human beings from living with hope. A man who incarnates God in order to save God's sons and daughters from evil.

Heinrich Böll saw that very clearly. «In the New Testament there is a theology of tenderness that always heals: with words, with hands, with caresses, with kisses, with a shared meal... This element of the New Testament, its tenderness, has yet to be discovered; everything has turned into quarrels and cries; yet there are some people who can be healed just by a voice, or by a shared meal... Then we can imagine something like a socialist tenderness».

Perhaps we should look more closely at the words of the German writer. Sometimes we hastily dismiss any gesture of acceptance, personal service or solidary presence with disadvantaged people as a suspiciously «reformist» attitude, incapable of renewing our society. We naïvely think that a «new, liberated and solidary people» can only be born out of confrontation, struggle, and violence.

We need to struggle firmly and tenaciously against every kind of injustice and oppression, unmasking all the social mechanisms that cause it. But that is not enough to bring about a «new humanity».

Some things cannot be resolved, by even the deepest reform or the most radical revolution: the love that is lacking in so many lives, the loneliness, the crisis of a meaningless life, the inner emptiness, the alienation, the despair felt by so many people. There is no assurance of love for each person, friendly presence, respect and a listening ear for every human being, acceptance and understanding, unless these things well up in the heart of men and women enlivened by the Spirit of Jesus.

3. LOVE OF LIFE

In the face of the destructive tendencies of today's society (necrophilia), Erich Fromm has raised a vigorous call to develop love of life (biophilia). Without it, we will slip into what the famous psychologist calls a «syndrome of decadence».

It is true that we need to be watchful for the different forms of aggressiveness, violence and destruction that have arisen in modern society. Some sociologists speak of an authentic «culture of violence». But there are more subtle, and therefore more effective, ways of destroying people's growth and life.

The mechanization of labor, the massification of life styles, the bureaucratization of society, and the reification of relationships, are among the other factors that lead many people to think of themselves, not as living beings but as small pieces of a social machine.

Millions of individuals in the West are living comfortable but monotonous lives, in which the lack of meaning and purpose can suffocate all truly human growth.

Some people end up losing contact with everything that is alive. Their lives are filled with things. They only feel vibrant when they are acquiring new things. They get with the program dictated by society.

Others look for any kind of stimulation. They have to work, produce, move around, be entertained. They are always looking for new emotions to feel. Something exciting that makes them feel they're still alive.

Nothing is more characteristic of Jesus than his passionate love for life, his biophilia. The gospel stories show him struggling against everything that blocks off, mutilates, or diminishes life. He is always looking for what makes people grow. Always spreading life, health, meaning.

He describes his own mission with expressions taken from Isaiah: «the blind receive their sight, the lame walk, the lepers are cleansed, the deaf hear, the dead are raised, and the poor have good news brought to them. And blessed is anyone who takes no offense at me».

Blessed indeed are those who discover that believing does not mean hating life but loving it, not blocking off or mutilating our humanity, but opening it up to all its best possibilities. Many people today have given up their faith in Jesus Christ without ever truly experiencing the truth of his words: «I came that they may have life, and have it abundantly» (John 10:10).

4. DEEDS, NOT WORDS

Sociologists have pointed out a curious linguistic phenomenon in our time. In recent years the industrialized world has adopted a technical, sterile, and euphemistic vocabulary to describe people who are suffering problems or illness. In America there is a dictionary of politically correct terms for certain people and groups.

For example in modern society there are no poor people, but the «economically challenged»; no old people, but those who have reached the «third age»; not blind, but «unsighted»; no one dying, but «terminally ill»; those without a roof over their heads have become «transients»; black people are «people of color»; and housemaids have become «domestic helpers».

This language certainly reflects a more respectful and polite attitude toward people, but at the same time it is more sterile, distant and reassuring, since it is an attempt to disguise suffering and tragedy. They're nothing for us to worry about; the Administration, Social Security, and other institutions will take care of them.

So we need to remember the warning of the early Christians: love for people who suffer does not mean using the right words, but helping them with our works. A first century writer put it this way: «Little children, let us love, not in word or speech, but in truth and action» (I John 3:18).

The gospel story conveys a lesson. The prophet John sends his disciples to ask Jesus a decisive question: «Are you the one who is to come, or are we to wait for another?» Jesus doesn't answer with a theoretical explanation. To describe his identity he uses deeds, not words: «the blind receive their sight, the lame walk, the lepers are cleansed, the deaf hear, the dead are raised, and the poor have good news brought to them».

The true Messiah is known to his followers, not by his words but by his deeds. The Danish philosopher Søren Kierkegaard began one of his essays this way: «These are Christian reflections. Therefore we will not talk about love, but about the works of love». It's that simple. Christian love for the suffering is not an explanation of love, a song of love, or praise for love. True love is not found in words, but in deeds.

5. ON NOT BEING DISAPPOINTED IN JESUS

In these days of religious crisis and inner confusion, it is important to remember that Jesus is not the Church's private property. He belongs to everyone. Those who confess him as the Son of God can come to him; so can those who are looking for more human meaning in their lives.

Some years ago the famous thinker Roger Garaudy, then a convinced marxist, cried out to Christians: «You have collected and preserved the hope that is Jesus Christ. Give it back to us; it belongs to everyone».

Around the same time, Jean Onimus published a passionate book on Jesus with the provocative title, *Le Perturbateur*. The French writer says to Jesus: «Why should you remain the private property of the preachers, doctors, and a few erudite people—you who said things so simply, in direct words, words that stay with people, words of eternal life?»

For the same reason, nothing gives me greater joy than to know that men and women who have turned away from practicing religion, are now looking for an encounter with Jesus in my writings. I am convinced that for many people, he is the best way to find God as a Friend, and to give more hopeful meaning to their lives.

No one who comes to Jesus can go away indifferent. In him we find someone truly alive, someone who knows why we live and why we die. We sense that this way of living, so typical of Jesus, is the best and most human way to face life and death.

Jesus heals. His passion for life unmasks our superficiality and conformism. His love for the helpless unmasks our selfishness and mediocrity. His truth lifts the curtain on our self-deception. But above all, his unconditional faith in the Father invites us to come out of our incredulity and place our trust in God.

People who today are leaving the Church because it makes them uncomfortable, or because they disagree with some of its specific actions or instructions, or simply because the Christian liturgy has become meaningless to them, should not automatically turn away from Jesus for that reason.

When we have lost our other points of reference, and feel that «something» is dying inside us, it may be especially important not to lose touch with Jesus. The gospel story reminds us of that: «Blessed is anyone who takes no offense at me!» Blessed is everyone who understands what Christ can mean for their lives.

17

The Father is Revealed to the Simple Folk

At that time Jesus said, «I thank you, Father, Lord of heaven and earth, because you have hidden these things from the wise and the intelligent and have revealed them to infants; yes, Father, for such was your gracious will. All things have been handed over to me by my Father; and no one knows the Son except the Father, and no one knows the Father except the Son and anyone to whom the Son chooses to reveal him».

«Come to me, all you that are weary and carrying heavy burdens, and I will give you rest. Take my yoke upon you, and learn from me; for I am gentle and humble in heart, and you will find rest for your souls. For my yoke is easy, and my burden is light» (Matthew 11:25-30).

1. GOD IS REVEALED TO THE SIMPLE FOLK

One day Jesus surprised everybody, by thanking God for his success with the simple folk of Galilee and for his failure among the teachers of the law, scribes, and priests. «I thank you, Father… because you have hidden these things from the wise and intelligent and have revealed them to infants». That seems to make Jesus happy. «Yes, Father, for such was your gracious will». That is God's way of revealing his «things».

The simple and ignorant folk, those who have no access to great knowledge, those who don't count in the religion of the temple, are opening themselves up to God with a clean heart. They are ready to let Jesus teach them. The Father is revealing his love to them through Jesus. They understand Jesus better than anyone else does.

The «wise and intelligent» understand nothing. They have their own scholarly vision of God and of religion. They think they know it all. They have nothing new to learn from Jesus. Their closed-off vision and their hard hearts keep them from opening up to the revelation of the Father through his Son.

Jesus finishes his prayer, but he goes on thinking about the «simple folk». They are oppressed by the powerful and do not find any comfort in the temple religion. Their life is hard, and the doctrines of the «intelligent» make it even harder. Jesus calls to them three times.

«Come to me, all you that are weary and carrying heavy burdens». This is the first call. It is addressed to all those who feel religion as something heavy, and those who are wearied by norms and doctrines that keep them from grasping the joy of salvation. If they are vibrantly in touch with Jesus, they will feel immediate relief: «I will give you rest».

«Take my yoke upon you… For my yoke is easy, and my burden is light». This is the second call. We have to change yokes. Take off the yoke of the «wise and intelligent», because it isn't light, and carry the one Jesus offers, which makes life easier to bear. Not because Jesus is less demanding. He expects more of us, but in a different way. He demands what is essential: liberating, life-giving love.

«Learn from me, for I am gentle and humble in heart». This is the third call. We have to learn to fulfill the law and live our religion with his spirit. Jesus doesn't «complicate» our life; he makes it simple and humble. He doesn't oppress; he helps us to live in a more worthy, human way. It is «restful» to come to him.

2. LEARNING FROM THE SIMPLE PEOPLE

Jesus didn't have problems with the simple people of the villages. He knew they understood him. What worried him was that someday the religious leaders, the specialists in the law, the great teachers of Israel might start to understand his message. It was becoming increasingly clear that what filled the simple people with joy, left the religious leaders indifferent.

The peasants who spent their lives staving off hunger and the powerful landowners understood him very well: God wanted them to be happy, without hunger and without oppressors. The sick trusted him, and bolstered by faith, they started believing again in the God of life. The women who dared to come out of their houses to hear him, understood that God loves —as Jesus said— the way a mother does, from the womb. The simple folk were attuned to him. The God he proclaimed was the God they yearned for, and needed.

The «wise and intelligent» had a different attitude. Caiaphas and the priests in Jerusalem saw him as a threat. The teachers of the law couldn't understand why he was so concerned with people's suffering, rather than with the requirements of religion. That is why there were no priests, scribes, or teachers of the law among his followers.

One day Jesus shared what he was feeling with everyone. Full of joy, he prayed to God: «I thank you, Father, Lord of heaven and earth, because you have hidden these things from the wise and the intelligent and have revealed them to infants».

It has always been like that. The simple people usually see things with clear eyes. There is not so much twisted self-interest in their hearts. They go straight to the point. They know what it's like to suffer, to feel bad, to live without security. They are the first to understand the gospel.

These simple people are the best thing the Church has. We all need to learn from them: bishops, theologians, moralists, the wise people of religion. God shows them things that we can't see. We ecclesiastics are in danger of rationalizing, theorizing, and «complicating» faith too much. Two questions: why are our words so far from the life of the people? Why is our message almost always more obscure and complicated than Jesus' message?

3. GOD BELONGS TO THE SIMPLE FOLK

Many years ago, in the École Biblique de Jérusalem, a teacher of exegesis was introducing us to the difficult art of interpreting the gospel of Matthew. Whatever we did —textual criticism, literary analysis, the structure of the passage— fell short of grasping the ultimate meaning of the text. One day we came across the verses in which Jesus exclaims: «I thank you, Father, Lord of heaven and earth, because you have hidden these things from the wise and the intelligent and have revealed them to infants». The professor paused for a long time. Then he said very slowly: «Never forget these words. You can forget everything else». That was probably the best exegesis lecture I have ever heard. Years later, I have seen how right he was.

Whenever I feel the person I am with is close to God, it is always someone with a simple heart. The person may not have a lot of knowledge, or it may be a very cultured person, but it is always a man or woman with a pure and humble heart.

More than once I have seen that talking about God is not enough to awaken faith. For many people, certain religious concepts seem very trite; no matter how we work to convey their original life and flavor, God stays «fossilized». But I have seen simple people who don't seem to need great ideas or reasoning. They immediately understand that God is «a hidden God», and a spontaneous invocation wells up in their heart: «Lord, show me your face».

I have also seen people who are mainly concerned with usefulness. Some turn away from God because he seems useless to them; others worship because it serves their interests to do so. But I have known simple people who spend their lives giving thanks to God. They enjoy the good that life offers, and patiently bear its misfortunes; they know how to live and give life. I don't know how they do it, but praise to the Creator seems to be always flowing from their hearts. They are always on the right track.

I often give talks on religious themes, and I have spoken about God to different kinds of people. Some people ask one question after another about all sorts of theological issues, without ever showing any interest in meeting God. But I have seen simple people whose eyes shine with a special light when I read them words like these from Isaiah: «I am the Lord your God… Because you are precious in my sight, and honored, and I love you… Do not fear, for I am with you» (Isaiah 43:3-5). Or when I recite Psalm 103: «As a father has compassion for his children, so the Lord has compassion for those who fear him. For he knows how we were made; he remembers that we are dust» (Psalm 103:1-14). Yes, God reveals himself to the simple folk.

4. THE ART OF RESTING

Many of us subject ourselves to a tough work schedule, which wears us out over a period of months. So in the summer we all try to set aside a time for rest which can help us get rid of the tension, the weariness and exhaustion that we have built up day after day.

But what does it mean to rest? Is it enough to recover our physical strength, by basking in the sun for hours and hours beside some ocean? It it enough to forget our problems and conflicts by plunging into parties and festivities? People often come back from vacation with an inner feeling that it was a waste of time. On vacation we can also fall under the tyranny of agitation, noisiness, superficiality and anxiety caused by easy, exhausting entertainment. We don't all know how to rest. Perhaps modern men and women urgently need to learn the art of true rest.

First we need to get more deeply in touch with ourselves and search for the silence, calm and serenity that we so often find missing during the year, in order to listen to the best that is within us and around us.

We need to remember that an intense life is not the same as an agitated life. We want to have everything, accumulate and enjoy everything. We surround ourselves with a thousand superfluous, useless things that suffocate our freedom and spontaneity.

We need to rediscover nature, contemplate the life springing up around us, stop to look at small things and at simple, good people. We need to realize how little happiness has to do with wealth, success, and easy pleasure.

We need to remember that the ultimate meaning of life is not found in effort, labor, and struggle. On the contrary, meaning reveals itself more clearly in celebration, shared joy, friendship, and life together as brothers and sisters.

But we also need to root our lives in the God who is a «friend of life», a source of true and authentic rest. How can the human heart rest without finding God? Let us hear Jesus' words with ears of faith: «Come to me, all you that are weary and are carrying heavy burdens, and I will give you rest».

5. WE NEED SOMETHING MORE THAN VACATIONS

There are types of weariness in today's world that vacations will not cure. They don't go away just because we take a few days off. The reason is simple. Vacations can help to refresh us a bit, but they cannot give us the inner rest, the peaceful heart and the tranquil spirit that we need.

One type of weariness comes from exhausting activism. We don't respect the natural rhythm of life. We keep doing more things, in less time. Our life is accelerated, constantly exhausted, wearing down day by day. We expect a vacation to «recharge our batteries».

That is a mistake. Vacations do nothing to resolve that kind of weariness. Completely «disconnecting» doesn't help. When we come back from vacation, everything goes on as usual. What we need is to stop accelerating our life, to learn a more human rhythm, stop doing some things, live more slowly and more restfully.

Another type of weariness comes from saturation. Our life is too full of activities, relationships, appointments, meetings, lunches. The answering machine, the cell phone, the computer, and electronic mail can make our work easier, but they bring saturation to our lives. We are everywhere at once, always on call, always «connected».

That is a mistake. What we need is to set priorities in our life: take care of what is important, set aside what is peripheral, devote more time to the things that give us inner peace and assurance.

Another type of weariness is more diffuse, harder to identify. We are tired of ourselves, full up with our own mediocrity, and unable to find what our hearts yearn for. What good will it do to take a vacation? Listen again to Jesus' words: «Come to me, all you that are weary and are carrying heavy burdens, and I will give you rest». That kind of rest can only be found when we accept the mystery of God in our heart, following in Jesus' footsteps.

18

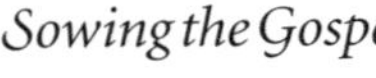

Sowing the Gospel

That same day Jesus went out of the house and sat beside the sea. Such great crowds gathered around him that he got into a boat and sat there, while the whole crowd stood on the beach. And he told them many things in parables, saying, «Listen! A sower went out to sow. And as he sowed, some seeds fell on the path, and the birds came and ate them up. Other seeds fell on rocky ground, where they did not have much soil, and they sprang up quickly, since they had no depth of soil. But when the sun rose, they were scorched; and since they had no root, they withered away. Other seeds fell among thorns, and the thorns grew up and choked them. Other seeds fell on good soil and brought forth grain, some a hundredfold, some sixty, some thirty. Let anyone with ears listen!»

Then the disciples came and asked him, «Why do you speak to them in parables?» He answered, «To you it has been given to know the secrets of the kingdom of heaven, but to them it has not been given. For to those who have, more will be given, and they will have an abundance; but from those who have nothing, even what they have will be taken away. The reason I speak to them in parables is that "seeing they do not perceive, and hearing they do not listen, nor do they understand"». With them indeed is fulfilled the prophecy of Isaiah that says:

«You will indeed listen, but never understand,
and you will indeed look, but never perceive.
For this people's heart has grown dull,
and their ears are hard of hearing,
and they have shut their eyes;
so that they might not look with their eyes,
and listen with their ears,
and understand with their heart, and turn—
and I would heal them» (Matthew 13:1-15).

1. LEARNING TO SOW LIKE JESUS

It was not easy for Jesus to carry out his project. He faced criticism and rejection from the beginning; his word didn't receive the response he might have wished for. His closest followers were beginning to feel discouraged and doubtful. Was it worth it to go on working beside Jesus? Wasn't it all a utopian dream?

Jesus told them what he was thinking. To help them see that his work was both realistic and inspired by an unshakable faith, he told a parable about a farmer sowing seeds. Certainly some of the work may be wasted, but God's great project will not fail. They must not give in to discouragement. They must keep spreading the seeds. In the end there will be an abundant harvest.

The people who heard the parable knew that he was talking about himself. That was his way. He planted his word wherever he saw a chance that it might germinate. He planted acts of kindness and mercy even in places one wouldn't expect them to grow, among people far removed from religion.

Jesus planted with realism and trust, just as the Galilean farmers did. They knew that not all their land was equally fertile; some of the planting would be lost. But that didn't keep any of them from planting. The important thing was the final harvest. The reign of God was like that. There were many obstacles and struggles, but God's power would produce results. It wouldn't make sense to stop planting.

In the Church of Jesus we don't need harvesters. It's not our job to reap success, conquer the streets, take charge of society, fill the churches, impose our religious faith on others. We need more sowers, followers of Jesus who will spread Jesus' words of hope and acts of compassion wherever they go.

That is the kind of conversion we need today: from our obsession with «harvesting» to the patient work of «sowing». Jesus' enduring gift to us is the parable of the sower, not the harvester.

2. THE HIDDEN POWER OF THE GOSPEL

The parable of the sower is an invitation to hope. There is an irrepressible power in planting the gospel, no matter how many problems and how much opposition it causes. In spite of all the obstacles and difficulties, and no matter how uneven the results seem, it leads to a harvest so abundant that past failures are soon forgotten.

We mustn't lose hope on account of the apparent powerlessness of the reign of God. It always seems as if God's «cause» is falling apart, or that the gospel has no relevance and no future. But that's not true. The gospel is not a moral or political philosophy, not even a religion, whose future ebbs and flows. The gospel is the saving power of God, «planted» by Jesus in the heart of the world and in the life of human beings.

We are so influenced by the sensationalism of today's news media, that it seems we can see nothing but evil. We can no longer imagine the power of life that is hidden behind such apparently terrible events.

If we could see inside people's lives, we would be surprised by the kindness, commitment, sacrifice, generosity, and true love we'd find. There is violence and bloodshed in the world, but in many people there is a growing eagerness for real peace. Selfish consumerism is spreading through our society, but many people are discovering the joy of simple, shared living. Religion seems to have been stifled by indifference, but many people are feeling a yearning for God and a need for prayer.

That is where we see the transforming power of the gospel, working in human beings. The thirst for justice and love is growing. What Jesus has planted will not end in failure. What he asks of us is to accept the seed. Can we see in ourselves the power that doesn't come from us but invites us to keep on growing, to be more human, to transform our lives, to weave new relationships with other people, to live more transparently, to open ourselves more truly to God?

3. SOWING WITH FAITH

In just a few years we have changed from a deeply religious society, where Christianity played an important role in individual and social life, to a more laicized and unbelieving way of life, where religion is losing its importance.

Many believers —accustomed to a «Christendom» society in which religion was visible in the streets, plazas, schools and homes— are feeling discomfort and pain in the new situation.

Worse yet: we may slip into thinking that the gospel itself has lost its importance, that Jesus' message has lost its grip and its persuasive power in modern humanity.

So we need to listen attentively to the parable of Jesus. As simple and insignificant as it seems, the gospel still has the power to «save» people from what dehumanizes them. We will hardly find anyone or anything else that gives more human and liberating meaning to our lives.

It is true that in order to exert this liberating power, the gospel has to be presented faithfully, with all the truth, the challenges, and the hope that lie within it. Without distortion or evasiveness. Without self-serving partiality or manipulation.

It is also true that the gospel must be accepted sincerely, with total commitment. Many things —wealth, self-interest, cowardice— can stifle Jesus' word and make it ineffective.

But the gospel still has more humanizing force than we think. Modern society will be making a terrible mistake if it forgets that. In any case, we Christians must remember that this is not «harvest» time, but a time to sow the seed with faith in the power of renewal hidden in the gospel.

4. INSPIRING CREATIVITY

Pre-modern societies developed through many centuries by following tradition. Each generation learned how to live by looking to the past. Tradition gave them a code of knowledge, values, and customs, passed on from parents to children. The life of each person and the whole society was governed by the wisdom of the past.

It is no longer that way. Tradition is in crisis. Modern society is changing so rapidly that the past has almost no authority unless we can see a future use for it. We live facing forward. We don't want to do things the way we always did. Solutions from the past are no use for the new problems of our time. It's not enough to look to tradition. We have to learn to live creatively.

This is not usually the attitude of today's Church. It's hard to find creativity in the Church's magisterium, which addresses most issues on the basis of tradition. But a Church without creativity is a Church doomed to stagnation. If people see Christianity as a «relic of the past», they will keep losing interest.

We in the Church are afraid of promoting creativity. There are reasons for that fear; some people think of creativity as spontaneity, improvisation, or arbitrary action. But to suppress creativity, to systematically oppose new responses to new problems, can lead the Church to a paralysis that is far from the spirit of Jesus.

The Church in the first centuries was surprisingly creative, responding boldly to the new situations it faced. It was amazingly bold, for example, in moving out of the cultural and religious context of the Jewish world and putting down roots in the Greek and Latin culture. Don't today's Christians have a right to be as creative as Christians were in other ages?

The parable of the sower is a challenge to us all: what fruits might the word of Jesus produce, if we accept it faithfully in our hearts?

5. HAVING EARS AND NOT HEARING

Jesus' parables have always captivated his listeners. About forty parables are recorded in the gospels—probably the ones he told most often, or the ones that were most forcefully engraved in the heart and memory of the disciples. How should we read those parables? How shall we hear their message?

Matthew begins by reminding us that the parables were planted in the world by Jesus. «Jesus went out of the house» to teach the people, and his first parable begins, «A sower went out to sow». Jesus is the sower. His parables are a call to understand and live life the way he understood it and lived it. If we aren't attuned to Jesus, it will be hard for us to understand his parables.

What Jesus sows is «the word of the kingdom», Matthew tells us. Each parable is an invitation to move out of an old, conventional, and barely human world, into «a new country», full of life, which is what God wants for his sons and daughters. Jesus called it «the reign of God». If we're not following Jesus, working for a more human world, how are we going to understand his parables?

Jesus sows his message «in the heart», that is, in the inner person. That is where real conversion takes place. It's not enough to preach the parables. Unless our heart is open to Jesus, we will never grasp their transforming power.

Jesus doesn't discriminate when he proclaims the gospel. He does say that God has «given to know the secrets of the kingdom» to those who are his disciples and follow in his footsteps, and not to others. The disciples have the key to understanding the parables; their knowledge of God's project will keep growing deeper. But those who do not take that step, who live their lives without making a choice for Jesus, will not understand his message—and they end up losing what they have heard.

Our problem is that we end up with «dullness of heart». What happens then is inevitable. We have ears, but we don't hear any message. We have eyes, but we aren't looking at Jesus. Our hearts don't get it. How shall we plant the seed of the gospel in our Christian communities? How shall we awaken in them an acceptance of the Sower?

He put before them another parable: «The kingdom of heaven may be compared to someone who sowed good seed in his field; but while everybody was asleep, an enemy came and sowed weeds among the wheat, and then went away. So when the plants came up and bore grain, then the weeds appeared as well. And the slaves of the householder came and said to him, "Master, did you not sow good seed in your field? Where, then, did these weeds come from?" He answered, "An enemy has done this". The slaves said to him, "Then do you want us to go and gather them?" But he replied, "No; for in gathering the weeds you would uproot the wheat along with them. Let both of them grow together until the harvest; and at harvest time I will tell the reapers, Collect the weeds first and bind them in bundles to be burned, but gather the wheat into my barn"».

He put before them another parable: «The kingdom of heaven is like a mustard seed that someone took and sowed in his field; it is the smallest of all the seeds, but when it has grown it is the greatest of shrubs and becomes a tree, so that the birds of the air come and make nests in its branches».

He told them another parable: «The kingdom of heaven is like yeast that a woman took and mixed in with three measures of flour until all of it was leavened».

Jesus told the crowds all these things in parables; without a parable he told them nothing. This was to fulfill what had been spoken through the prophet:

«I will open my mouth to speak in parables;
I will proclaim what has been hidden from the foundation of the world».

Then he left the crowds and went into the house. And his disciples approached him, saying, «Explain to us the parable of the weeds of the field». He answered, «The one who sows the good seed is the Son of Man; the field is the world, and the good seed are the children of the kingdom; the weeds are the children of the evil one, and the enemy who sowed them is the devil; the harvest is the end of the age, and the reapers are angels. Just as the weeds are collected and burned up with fire, so will it be at the end of the age. The Son of Man will send his angels, and they will collect out of his kingdom all causes of sin and all evildoers, and they will throw them into the furnace of fire, where there will be weeping and gnashing of teeth. Then the righteous will shine like the sun in the kingdom of their Father. Let anyone with ears listen!» (Matthew 13:24-43).

1. LIFE IS MORE THAN WHAT WE SEE

We usually expect to see God in the large and spectacular, not in the small and insignificant. So the Galileans had a hard time believing Jesus when he said that God was already acting in the world. Where could one feel his power? Where were the «signs and wonders» that the apocalyptic writers talked about?

Jesus had to show them another way to understand the saving presence of God. He shared with them his great conviction: that life is more than what we see. While we go about our distracted lives without noticing anything special, something mysterious is going on inside life.

Jesus lived with this faith: we may not experience anything unusual, but God is at work in the world. His power is irresistible. It takes time to see the final result. Above all, it takes faith and patience to look at the very depth of life and sense God's secret action within it.

Perhaps the parable that surprised them most was the one about the mustard seed. It is the smallest of all seeds, the size of a pinhead, but in time it grows into a beautiful shrub. Around April, everyone can see flocks of finches nesting in its branches. The reign of God is like that.

There was surely a general sense of bewilderment. He wasn't talking like a prophet. Ezekiel had spoken of a «noble cedar», planted on a «high and lofty mountain», that would spread its branches and give shade to all the winged creatures of the sky. For Jesus, the true metaphor for God is not something great and powerful like a cedar, but something as small and insignificant as a mustard seed.

Jesus doesn't want his followers to dream of great things. They would be wrong to work for a powerful, strong Church that can impose itself on everyone. The ideal is not a cedar on a high mountain, but a mustard shrub that grows beside the roads, and gives shelter to the finches every April.

God is not to be found in success, power, or superiority. In order to discern his saving presence we have to be attentive to small, ordinary, everyday things. Life is more, much more, than what we see. That is the way Jesus saw it.

2. THE TRANSFORMING POWER OF THE YEAST

Jesus said over and over: God is already here, trying to transform the world; God's reign is arriving. It was hard to believe him. People were hoping for something more spectacular. Where could they see God's power, bringing in his reign at last?

Jesus still remembered a scene that he must have watched as a child in the patio of his house. His mother and the other women rose early on the morning before the sabbath, to bake bread for the week. Now that scene made him think of God's motherly act, kneading «yeast» into the world.

The same thing happens with the reign of God as with the yeast that a woman «hides» in the dough so that «all of it» will be fermented. That is how God works. He doesn't come to impose his power, like the Roman emperor. He comes to transform life from within, in quiet, hidden ways.

That is how God acts: he doesn't impose but transforms; he doesn't control but attracts. And that is how the people must act who share in his project: like yeast, introducing God's truth, justice and love into the world, with humility but with transforming power.

As Jesus' followers we cannot come into this society «from outside», trying to dominate and control people who don't think as we do. That is not how we should prepare the way to the reign of God. We have to live «inside» society, sharing the uncertainty, the crises, and the contradictions of today's world, and contributing to it our life transformed by the gospel.

We have to learn to live our faith as a «minority», and as faithful witnesses to Jesus. What the Church needs is not more social or political power, but the humility to let itself be transformed by Jesus and to become the ferment of a more human world.

3. FERMENT OF A MORE HUMAN WORLD

It is surprising how often Jesus warns his disciples against a false «messianic zeal» that does not respect the rhythm of God's quiet, but vigorous, action.

To people who hope he will lead a decisive, momentous movement capable of putting an end to other currents and alternatives, Jesus speaks about God's humbler, more respectful way of acting. The world is a field of competing crops; that is where the reign of God is growing, in the density of life that is sometimes so ambiguous and complex.

That is where God is saving humanity. In the midst of that kind of behavior, sometimes motivated by high ideals, sometimes by obscure self-interest. In the thousand things we do every day, partly out of generosity and partly out of shameful pettiness.

To people who are hoping for a spectacular display of power, Jesus speaks about a simpler, more discreet reign of God. Not something that will unleash great mass movements. The reign of God is already present—in the same humble way a tiny, almost laughable mustard seed germinates, or the way a tiny lump of yeast gets lost in the dough and begins to ferment it from within.

We will never prepare the way for the reign of God by excommunicating other groups, parties or ideologies, or by condemning everything that doesn't agree with our way of thinking. We will not plant the reign of God in society by gathering masses of people, or by winning a moment of applause from the multitudes.

The reign of God is a «human ferment» that can grow in any dark corner of the world, wherever people love their brothers and sisters and fight for a life of dignity. We prepare the way of the reign of God by letting the power of the gospel transform our way of living, loving, enjoying, struggling, and being.

4. CONDEMNING NO ONE

In today's society we often see what some writers call «religious diversity». There are pious believers and convinced atheists among us, people with no interest in religion and followers of new religions, people who vaguely believe in «something» and others who have assembled an «a la carte religion» to fit their particular needs, people who don't know whether they believe or not and others who want to believe but don't know how.

But although we live together and see each other at work, in leisure activities and in everyday life, we know little about one another's thinking about God, faith, or the ultimate meaning of life. Sometimes even couples know nothing about their partners' inner life. We don't know what questions, doubts, uncertainties, and searches are hidden in their hearts.

We think of those who have abandoned religious faith as «nonbelievers», which doesn't seem like a very useful term. It is true that they have abandoned «something» that they once lived by, but their lives today are not defined by that rejection or abandonment. They have gone on to live by other convictions, which they sometimes cannot articulate, but which help them to live, struggle, suffer, and even die with a certain sense of meaning. In every life there are convictions, commitments, and loyalties that give consistency to that person.

It's hard to tell how God is working in each person's consciousness. The parable of the wheat and the weeds suggests that we shouldn't be in a hurry. It's not up to us to judge each person. We certainly should not excommunicate those who don't fit the «ideal Christian» profile that we construct out of our own understanding of the faith, and which probably is not as ideal as we think it is.

«Only God knows his own», said St. Augustine. Only God knows who is living with a heart open to God's Mystery, responding to his deep desire for peace, love, and solidarity among human beings. We who call ourselves Christians should be attentive to people outside religious faith, because God is also living and working in their hearts. We will find in them a lot that is good, noble, and sincere. We will find, especially, that God is always ready for everyone to seek him.

5. LEARNING TO LIVE WITH NONBELIEVERS

In spite of Jesus' warning, we Christians keep falling into the old temptation of separating the wheat from the weeds, always naturally assuming that we are «good wheat».

It is surprising how harshly some «believers» dare to judge those who for various reasons have turned away from faith and from the Church.

Belief and unbelief, like the wheat and the weeds in the parable, are mixed together in each one of us. It would be more honest to acknowledge the unbeliever within us, and the believer that still lives within many people who have left the faith.

Rather than reacting to them with condemnation or anger, we can learn from them better ways to understand and live our own faith. Let me give an example from my own experience.

From the fact that some men and women can live without believing in God, I learn that I can believe freely. My faith has not been imposed on me. Nothing and no one is forcing me. My faith is an act of freedom. It comes from within me.

Nonbelievers also teach me to be more rigorous in living my faith. I often see people rejecting a ridiculous, false God. That God doesn't really exist, but it may be the kind of God they see in the lives of people like us who call ourselves believers.

Let us not forget the words of Vatican II: «For, taken as a whole, atheism is not a spontaneous development but stems from a variety of causes, including a critical reaction against religious beliefs, and in some places against the Christian religion in particular. Hence believers can have more than a little to do with the birth of atheism. To the extent that they neglect their own training in the faith, or teach erroneous doctrine, or are deficient in their religious, moral or social life, they must be said to conceal rather than reveal the authentic face of God and religion» (*Gaudium et Spes* 19).

Nonbelievers also remind me of the unbelief within me. It is true that there is a difference between believers and nonbelievers, but sometimes we get too comfortable with the distinction. The line between faith and unbelief runs through each of us. Remembering that helps me learn not to be an arrogant, conceited, or fanatical believer, but to continue walking humbly before the mystery of God.

I am not uncomfortable in the presence of nonbelievers. I believe God is in them, and cares for their life with infinite love. I cannot forget God's comforting words:

> I was ready to be sought out by those who did not ask,
> to be found by those who did not seek me.
> I said, «Here I am, here I am»,
> to a nation that did not call on my name (Isaiah 65:1).

20

A Treasure Waiting to Be Found

«The kingdom of heaven is like treasure hidden in a field, which someone found and hid; then in his joy he goes and sells all that he has and buys that field».

«Again, the kingdom of heaven is like a merchant in search of fine pearls; on finding one pearl of great value, he went and sold all that he had and bought it» (Matthew 13:44-46).

1. A HIDDEN TREASURE

Not all Jesus' listeners were enthusiastic about his project. Many of them had serious doubts and questions. Did it make sense to follow him, or was this craziness? The Galileans were raising those questions, and so does everyone who listens to Jesus with any degree of seriousness.

Jesus told two short parables to entice the people who remained indifferent. He wanted to plant a decisive question in everyone's mind: Is there a «secret» to life that we have not yet discovered?

Everyone could understand the parable of the poor worker who was digging in someone else's land, and found a treasure hidden in a clay jar. He didn't have to think twice. It was the chance of a lifetime; he wasn't going to let it pass. He sold everything he had, and joyfully made the treasure his own.

The same thing happened to a rich pearl merchant when he discovered one incredibly valuable pearl. He had never seen another like it. He sold everything he owned, and bought the pearl for himself.

These were seductive words. Is God like that? Would it be like that to find God? Would it be like discovering a «treasure» more beautiful, more solid and true, than everything we are living and enjoying?

Jesus is talking about his experience of God: it has completely transformed his life. Could he be right? Would it be like that to follow him? Could this be the great good fortune of finding the essence of life, the one thing human beings have always wanted most?

Many people today are turning away from religion without ever having tasted God. I know how they feel; I would turn away, too. If we never get a taste of the experience of God that Jesus lived, religion is boring. It's not worth the trouble.

It is sad to see so many Christians whose lives have never been touched by the joy, the wonder, or the surprise of God. Never. They are closed in on their religion, and have never discovered a «treasure». For Jesus' followers, taking care of our inner life is not just one thing more to do.It is an indispensable part of opening up to the surprise God has in store.

2. DISCOVERING JESUS' PROJECT

It was not easy to believe Jesus. His words appealed to some people. For others they raised many doubts. Did it make sense to follow Jesus, or was it craziness? We have the same questions today: is it worth while to commit ourselves to his project of humanizing life, or is it more practical to go on taking care of our own well-being? We can spend our lives thinking about it, without ever making a decision.

Jesus tells two parables. In each one the protagonist finds something extremely valuable, a treasure or a pearl of great price. They both react the same way: they sell everything they have and get the treasure or the pearl. Of course that is the sensible thing to do.

The reign of God is «hidden». Many people still have not discovered God's great project for a new world. Yet it is not an inaccessible mystery. It is «hidden» in Jesus, in his life and his message. A Christian community that has not discovered the reign of God really doesn't know Jesus well, and cannot follow in his footsteps.

Discovering the reign of God is a life-changing experience. It brings us a joy unlike any other. We have found the most essential thing, the best that Jesus offers, something that can transform our lives. If we Christians do not discover Jesus' project, there will be no joy in the Church.

The two people in the parables make the same decision: they sell everything they have. Nothing is more important than seeking «the kingdom of God and his righteousness». Everything else can wait; everything else is relative, and must take a back seat to God's project.

This is the most important decision facing the Church and the Christian communities: to liberate ourselves from everything secondary and commit ourselves to the reign of God. Get rid of everything superfluous. Forget our other interests. Learn how to «lose» in order to «win» our own authenticity. If we do that, we are collaborating in the conversion of the Church.

3. SEEKING GOD

According to the sociologists, the religious crisis in Europe is leading to increasing levels of indifference. It is a comfortable indifference, with no need to talk about God. Yet more and more people, moved by a «yearning for God», are feeling a need to search for «something different», a new way of believing in him. How shall we look for God?

Certainly we all have to start with our own experience. We don't need to copy anyone else. We don't need to do anything under pressure, or for the sake of appearance. Each of us knows our own desires and miseries, our empty places and our fears. We know our own «need» for God. Our needs constantly make themselves heard. They don't cry out loud, but they whisper in our hearts.

So it doesn't help to look for God outside us, in books, discussions, or debate. «Discussing religion» is very different from seeking God with a sincere heart. We ourselves know when we are running away from God, and when we are truly seeking him. St. Augustine said: «Don't scatter yourself around. Look to your intimate being. Truth resides in the inner man».

Seeking God takes effort, but finding God is never the result of a willful choice or edgy asceticism. God is a gift, and the gift must be accepted with «simplicity of soul». We remember the reflection of the old prioress in *Dialogues of the Carmelites* by Georges Bernanos: «Once we grow out of childhood, we have to suffer in order to return to it, just as the dawn only returns after a long night. Have I become a child again?»

Our own intuitions are not the best guide in seeking God. There are many ways to deceive ourselves, or to run in circles around ourselves, our feelings and our ideas. It is better to share and compare our experience with someone who can guide us on the basis of his or her own life with God. That mutual sharing may also give us the encouragement we need to keep searching for God.

In the parable of the hidden treasure, Jesus says that the man went «in joy» to sell everything and gain the treasure. Our search for God doesn't cause sadness or bitterness; on the contrary it brings joy and peace, because we begin to see where true happiness lies. In the words of St. Augustine: «Only what makes people good can make them happy».

4. WHERE DO WE START?

Some time back I was giving a talk to a young audience in San Sebastián. Afterward there was a lively debate on faith. At some point a young woman, who along with others had declared herself an agnostic, said something like this: «Today I am still an agnostic, but I am starting to feel a desire or a need to believe. Where should I start?»

Her question really got to me: «Where do we start?» I had to reply that I don't know from experience how to move away from agnosticism and begin to recover a living faith in God. I believe there are different ways to do it. But the question made me think about how my experience as a believer can help people who seek to recover or «re-establish» their faith.

First, I believe that nobody outside ourselves can help us to believe, just as no one can teach us to feel, to cry, or to be joyful. I can share my experience with people, and show them how I live the mystery of life, but each one has to walk his or her own path, secretly «pulled along» by God.

I also believe that faith is not a matter of reasoning and discussion. Believing is different. What we need is not to verify a «hypothesis» of God by using our reason. The real problem lies somewhere else. Whenever I have discussed theoretical issues of faith with someone, I have had the impression that we're not getting to the «important» point.

Perhaps the first thing is to be sincerely in touch with oneself and to go down into one's «heart», that symbolic, secret place where fundamental decisions are made. We are usually so distracted and busy that we can never think about life in terms of the ultimate mystery of existence. That sincere, inward attitude seems decisive to me.

For that reason, prayer is also important. Do you pray, or not? I think that is a very important question. Prayer is not theory, or discussion, or reflection. It is a free and responsible approach to the ultimate mystery of life. When I pray, I am thinking about the most decisive questions: can I trust someone, or am I the absolute center of my existence? Does my life begin and end with me, or can I place my hope in God?

The most honest and courageous position a man or woman can take is one that says, in a sincere attitude of searching, «God, if you exist, help me believe in you». The mystery of God, says Jesus, is like a treasure hidden in the field. The person who finds it lets go of everything else in order to make it his or her own.

Many Christians today are living in some intermediate state, between the traditional Christianity of their childhood and the de-christianization that is gradually invading everything.

Perhaps without saying so in words, some people are secretly afraid that the social and cultural changes we see today are threatening to eliminate Christian faith as we know it from our society.

It is natural in that case that many believers live their Christianity «on the defensive», disconcerted by customs and attitudes that leave Christian meaning out of life, and by so much mockery and disrespect toward the faith.

A faith exposed to so much criticism, and challenged on so many fronts, can only be lived authentically by people who have discovered the joy of encountering the reality of the living God. We all have to build our own experience. Belonging to the Church, confessing Christian doctrine with our lips, does not automatically protect us from unbelief. Today more than ever, we need «religious experience».

It does Christians little good to confess our beliefs unless we have discovered faith as a joyful, warm and revitalizing experience. The important thing is always to find the «treasure hidden in the field». We have to meet the God of Jesus Christ, and discover for ourselves that God alone can fully respond to people's most vital questions and deepest desires.

More than ever we need to pray, to be silent, to overcome our great haste and superficiality, to stand before God, to open ourselves more sincerely and trustingly to God's unfathomable mystery. One can no longer be a Christian by birth, but only by a decision nourished by each person's personal experience.

21

You Give Them Something to Eat

Now when Jesus heard [about the death of John the Baptist], he withdrew from there in a boat to a deserted place by himself. But when the crowds heard it, they followed him on foot from the towns. When he went ashore, he saw a great crowd; and he had compassion for them and cured their sick.

When it was evening, the disciples came to him and said, «This is a deserted place, and the hour is now late; send the crowds away so that they may go into the villages and buy food for themselves». Jesus said to them, «They need not go away; you give them something to eat». They replied, «We have nothing here but five loaves and two fish». And he said, «Bring them here to me». Then he ordered the crowds to sit down on the grass.

Taking the five loaves and the two fish, he looked up to heaven, and blessed and broke the loaves, and gave them to the disciples, and the disciples gave them to the crowds. And all ate and were filled; and they took up what was left over of the broken pieces, twelve baskets full. And those who ate were about five thousand men, besides women and children (Matthew 14:13-21).

1. YOU GIVE THEM SOMETHING TO EAT

Matthew the evangelist is not concerned with the details of the story. His only interest is in setting the scene; he shows us Jesus, feeling «compassion» in the midst of the «great crowd». We see the same compassion on other occasions. Everything he does comes from that compassion.

Jesus does not live with his back to the people, focused on his religious activities and indifferent to the suffering of the people. He «sees a great crowd; and he has compassion for them and cures their sick». His experience of God leads him to live by alleviating the suffering and hunger of those poor people. That is how the Church must live if it wants to make Jesus present in today's world.

Time goes by and Jesus is still curing the sick. The disciples interrupt him with a proposal: it's getting late; the best thing would be to send the crowds away so they can buy food. They haven't learned from Jesus. They aren't concerned with the hungry people, but leave them to buy food for themselves. What will the people do who can't buy it?

Jesus replies with a clear order, which comfortable Christians in the rich countries don't want to hear: «You give them something to eat». Not «send them to buy», but «give them food». He couldn't have said it more clearly. Jesus was constantly calling out to the Father: «Give us this day our daily bread». God wants all his sons and daughters to have bread, even those who can't buy it.

The disciples are still skeptical. They can only find five loaves and two fish among all those people. For Jesus that is enough: if we share what we have, there will be enough for everyone; there may even be twelve baskets of bread «left over». This is his alternative: in a more human society, one that can share its bread with the hungry, there will be enough resources for everyone.

In a world where millions of people are dying of hunger, we Christians must surely live in shame. Europe has no Christian soul; it calls the people illegal who live in search of bread, and «sends them away». Meanwhile in the Church, who is following the direction laid out by Jesus? Most of us are deaf to their cries, distracted by our own interests, debates, doctrines, and celebrations. How can we call ourselves followers of Jesus?

2. SHARING WITH PEOPLE IN NEED

The two most painful problems in the Galilean villages were hunger and debt. Jesus suffered over both of them. When his disciples asked him to teach them to pray, those two petitions came from his heart: «Father, give us this day our daily bread», and «Father, forgive us our debts, as we also have forgiven our debtors».

What could they do about the hunger that was destroying them, and about the debts that caused them to lose their land? Jesus saw God's will very clearly: they must share what they had, and forgive one another's debts. That was the only way for a new world to be born.

The early Christian sources have preserved the record of a memorable meal with Jesus. It was out in the countryside, and many people took part. It is hard to reconstruct the actual event. This is the memory that remained: they could only find five loaves and two fish among the people, but everyone shared what little they had, and with Jesus' blessing, they were all able to eat.

The opening dialogue tells us a lot. When they see the people are hungry, the disciples offer the simplest and least demanding solution: «let them go into the villages and buy food for themselves»; let each one solve the problem as best they can. Jesus replies by giving them the responsibility: «You give them something to eat»; don't abandon the hungry to their fate.

We must never forget that. When we turn our backs to the world's hungry, we lose our identity as Christians; we are not being faithful to Jesus; his sensitivity and his vision, and his compassion, are missing from our eucharistic meals. How can we transform a religion like ours into a movement of more faithful followers of Jesus?

The first thing is to hold on to his fundamental perspective: to let ourselves be affected more and more by the suffering of those who have never experienced a life with bread and dignity. The second is to get involved in small initiatives: specific, modest, partial solutions that can teach us how to share and help us become more identified with Jesus' way of life.

3. BUILDING A FAMILY OF BROTHERS AND SISTERS

According to an oriental proverb, «when the prophet points his finger at the moon, the fool keeps looking at the prophet's finger». Something like that happens when we focus on the wondrous character of Jesus' miracles, without looking at the message they carry.

Jesus was not a miracle maker who performed propagandistic stunts. His miracles are signs that break through this sinful world and point to a new reality, the final destiny of human beings.

Specifically, the miracle of the loaves and fish invites us to discover that Jesus' project was to nourish human beings, and bring them together in a real family where people know how to share their bread and fish as brothers and sisters. For Christians, brotherhood is not one moral requirement among others. It is the only way to build the reign of the Father among human beings. This brotherhood can be deceptive. Too often we confuse it with «a devious selfishness that knows how to behave with decency» (Karl Rahner).

We think we are loving our neighbors when we haven't done anything especially bad to them, even though our attitude is mean and selfish, uncaring toward everyone, motivated only by self-interest.

The Church as a «sacrament of brotherhood» is called, at every moment in history, to inspire new forms of close brotherhood among human beings. We believers have to learn to live a more brotherly and sisterly way of life, listening to the new needs of the people in our own time.

The struggle for military disarmament, protection of the environment, solidarity with hungry peoples, sharing the effects of the economic crisis with people on strike, the rehabilitation of drug addicts, concern for the lonely and neglected elderly... These are some of the things we must do in order to be brothers and sisters who can «feed the crowds» the bread they need to live.

4. A NEW EUROPEAN WALL

The gospel story reminds us that we cannot eat our bread and fish in peace, in the presence of men and women threatened by so many «hungers». We who live in peace and comfort must listen to Jesus' words: «you give them something to eat». A great parade of Africans, Latin Americans, and people from the East have been coming to Europe in recent years, pushed by hunger and misery. There were fourteen million in 1989; today there are many more.

But Europe is not prepared to respond in solidarity to the great challenge of our time. This European society, which established its prosperity during centuries of colonial exploitation, is living so comfortably that it is afraid to accept these men and women who seek to survive in our midst.

Now we are seeing a resurgence of racist and anti-foreign sentiment. The communications media are encouraging public opinion to see immigrants as dangerous criminals who will take away our relatively scarce employment opportunities.

What is worse, a great wall is being built to defend us from these perceived dangers. Firm measures are established to control the movement of foreigners. Deportation and expulsion policies are tightened. There are widespread calls to reduce the opportunities for immigrants and refugees to legalize their status. These restrictions are justified as a «threshold of tolerance» which must be protected in order not to lose our socio-economic balance.

We have a lot to learn from the gospel story. The disciples, figuring that there is not enough bread for everyone, think the problem can be solved by sending the crowd to «buy» bread. Jesus' answer to this «buy», governed by the laws of economics, is a free and generous «give»: «You give them something to eat».

Then Jesus gathers all the provisions that people have brought, and pronounces the words of thanksgiving over them. In this way the bread is released by the people who brought it, treated as a gift of God, and generously shared among everyone who is hungry. This is the deepest lesson of the story: «When creation is set free from human selfishness, there is more than enough to meet the needs of all».

Europe needs to be reminded that the earth belongs to everyone, and that we cannot deny bread to a hungry person. There is enough bread for everyone, if we can learn to share it in solidarity. Instead of giving in to racism and xenophobia, we have to educate public opinion in the practice of solidarity; and above all we need to promote programs of assistance and cooperation that can gradually bring countries out of their hunger and economic despair.

5. HOW SHOULD WE BLESS THE TABLE?

Gradually, almost unconsciously, pushed by a variety of factors, we are dehumanizing the wonderful, human act of sitting down together at the table to eat.

For many people, meals have become something purely functional; we have to fit them quickly and precisely into the work schedule. The privileged moment of gathering around the family dinner table is becoming increasingly rare. In many homes the table no longer serves as a place for parents and children to share their lives, talk to one another, and relax together.

Some people are accustomed to «feeding the organism» in impersonal meals at a restaurant, or in a corner of a fast food outlet. Some are required to participate in official or working dinners, where the friendly act of eating together is set aside in favor of self-interest, pragmatism, or ostentation.

Jesus' way of inviting people to recline around a table for a simple meal, blessing God for the bread we receive, can be a reminder for us. As Xabier Basurko commented in his study *Compartir el pan,* eating is much more than «introducing a prescribed ration of calories into the organism».

Above all, our need for food is a sign of our radical dependency. In some obscure way, we humans realize that we do not construct ourselves. In reality we live by receiving: by nourishing ourselves with a life that is given to each of us, day by day, from the earth. For this reason it is a profoundly human gesture to bow down before eating and give God thanks for this food, the fruit of human effort and labor, but at the same time a gift from the God who creates and sustains life.

Eating is more than an individual, biological act. Human beings are made to eat together, sharing their table with family and friends. Eating together is a way of building brotherhood, dialogue and friendship, a way of sharing the gift of life.

It is hard to give thanks to God when some of us have more food than we need, while others are suffering misery and hunger. Gandhi's words come to us as an accusation: «Whatever you eat without need, you are stealing from the stomach of the poor». Perhaps we in the affluent countries should learn to bless the table in a different way: by giving thanks to God, but at the same time asking God to forgive our lack of solidarity, and acknowledging our responsibility for the world's hungry people.

22

Do Not Be Afraid

Immediately he made the disciples get into the boat and go on ahead to the other side, while he dismissed the crowds. And after he had dismissed the crowds, he went up the mountain by himself to pray. When evening came, he was there alone, but by this time the boat, battered by the waves, was far from the land, for the wind was against them. And early in the morning he came walking toward them on the sea. But when the disciples saw him walking on the sea, they were terrified, saying, «It is a ghost!» And they cried out in fear. But immediately Jesus spoke to them and said, «Take heart, it is I; do not be afraid».

Peter answered him, «Lord, if it is you, command me to come to you on the water». He said, «Come». So Peter got out of the boat, started walking on the water, and came toward Jesus. But when he noticed the strong wind, he became frightened, and beginning to sink, he cried out, «Lord, save me!» Jesus immediately reached out his hand and caught him, saying to him, «You of little faith, why did you doubt?» When they got into the boat, the wind ceased. And those in the boat worshiped him, saying, «Truly you are the Son of God» (Matthew 14:22-33).

1. THE CHURCH HAS BECOME FEARFUL

As they went back and forth across the lake of Galilee, Jesus must surely have used the difficult moments in their journeys to teach his disciples how to face the more dangerous storms that were coming. Here Matthew is «re-creating» one of those moments, to help the Christian communities overcome their «fears» and their «little faith».

The disciples were alone. This time Jesus was not with them. Their boat was «far from the land», a long way from Jesus, and because «the wind was against them», they could not return to him. What could they do, alone in the storm, without Jesus?

The boat is in a desperate situation. Matthew describes the dark night, the strong wind, the battering waves. This is biblical language, well known to his readers in the Christian communities. Matthew uses it to describe their situation, threatened from without by hostility, and from within by their fear and little faith. Don't we face the same threats today?

Somewhere between three and six o'clock in the morning, Jesus comes «walking toward them on the sea», but the disciples are unable to recognize him. Because of their fear, they think he is «a ghost». More than anything else, fear keeps us from recognizing, loving, and following Jesus as the «Son of God» who walks with us and saves us in times of crisis.

Jesus says the words they need to hear: «Take heart, it is I; do not be afraid». He wants to give them his strength, his security, his absolute trust in the Father. Peter reacts first. As always, Peter's behavior is both a model of trusting commitment and an example of fear and weakness. He walks confidently over the water until he «becomes frightened»; then he forgets Jesus' Word, feels the power of the wind, and begins to sink.

The Church of Jesus has become fearful, and we don't know how to overcome it. We are afraid of losing prestige and power, and of being rejected by society. We are afraid of one another: the hierarchy hardens its stance, theologians are losing their freedom, pastors would rather not take any risks, the faithful look fearfully at the future. Behind these fears is our fear of Jesus, our little faith in him, our reluctance to follow in his footsteps. He says so himself: «You of little faith, why did you doubt?»

2. BEFORE WE SINK

The story of the storm on Lake Galilee is surprisingly relevant to our present situation of religious crisis. Matthew describes it accurately: Jesus' disciples are alone and insecure, «far from the land»; their boat is «battered by the waves», overrun by adverse forces; «the wind is against them», and in the darkness they cannot see the horizon.

Many believers are feeling that way today. There is no security, no religious certainty; everything has turned dark and doubtful. Religion is subjected to all kinds of accusations and suspicions. People talk about Christianity as a «terminal religion» that belongs to the past; we are said to be living in a «post-Christian age» (E. Poulat). Some wonder: Isn't religion an unreal dream, a naïve myth that will soon fade away? That is what the disciples thought when they first saw Jesus in the storm: «It is a ghost!».

Jesus responds quickly: «Take heart, it is I; do not be afraid». Inspired by his words, Peter makes a strange request: «Lord, if it is you, command me to come to you on the water». He doesn't know if Jesus is a ghost or a real person, but he wants to see if he can walk toward him —not on land but on the water, not on the basis of firm arguments but in the weakness of his faith.

That is how believers live their commitment to Christ in times of crisis and darkness. We don't know if Christ is a ghost or a real, living person, raised up by the Father for our salvation. We don't have scientific arguments to prove it, but we know from experience that we can walk through life with the support of faith in him and in his word.

It is not easy to live by naked faith. The gospel story tells us that Peter felt the power of the wind, became frightened, and started to sink. That is a familiar process: when we look only at the power of evil, we become paralyzed by fear and sink into despair.

Peter reacts in time; before he sinks completely, he cries «Lord, save me!» Faith is often a cry, an invocation, a way to call on God: «Lord, save me!» Then without knowing how or why, we can see Christ as a hand held out to sustain our faith; to save us, while saying at the same time: «You of little faith, why did you doubt?».

3. WALKING ON THE WATER

Many believers today feel left out in the elements, abandoned in the midst of crisis and general confusion. The traditional pillars of their faith have been violently shaken, from top to bottom. The authority of the Church, the infallibility of the pope, the magisterium of the bishops can no longer uphold them in their religious convictions. The strange new language they hear is creating a sense of discomfort and confusion that they have never felt before. The «lack of agreement» among priests and even bishops has plunged them into despondency.

Many people are wondering, with varying degrees of sincerity, what can we believe? Who should we listen to? What dogmas should we accept? What morality should we follow? And when they can no longer answer with the certainty of other times, many feel as if they are «losing their faith».

But we must never confuse faith with the mere affirmation of theoretical truths or principles. Certainly faith is a vision of life and a unique concept of humanity, its task and its ultimate destiny. But to be a believer is more profound and radical than any concept. More than anything else, it is a trusting openness to Jesus Christ as the ultimate meaning of our life, the definitive criterion of love for our brothers and sisters, our ultimate hope for the future.

So one can be a true believer without being able to express every aspect of the Christian understanding of life with certainty. Conversely, one can affirm the various Christian dogmas with great certainty, and still not faithfully live a life committed to God.

Matthew was describing true faith when he showed Peter «walking on the water» toward Jesus. That is what believing means. Walking on the water, and not on firm ground. Looking to God, not to our own reason, arguments, and definitions, to support our existence. Being upheld, not by our own certainty, but by trust in God.

4. MOVING FROM DOUBT TO BELIEF

It is not easy to answer the question Jesus asked Peter as he was saving him from the water: «Why did you doubt?»

Sometimes our deepest convictions suddenly fade away, the eyes of our soul grow dim, and we don't know exactly why. The principles we thought were unshakable, begin to fall apart. Then we are tempted to give it all up, without building anything new in its place.

Sometimes we feel overwhelmed by the mystery of God. I can't get hold of the meaning of life, and it is hard to surrender to the mystery: my reason keeps looking for a clear and steady light, which it can't find and never will.

Sometimes the shallow superficiality of everyday life, and our secret worship of idols, plunge us into such a long crisis of indifference and inner skepticism that we come to feel we really have lost God.

Often, when our faith crumbles and weakens because we have turned away from God, it is our own sin that finally breaks it up. If we are honest, we must confess how far we really are from the believers we claim to be. What do we do when we notice how weak and vacillating our faith is?

First, we must not let our doubts and vacillation surprise or defeat us. The search for God almost always takes us through insecurity, darkness, and risk. We have to «grope» for God. Let us remember how often «genuine faith comes by overcoming doubt» (Ladislao Boros).

The important thing is to accept the mystery of God with an open heart. Our faith depends on a true relationship with God. We don't have to wait until our questions and doubts are resolved, in order to live in truth before the Father.

So we learn to cry out as Peter did: «Lord, save me!» We learn to hold up our empty hands to God, not only as a gesture of supplication, but also in trusting commitment as small, ignorant men and women in need of salvation. Let us remember that faith means «walking on water», always expecting a hand to save us when we begin to sink.

5. THE DOUBTS OF THE BELIEVER

Christians used to think of unbelief as something that happened only to atheists and skeptics, not an imminent danger for us. Today we have lost that sense of immunity. We know now that unbelief isn't «someone else's» problem, but a challenge to the believer's faith as well.

First we need to remember that faith is not a fixed resource that we can always draw on when we need it. Faith is a gift of God that we need to accept and faithfully care for. The danger of losing our faith doesn't come from outside us, but from our own personal attitude toward God.

Many people today talk about their «doubts of faith». In reality these are the problems we face in understanding certain ideas and concepts of God and the Christian mystery in a coherent and rational way. These «doubts of faith» are less threatening to the Christian who lives in a trusting, loving relationship with God. As Cardinal Newman used to say, «ten problems don't make a doubt».

The ancient Hebrews used a very expressive word for faith: *'amán*. That's where we get the word «amen». The verb means to «lean on», «rest on», «trust in» someone more solid than ourselves.

That is the very heart of faith. To believe means to live supported by God. To wait on him trustingly, in an attitude of absolute, trusting, faithful commitment.

This is the experience that the great believers have always lived in their times of crisis. St. Paul described it graphically: «I know the one in whom I have put my trust» (2 Timothy 1:12).

It was also Peter's attitude, when he cried out from his heart as he began to sink, «Lord, save me!» As he felt Jesus' hand grasping him, he heard him say, «Why did you doubt?».

Our moments of doubt may be an opportunity to purify our faith, to deepen and renew its roots in God. They are a time to lean on God more trustingly, and to pray more truly than ever.

For those who are «Christians by birth» there is always a time when we must ask whether we really believe in God, or if we have simply gone on believing in those who told us about him when we were children.

23

Jesus and The Pagan Woman

Jesus left that place and went away to the district of Tyre and Sidon. Just then a Canaanite woman from that region came out and started shouting, «Have mercy on me, Lord, Son of David; my daughter is tormented by a demon». But he did not answer her at all. And his disciples came and urged him, saying, «Send her away, for she keeps shouting after us». He answered, «I was sent only to the lost sheep of the house of Israel». But she came and knelt before him, saying, «Lord, help me». He answered, «It is not fair to take the children's food and throw it to the dogs». She said, «Yes, Lord, yet even the dogs eat the crumbs that fall from their masters' table». Then Jesus answered her, «Woman, great is your faith! Let it be done for you as you wish». And her daughter was healed instantly (Matthew 15:21-28).

1. THE WOMAN'S CRY

When Matthew wrote his gospel sometime after 80 A.D., the Church was facing a serious question: What should Jesus' followers do? Should they remain entirely within the Jewish people, or open up to pagans too?

Jesus' activity had been carried out exclusively within the borders of Israel. He was so quickly eliminated by the Roman representative and the temple leadership, that he was never able to go further afield. But as they looked back over his life, the disciples remembered two important things. First, Jesus could see a greater faith in some pagans than among his own followers. Second, he had never kept his compassion for Jews only. The God of compassion belonged to everyone.

It is a moving scene. A woman comes out to meet Jesus. She does not belong to the chosen people. She is a pagan. She is a Canaanite, from a people condemned by God for its struggles against Israel. She is a woman alone, without a name. Perhaps she is a single mother, a widow, or someone rejected by her family.

Matthew only tells us about her faith. Her whole life is summed up in one cry, which expresses the depth of her misfortune. She comes after the disciples, «shouting». She is not turned away by Jesus' silence, nor by his disciples' annoyance. The tragedy of her daughter, «tormented by a demon», has become her own sorrow. «Have mercy on me, Lord!»

At some point the woman catches up with the group, kneels before Jesus, and begs him: «Lord, help me!» She is not deterred by Jesus' explanation, that he was sent only to the people of Israel. She refuses to accept the ethnic, political, religious, and gender exclusion that forces so many women into loneliness and marginalization.

That is when we see the humility and greatness of Jesus: «Woman, great is your faith! Let it be done for you as you wish». The woman is right. There is nothing left to say. The important thing is to relieve suffering. Her plea reflects God's will.

What do we Christians do today about the cry of so many women alone, marginalized, abused, and neglected by the Church? Do we push them aside, justifying their abandonment by saying we have more important things to do? That's not what Jesus did.

2. ALLEVIATING SUFFERING

Jesus is always attentive to life. That is where he discerns God's will. He looks deeply into creation and grasps the mystery of the Father, who invites him to care tenderly for the smallest of his creatures. He opens his heart to people's suffering, and hears in it the voice of God calling him to alleviate their pain.

The gospels have preserved the memory of Jesus' encounter with a pagan woman in the region of Tyre and Sidon. It is a surprising story, showing us how Jesus learned to be faithful to God.

A woman, alone and in despair, comes out to meet him. She can only do one thing: shout and beg for mercy. Her daughter is not only sick and out of her mind, but «tormented by a demon». Her home has become a hell. The cry rises up from her broken heart: «Lord, help me!»

Jesus answers with a surprising coolness. He has a very specific, well-defined mission: he was «sent only to the lost sheep of the house of Israel». The pagan world is not part of his mission: «It is not fair to take the children's food and throw it to the dogs».

It is a harsh thing to say, but the woman does not take offense. She knows her request is right, and she throws Jesus' image back to him with these admirable words: «Yes, Lord, yet even the dogs eat the crumbs that fall from their masters' table».

Suddenly Jesus sees everything in a new light. The woman is right: what she wants is in line with the will of God, who wants no one to suffer. With compassion and admiration he replies: «Woman, great is your faith! Let it be done for you as you wish».

Jesus, who always seemed so sure of his own mission, is letting this pagan woman teach him and correct him. Suffering knows nothing of boundaries. It is true that his mission is to Israel, but God's compassion extends to anyone who suffers.

When we meet someone who suffers, there God's will shines in all its brilliance. God wants us to alleviate their suffering. That comes first. Everything else is secondary. This is the path Jesus followed out of faithfulness to the Father.

3. NOT TO CONQUER BUT TO LIBERATE

Apparently Jesus never did proclaim his message in the pagan cities around him. He did not see himself as a «religious conqueror». He felt he had been sent to the people of Israel, which would one day become «a light to the gentiles» in the words of the prophet Isaiah. Within Israel he was sent to the «lost sheep», the poorest, most forgotten people, most despised and abused by life and by society.

But at a time when he has withdrawn into the region of Tyre and Sidon, Jesus meets a pagan woman who brings her great suffering to him: «My daughter is tormented by a demon». Something sinister and disturbing has taken possession of her; she cannot communicate with her beloved daughter; her life has become a hell. This pagan woman can only cry out to Jesus: «Have mercy on me!».

Jesus' reaction is always the same. He only pays attention to people's suffering. He is moved by the woman's sorrow and her faithful struggle for her daughter. Human suffering has no boundaries, recognizes no religious differences; therefore compassion also cannot be enclosed in a particular religion. Jesus knows that God wants no one to suffer. He has always prayed to God, «Your will be done»; now he tells the woman, «Let it be done to you as you wish», because that is God's will.

The relationship between Christianity and other religions has often been invasive and controlling. Aware of its power, the Church has tried to impose its faith and implant its religious system, and thus contributed to the destruction of cultures and the uprooting of whole populations. This «colonizing» operation certainly grew out of a sincere desire to make Christians of all the nations, but it was not the evangelical way to make the Spirit of Christ present in pagan lands.

Things are different today. Christians have learned to move toward human suffering in order to alleviate it. The work of missionaries has been profoundly transformed. Their mission is not to «conquer» peoples for the faith, but to work tirelessly for the liberation of people from hunger, misery, or sickness. They are

Christ's best witnesses on Earth. Their service can lead to true faith in Jesus Christ.

4. WHY DO WE ASK GOD FOR HELP?

We have gotten used to taking our requests to God in such a superficial, self-interested way that we probably need to learn the meaning and the greatness of Christian prayer all over again.

Some people are too proud to ask for anything. People are responsible for themselves and their own history. That is true, but it is also true that we live by the love of God. By acknowledging that need, we come closer to the truth of our own lives.

Others see God as something unreal. A distant being, unconcerned with the world. We are here, caught up in «the labyrinth of earthly things», and God is out there in his eternal world. Yet by praying to God we can see that he is on our side, against the evil that threatens us. To ask for help is to invoke God as grace, liberation, and strength for living.

But that is just when God seems weakest and most powerless, because he doesn't act or intervene. And it's true that God can't do everything. He has created the world and respects it as it is; he doesn't enter into conflict with it. He has made us free, and doesn't override our decisions.

But events in the world and in our own life are not a closed book. Supplication itself is fruitful, because it opens us up to the God who is working out our definitive salvation beyond the power of evil. We pray to God, but not to make God love us more and pay more attention to us. God cannot love us more than he does. It is we, by praying, who discover life from the horizon of God's love and open ourselves up to his saving will. It is not God who needs to change, but we ourselves.

The humble Canaanite woman, kneeling in faith at Jesus' feet, can be a call and invitation for us to recover the meaning of trustful supplication to the Lord.

5. ASKING IN FAITH

Petitionary prayer has been strongly criticized in recent years. Educated people in the modern age know better than to ask God for help; they know that God isn't going to change the natural course of events in order to fulfill our desires.

In this view, nature is like a machine that functions according to certain natural laws. Only human beings can change the world and history —and that only in part— by what they do.

So petitionary prayer is set aside in favor of other forms of prayer, like praise, thanksgiving or adoration, that fit more comfortably with modern ways of thinking.

Or sometimes creaturely supplication to the Creator is replaced by meditation, or by the immersion of the soul in God, the ultimate mystery of existence and the source of all life.

But prayers of supplication, despite all our possible misunderstandings, are an effective way to express and live our creaturely dependence on God from a viewpoint of faith.

It is not surprising that Jesus praised the great faith of a simple woman who knew how to pray urgently for his help. We can call on God in any situation—in happiness and adversity, in well-being and in suffering.

The man or woman who raises a petition to God is not addressing an apathetic Being, indifferent to creaturely suffering, but a God who comes out of his hiddenness and shows his nearness to those who ask.

That is what prayer is about. Not about using God to get what we want, but seeking and begging for God's nearness in that situation. And our experience of God's nearness does not depend mainly on the fulfillment of our wishes.

Believers can feel the nearness of God in many ways, regardless of how our problems are resolved. We remember the wise words of St. Augustine: «God listens to your call if you look for him. He doesn't listen if you're looking, through him, to get something else».

It is not yet time for the final fulfillment. Evil is not yet totally overcome. The person who prays senses a contradiction between his or her suffering and the definitive salvation that God has promised. For that reason all our specific requests and petitions to God are wrapped up in the great supplication that Jesus taught us: «Your kingdom come», the reign of salvation and definitive life.

24
Who Do You Say that I am?

Now when Jesus came into the district of Caesarea Philippi, he asked his disciples, «Who do people say that the Son of Man is?» And they said, «Some say John the Baptist, but others Elijah, and still others Jeremiah or one of the prophets». He said to them, «But who do you say that I am?» Simon Peter answered, «You are the Messiah, the Son of the living God». And Jesus answered him, «Blessed are you, Simon son of Jonah! For flesh and blood has not revealed this to you, but my Father in heaven. And I tell you, you are Peter, and on this rock I will build my church, and the gates of Hades will not prevail against it. I will give you the keys of the kingdom of heaven, and whatever you bind on earth will be bound in heaven, and whatever you loose on earth will be loosed in heaven». Then he sternly ordered the disciples not to tell anyone that he was the Messiah (Matthew 16:13-20).

1. A DECISIVE QUESTION

«But who do you say that I am?» Jesus' question is not addressed only to his first followers. It is the fundamental question that we must answer whenever we call ourselves Christians.

Our first reaction may be to look for a quick, doctrinal answer, and recite it routinely: Jesus is the «Son of God incarnate», the «Redeemer» of the world, the «Savior» of humanity. These are all solemn, orthodox answers to be sure, but they can be recited with no vital content whatsoever.

Jesus is asking for more than an opinion. He wants to know, especially, about our attitude toward him. Not only in words, but in our specific ways of following him. Some theologian has written: «The short proposition, "I believe that Jesus is the Son of God", means something completely different when Francis of Assisi says it than when one of our South American dictators says it. The God of these two men, or at least the God that each one calls on to direct his behavior, is not the same God».

Jesus is asking for a radical choice. Either he is just another historic figure for us, or he is the One who gives ultimate meaning to our existence, provides decisive guidance for our life, and offers us definitive hope.

Thus the question, «who do you say that I am?» takes on new meaning. It is no longer a question about Jesus, but about ourselves. Who am I? In whom do I believe? Where is the North on my compass? What is the essence of my faith?

We can all remember a time when our faith didn't fit with the formulas we were reciting. In order to understand «what I believe», we have to look at how I live, what I aspire to, what commitments I undertake.

For that reason Jesus' question, more than a test of our orthodoxy, is a call to a Christian way of life. Of course we can't just say or believe whatever we want about Christ. But we also can't just make solemn professions of orthodox belief and then live apart from the spirit that those professions demand and imply.

2. A LIVING ACCEPTANCE OF JESUS CHRIST

It is not easy to respond sincerely to Jesus' question: «Who do you say that I am?» Who is Jesus for us, really? What we know of him has come through two thousand years of images, formulas, devotions, experiences, cultural interpretations—all of which both conceal and reveal his unfathomable richness.

Moreover, we each clothe Jesus in our own self. We project on him our wishes, aspirations, interests and limitations. We unconsciously diminish and reshape him, even when we are trying to exalt him.

But Jesus still lives. We haven't been able to wear him down with our mediocrity. He refuses to wear our disguises. He won't let us label him or reduce him to our own rites, formulas, or customs.

Jesus is always a puzzlement to those who come to him with an open, sincere attitude. He is always different from what we expect. He keeps making new openings in our life, breaking our molds, drawing us toward a new life. The better we know him, the better we know how little we know.

Jesus is dangerous. In him we see a commitment to human beings that unmasks our own selfishness. A passion for justice that shakes up our certainties, privileges, and self-interest. A tenderness that puts our pettiness to shame. A freedom that uncovers our thousands of bondages and servitudes.

Above all, we sense in him a mystery of openness, nearness, and intimacy with God that draws us in and invites us to open up our own existence to the Father. We come to know Jesus better as we become more committed to him. There is only one way to understand his mystery: by following him.

Following his steps in humility, opening ourselves to the Father with him, imitating his acts of love and tenderness, looking at life through his eyes, sharing his painful destiny, waiting for his resurrection. And of course, praying from the bottom of our heart: «I believe; help my unbelief!»

3. CONFESSING JESUS WITH OUR LIFE

«Who do you say that I am?» All three of the synoptic gospels include this question that Jesus asked his disciples in the region of Caesarea Philippi. To the first Christians it was very important to remember again and again whom they were following, how they were collaborating in his project, and for whom they were risking their lives.

When we hear the question today, we tend to recite the formulas that Christianity has built up through the centuries: Jesus is the Son of God made man, the Savior of the world, the Redeemer of humanity. Are those words enough to make us «followers» of Jesus?

Unfortunately these are often formulas that we have learned as children, accepted in a mechanical way, repeated without thinking about them, and affirmed verbally, rather than living them by following in Jesus' footsteps.

We confess Christ out of habit, piety, or discipline, but we often go through life without ever grasping the uniqueness of his life, without hearing the newness of his call, without being drawn in by his passionate love, without catching hold of his freedom, and without making the effort to follow in his way.

We worship him as «God», but he is not at the center of our life. We confess him as «Lord», but we live with our back turned to his project, never quite knowing who he was or what he wanted. We call him «Teacher», but we are not motivated by what motivated his life. We live as members of a religion, but that does not make us disciples of Jesus.

Paradoxically, the «orthodoxy» of our doctrinal formulas can give us security, which enables us to avoid a living encounter with Jesus. Some very orthodox Christians live an instinctive religiosity, but have never experienced what it means to be nourished by Jesus. They consider themselves the «owners» of the faith and are even proud of its orthodoxy, but have never felt the vitality of the Spirit of Christ.

Let's not fool ourselves. Each one of us needs to stand before Jesus, let him look us in the eyes, and hear his words from the depth of our being: Who am I for you, really? We have to answer that question with our lives, not only with beautiful words.

4. FACE TO FACE WITH JESUS

We Christians too often forget that faith is not about believing something, but about believing in Someone. It's not about faithful adherence to a creed, let alone blind acceptance of «a strange assortment of doctrines», but about meeting a living Someone who gives radical meaning to our existence.

What truly matters is to meet Jesus in person and to discover, by personal experience, that he alone can fully answer our most important questions, our deepest desires, and our ultimate needs.

In our day it is getting harder and harder to believe in something. The most solid ideologies, the most powerful systems, the most brilliant theories, crumble when we see their limitations and profound deficiencies.

Perhaps people today, turned off by dogmas and ideologies, are still willing to believe in someone who can help us to live by giving new meaning to our existence. Karl Lehmann used to say that «modern people will only believe when they have had an authentic experience of relationship with the person of Jesus Christ».

It is sad that some Catholic groups seem to care only about «conserving the faith», as a «deposit of doctrines» that must be defended from the onslaught of new ideologies and currents.

Believing is something altogether different. First, we Christians need to renew and deepen our relationship with Jesus Christ. Only when we are «seduced» by him and energized by the renewing power of his person, can we pass on his spirit and his vision of life. Otherwise we will be pronouncing beautiful doctrines with our lips, but we will go on living a mediocre and unconvincing faith.

We Christians have to respond sincerely to Jesus' challenging question: «But who do you say that I am?» Ibn Arabí wrote that «those who have been caught by the sickness called Jesus, can never be cured».

5. OUR IMAGE OF JESUS

Jesus' question, «Who do you say that I am?» still demands an answer from believers in our time. We don't all have the same image of Jesus. This is not only because of his inexhaustible personality, but because each of us has a personal image of Jesus based on our own interests and concerns, conditioned by our personal psychology and the social group we belong to, and by the religious formation we have received.

And yet each one's image of Christ has a decisive importance for our life, because it shapes our way of understanding and living the faith. This is why we have to avoid any possible distortion in our understanding of Jesus, and purify our relationship with him.

It is not true that we believe in Jesus Christ just because we «believe» a dogma, or because we believe «what the holy Mother Church believes». In fact each person's beliefs are based on what each of us is discovering by following Jesus Christ, even when we do it within the Christian community.

Unfortunately, many Christians understand and live their religion in such a way that they will probably never have a living experience of personal encounter with Christ.

Already as children they have developed a childish idea of Jesus, perhaps before they were ready to raise the issues and ask the questions that Christ can answer.

They did not go on to rethink their faith in Jesus Christ, either because they considered it trivial and unimportant for their lives, or because they were afraid to examine it seriously and rigorously, or because for them it was enough to hold on to it in an indifferent and apathetic way that never changes their lives.

Unfortunately they have no idea who Jesus could be for them. This comment by Marcel Légaut is harsh but may be true: «These Christians don't know who Jesus is, and their religion itself keeps them from ever discovering him».

25

Taking Up the Cross

From that time on, Jesus began to show his disciples that he must go to Jerusalem and undergo great suffering at the hands of the elders and chief priests and scribes, and be killed, and on the third day be raised. And Peter took him aside and began to rebuke him, saying, «God forbid it, Lord! This must never happen to you». But he turned and said to Peter, «Get behind me, Satan! You are a stumbling block to me; for you are setting your mind not on divine things but on human things».

Then Jesus told his disciples, «If any want to become my followers, let them deny themselves and take up their cross and follow me. For those who lose their life for my sake will find it. For what will it profit them if they gain the whole world but forfeit their life? Or what will they give in return for their life?»

«For the Son of Man is to come with his angels in the glory of his Father, and then he will repay everyone for what has been done» (Matthew 16:21-27).

1. WHAT PETER HAD TO HEAR

When Jesus appeared in Galilee, he caused surprise, admiration and enthusiasm among the people. The disciples dreamed of total success. Jesus, in contrast, was only thinking about the will of the Father. He wanted to do God's will to the end.

So he began explaining to the disciples what was coming. His plan was to go up to Jerusalem, despite the fact that there he would «undergo great suffering» at the hands of the religious leaders. In God's plan, his death would come as an inevitable consequence of his activity. But the Father would raise him up; God would not look on passively and indifferently.

Peter rebels against the very idea of Jesus being crucified. He doesn't want to see him fail. He wants to follow a victorious and triumphant Jesus. So he «takes him aside», and pressures and «rebukes» him to make him forget what he has just said: «God forbid it, Lord! This must never happen to you».

Jesus replies sharply: «Get behind me, Satan!» He doesn't want Peter in front of him, because Peter is a «stumbling block», an obstacle in his path. «You are setting your mind not on divine things but on human things». You don't think like the Father, who is seeking happiness for all his sons and daughters; you are like human beings, who only think about their own well-being. You are the incarnation of Satan.

When Peter opens himself with simplicity to the Father, and confesses Jesus as the living Son of God, he is a «Rock» on which Jesus can build his Church. When he follows human thinking and tries to pull Jesus away from the way of the cross, he becomes a satanic tempter!

The gospel writers emphasize Jesus' literal words to Peter: «Get behind me, Satan!» That is where you belong. Fall into line as my faithful follower. Don't try to lead me astray by directing my project toward power and triumph.

We cannot confess Jesus as «the Son of the Living God» without following the way of the cross. If today's Church continues to act like Peter, we too must hear what Peter heard from the lips of Jesus.

2. RISKING EVERYTHING FOR JESUS

It is hard to get into Jesus' inner world, but we can sense a double experience in his heart: his identification with the last and the least, and his total trust in the Father. On the one hand he suffers over the injustice, misfortune, and sickness that cause so much suffering to people. On the other he has total trust in God the Father, whose most important goal is to uproot everything in life that is evil and causes his children to suffer.

Jesus would do anything to carry out the will of God, his Father: a world of justice, dignity, and happiness for all. Naturally he wanted to see the same attitude in his followers. If they followed his way, they would have to share his passion for God and his total commitment to God's reign. He wanted to light in them the fire that was burning in him.

Some words are especially telling. The Christian sources have preserved one of Jesus' sayings to his disciples, in slightly different versions: «For those who want to save their life will lose it, and those who lose their life for my sake will find it». With these paradoxical words, Jesus is inviting them to live as he does. If they cling blindly to life they may lose it; by generously and bravely risking life they will save it.

Jesus' way of thinking is clear. Whoever follows him but keeps holding on to the security, goals, and expectations that life offers, may end up losing the greatest of all goods: a life lived according to God's saving plan. On the other hand, whoever risks everything to follow him, will find life by entering the Father's reign with him.

People who follow Jesus often have the feeling that they are «losing out on life» in search of an impossible dream: Are we losing the best years of our life, dreaming about Jesus? Are we wasting our energy on a hopeless cause?

What did Jesus do when he was troubled by dark thoughts like these? He identified even more with those who suffered, and went on trusting in the Father whose gift of life cannot be measured by our earthly experience.

3. JESUS AND SUFFERING

Whether we like it or not, suffering is deeply embedded in the human experience; it would be naïve to try to change that. Sometimes it is physical pain that wracks our body. Sometimes it is moral suffering, the death of a loved one, a broken friendship, conflict, insecurity, fear, or depression. It may be sudden, intense suffering that quickly passes, or chronic pain that consumes our being and destroys our joy in living.

People throughout history have adopted very different ways of looking at evil. The stoics thought that the most human response was to face suffering with dignity. The school of Epicurus took a pragmatic position: avoid suffering and enjoy life as much as we can, as long as we can. Buddhism attempts to uproot suffering from the heart by suppressing «desire».

In everyday life, people deal with it as best they can. Some rebel against the inevitable; some become resigned; some sink into pessimism; on the other hand, there are those who need to suffer to feel they are really alive. And Jesus? What was his attitude toward suffering?

For Jesus, suffering is not the axis around which everything else revolves. His suffering is a kind of solidarity, open to others, fruitful. He does not see himself as a victim. He doesn't feel sorry for himself, but listens to other people's suffering. He doesn't complain about his situation. Rather he is attuned to the cries and tears of the people around him.

He doesn't agonize over nightmares of future suffering. He lives each moment, accepting and passing on the life he receives from the Father. He lives by the wise saying: «Do not worry about tomorrow, for tomorrow will bring worries of its own. Today's trouble is enough for today» (Matthew 6:34).

Above all, he trusts in the Father and serenely puts himself in God's hands. Even when his heart is overcome by anguish, only one prayer comes to his lips: «Father, into your hands I commend my spirit» (Luke 23:46).

4. LEARNING FROM JESUS' ATTITUDE TOWARD SUFFERING

Few of Jesus' sayings have been so distorted as his call to «take up the cross». That has led to great confusion over the Christian attitude toward suffering.

Here are some things we need to remember, in order to follow the Crucified One more faithfully.

We don't see in Jesus the suffering that we so often feel, caused by our own sin or our wrong ways of living. Jesus wasn't affected by the suffering that comes from envy, resentment, inner emptiness, or selfish attachment to people and things. There is a kind of suffering in our lives (some experts say as much as 90%) that we ourselves have to overcome in order to follow Jesus.

Jesus doesn't love suffering, or seek it for himself or others, as if suffering was especially pleasing to God. It is not true that we can follow Christ more closely by suffering needlessly or arbitrarily. What pleases God is not our suffering, but the attitude we adopt toward suffering in faithfully following Christ.

Jesus commits all his energy to eliminating suffering from the world. His whole life was a struggle to free human beings from the suffering that comes from sickness, hunger, injustice, abuse, sin, or death.

Those who would follow him cannot ignore the people who suffer. On the contrary, our first task is to remove suffering from human life. As one theologian says, «we have no right to happiness without others, or against others (Ignacio Larrañeta).

Finally, when Jesus sees the suffering caused by those who oppose his mission, he does not back away but embraces it, in an attitude of total faithfulness to the Father and unconditional service to humankind.

More than anything else, «taking up the cross» means accepting the painful consequences that will surely come as a result of faithfully following Jesus. Christians will always have to take on that kind of rejection, pain, and hurt. This is the suffering that we can only avoid by ceasing to follow Christ. This is the cross that each of us must carry if we are following in his footsteps.

5. THE CROSS IS SOMETHING DIFFERENT

It is hard to hear Jesus' words again without feelings of distress and anxiety: «If any want to become my followers, let them deny themselves and take up their cross and follow me». We can surely understand the reaction of Peter, who «took him aside and began to rebuke him». The theologian and martyr Dietrich Bonhoeffer says that Peter's reaction «proves that from the beginning, the Church has been scandalized by the suffering Christ. The Church does not want its Lord to impose on it the law of suffering».

This scandal may be unbearable for those who live in what Leszek Kolakowsky calls «the analgesic culture», a society obsessed with eliminating suffering and discomfort through all kinds of drugs, narcotics, and evasions.

If we want to be clear about the Christian attitude, we have to understand what the cross means to Christians; we may be giving it a meaning that Jesus never intended.

We sometimes describe anything that makes us suffer as a «cross», including the suffering caused by our own sin and our misguided ways of living. We should not confuse the cross with just any misfortune, annoyance, or discomfort that comes into our life.

The cross is something different. Jesus calls his disciples to follow him faithfully in the service of a more human world: the reign of God. That is the important thing. The cross is what comes to us as a result, the painful fate that we have to share with Christ if we are really following him. To «deny ourselves» does not mean self-mortification, self-castigation, and especially not self-annulment or self-destruction. Self-denial means not focusing on oneself; it means setting aside one's own «ego» in order to build a new life around Jesus Christ. It means being free from our selves, and committing ourselves radically to him. In other words, «taking up the cross» means being willing to take on the insecurity, conflict, rejection, and persecution that the Crucified One had to suffer.

But believers do not experience the cross as a defeat; rather we become the bearers of an ultimate hope. Those who lose their life for Jesus' sake will find it. The God who raised Jesus will also raise us to a full life.

26

The Transfiguration of Jesus

Six days later, Jesus took with him Peter and James and his brother John and led them up a high mountain, by themselves. And he was transfigured before them, and his face shone like the sun, and his clothes became dazzling white. Suddenly there appeared to them Moses and Elijah, talking with him. Then Peter said to Jesus, «Lord, it is good for us to be here; if you wish, I will make three dwellings here, one for you, one for Moses, and one for Elijah». While he was still speaking, suddenly a bright cloud overshadowed them, and from the cloud a voice said, «This is my Son, the Beloved; with him I am well pleased; listen to him!» When the disciples heard this, they fell to the ground and were overcome by fear. But Jesus came and touched them, saying, «Get up and do not be afraid». And when they looked up, they saw no one except Jesus himself alone.

As they were coming down the mountain, Jesus ordered them, «Tell no one about the vision until after the Son of Man has been raised from the dead» (Matthew 17:1-9).

1. LISTENING ONLY TO JESUS

Jesus takes his closest disciples with him «up a high mountain». This is not the mountain to which the tempter took Jesus, to offer him the power and glory of «all the kingdoms of the world». It is the one where his closest friends will discover the way that leads to the glory of the resurrection.

The transfigured face of Jesus «shines like the sun», which shows what his true glory is made of. It doesn't come from the devil but from God, his Father. One doesn't get to it by the way of earthly power, but on the patient path of quiet service, suffering, and crucifixion.

Beside Jesus they see Moses and Elijah, apparently representing the law and the prophets. Their faces are not shining, but subdued. They don't start teaching the disciples; they are talking with Jesus. The law and the prophets are oriented to him, subordinate to him.

But Peter doesn't yet sense the uniqueness of Jesus. «If you wish, I will make three dwellings here, one for you, one for Moses, and one for Elijah». He thinks of Jesus on the same level with Moses and Elijah; to each one his own dwelling. He doesn't understand that Jesus isn't on the same level with anyone.

It is God who silences Peter. «While he was still speaking», overshadowed by a bright cloud, they hear God's mysterious voice: «This is my Son, the Beloved», the one whose face is glorified by the resurrection. «Listen to him!» Don't listen to anyone else. My Son is the only lawgiver, teacher, and prophet. Don't confuse him with anyone else.

The disciples «fell to the ground and were overcome by fear». They were afraid to listen only to Jesus, and to follow his humble way of service to God's reign, the way of the cross. It was Jesus himself who released them from their fears. «He came and touched them» as only Jesus would do, in the same way he touched the sick. Then he said, «Get up and do not be afraid» to listen only to me, to follow only me.

Christians today are also afraid to listen only to Jesus. We're afraid to put him in the center of our lives and our communities. We don't allow him to be the only and decisive Word. It is Jesus himself who can free us from all our fear, cowardice, and ambivalence if we let ourselves be transformed by him.

2. LISTENING TO JESUS IN TODAY'S SOCIETY

In past years most people looked to religion for the meaning of life, and the guiding principles for living sensibly and responsibility. Today many people feel they don't need God; they can face their life, their desires, their fears and expectations by themselves.

That's not easy to do. It has probably never been harder than it is today to stop and think, reflect, and make decisions about oneself and what matters in one's life. We live in the midst of a «culture of intranscendence», tied down to the «here and now», living only for today, unable to open up to the ultimate mystery of life. We live in an «entertainment culture» that pulls people out of themselves, forcing them to forget about the great questions they carry in their heart.

People today have learned many things. They know what's happening in the world around them, but they don't know themselves, or how to become free. Many would agree with this gloomy observation made a few years ago by the director of *La Croix*, G. Hourdin: «Human beings today are becoming incapable of loving, of being free, of judging for themselves, of changing their way of life. They are becoming trained robots who work to earn money, which they will then spend at vacation resorts. They read the same fashion magazines and watch the same television programs as everyone else. That is how they learn who they are, what they want, and how they should think and live».

More than ever we need to hear the evangelical call: «This is my Son, the Beloved; with him I am well pleased; listen to him!» We need to stop, be silent, and listen to the God revealed in Jesus. That inner listening helps us to live in the truth, to taste life rather than wasting it, not to skim over what is essential. By listening to God incarnate in Jesus we discover our own smallness and poverty, but also the greatness that comes from being infinitely loved by him.

Each of us is free to listen to God or turn away. Whatever we do, let us not forget this scandalous, countercultural truth: to live without ultimate meaning is to live a meaning-less life; to act without hearing the inner voice of our consciousness is to be un-conscious.

3. FEAR IN THE CHURCH

Fear is probably the main thing that keeps Christians from faithfully following Jesus Christ. There is sin and weakness in today's Church, but more than anything else there is a fear of taking risks. We have entered the third millennium without the courage to undertake a creative renewal of our life together in faith. It's not hard to identify some of those fears.

We are afraid of newness, as if «preserving the past» could automatically guarantee faithfulness to the Gospel. Vatican II strongly affirmed that the Church should be in a process of «constant reform», because «as a human institution it is always in need of reform». But what we see moving in the Church today is not so much a spirit of renewal as an instinct of conservation.

We are afraid to take on the tensions and conflicts that would arise from a search for faithfulness to the gospel. We fall silent when we should speak out; we are inhibited when we should intervene. We forbid debate on important questions, in order to avoid potentially conflictive discussions; we would rather go along than create problems or displease the hierarchy.

We are afraid of creative theological thinking. Afraid to revise liturgical rites and wordings that work against a lively celebration of the faith. Afraid to speak of «human rights» in the Church. Afraid to acknowledge women in practice, in roles that conform to the spirit of Jesus.

We are afraid to put mercy above all else, because we forget that the Church was not given a «ministry of judgment and condemnation» but a «ministry of reconciliation». There is a fear of embracing sinners as Jesus did. It would be hard to call today's Church a «friend of sinners», as people said of our Teacher.

In the gospel story, the disciples «fall to the ground and are overcome by fear» when the voice tells them, «This is my Son, the Beloved... listen to him!» It is scary to listen only to Jesus. But it is Jesus himself who comes near, touches them, and says: «Get up and do not be afraid». Only a living touch from Christ can free us from all that fear.

4. THE FEARS OF HUMANITY IN OUR TIME

What is happening to humankind today? We have never had so much knowledge, with which to control life; we have never had so many technical and scientific resources for resolving our problems. Yet according to recent studies, people today feel more insecure and threatened than in previous eras; we harbor more fears of all kinds within us, sometimes for no apparent reason. Why do we hear so many people saying, «It's all so scary!»

An esteemed psychiatrist, my good friend Vicente Madoz, has published an excellent study titled *Los miedos del hombre moderno*. With the clarity and simplicity of a true expert, he analyzes both the irrational fears of today's people and their specific fears of sickness, old age, death, failure, loss of love, or loneliness.

Certainly the anxiety and malaise of many people has to do with the radical, rapid changes that are taking place in our society. They also have to do with individualism, a lack of solidarity, and exaggerated pragmatism. But we can also see an existential anguish, sometimes subtle and hidden, that rises up from the great unknowns of life and comes to the surface in the face of sickness, old age, failure, loss of love, or death.

These specific fears, which so often cause needless and exaggerated suffering, have many different causes; each case requires individualized attention. But in many of them we can see «an existence emptied of content, scattered and disoriented». According to Dr. Madoz, «this is the perfect breeding ground in which to feed and nourish both the fundamental anguish of today's human beings and all sorts of neurotic, secondary fears».

Few sayings are more often repeated in the gospels than these words of Jesus: «Do not be afraid», «Trust», «Don't let your hearts be troubled». The story of the transfiguration conveys the same message. When the disciples fall to the ground in fear, overshadowed by the bright cloud, they hear Jesus' words: «Get up and do not be afraid». This is God's beloved Son; we need to listen. We should never reduce faith to a psychological prescription, but it is true that listening to the God revealed in Jesus and letting his Word enlighten us can heal human beings at our deepest roots, giving us meaning and inspiring us with an indestructible, fundamental trust.

5. THE RISK OF SETTLING DOWN

Sooner or later we all run the risk of settling down in life, looking for nothing more than a protected space in which to live comfortably, without any disruptions or great worries.

Having achieved a certain level of professional success, with a growing family and a more or less secure future, we easily fall into a comfortable routine that enables us to get along pretty well in life.

We want to live that kind of good life. To relax into a happy environment. To make our home a cheerful refuge, to sit in a corner reading and listening to good music. To enjoy a good vacation, an occasional weekend off.

But sometimes that is when we see more clearly than ever that happiness is not the same as well-being. Something is missing, leaving us with an empty, unsatisfied feeling. Something we can't buy with money, something that comfort doesn't provide. What's missing is the joy of sharing other people's problems and struggles, living together with people in need, coming close to the people mistreated by society.

Some ways of settling down can be falsely justified as a «Christian life». This is the temptation that believers always face. Just as Peter wanted to build dwellings on the high mountain, we want to establish our inner well-being in religion, evading our individual and collective responsibility of working for more human ways of living together.

But Jesus' message is clear. A religious experience is not truly Christian if it isolates us from our brothers and sisters, if it allows us to settle down comfortablyand neglect our duty of service to people in need.

If we listen to Jesus, we will feel encouraged to leave conformity behind, break away from the self-centered way of life that we have settled into, and begin paying attention to the challenge that comes to us from the marginalized sectors of our society.

27

Gathered in the Name of Jesus

Jesus said to his disciples:

«If another member of the church sins against you, go and point out the fault when the two of you are alone. If the member listens to you, you have regained that one. But if you are not listened to, take one or two others along with you, so that every word may be confirmed by the evidence of two or three witnesses. If the member refuses to listen to them, tell it to the church; and if the offender refuses to listen even to the church, let such a one be to you as a Gentile and a tax collector. Truly I tell you, whatever you bind on earth will be bound in heaven, and whatever you loose on earth will be loosed in heaven. Again, truly I tell you, if two of you agree on earth about anything you ask, it will be done for you by my Father in heaven. For where two or three are gathered in my name, I am there among them» (Matthew 18:15-20).

1. GATHERING IN THE NAME OF JESUS

The destruction of the Jerusalem temple in the year 70 A.D. led to a profound crisis among the Jewish people. The temple was «the house of God». God ruled from there by imposing his law. After the destruction of the temple, where could the people go to be in God's saving presence?

The rabbis responded by seeking God in their meetings to study the Law. The famous Rabbi Ananias, who died around the year 135, said it clearly: «Where two people meet to study the words of the Law, the presence of God (*shekinah*) is with them».

Jesus' Jewish followers had a very different response. Matthew attributes to Jesus these words, which were very important in keeping his presence alive among his followers: «Where two or three are gathered in my name, I am there among them».

These people are not meeting out of habit, for discipline, or in compliance with a rule. The atmosphere of these meetings is very different. Jesus' followers are «gathering in his name», drawn in by him, enlivened by his spirit. Jesus is the reason, the source, the encouragement, the life of these meetings. Jesus, the Resurrected One, is present there.

Everyone knows that the Sunday gathering of Christians is in a profound state of crisis. Many people find the weekly mass unbearable. They no longer have the patience to attend a service whose symbols have lost their meaning, and listen to words that don't always touch the reality of their lives.

Some have only experienced the mass as a social event, regulated and directed by ecclesiastical leaders, while the people remain passively enclosed in silence or mechanical responses, no longer attuned to language they don't always understand. Is this what it means to gather in the name of the Lord?

How can we allow the Sunday service to lose its meaning? Isn't the eucharist the center of Christianity? Why does the hierarchy prefer not to question, not to change anything? How can we Christians fail to speak up? Why so much passivity and disinterest? Where can we see the Spirit bringing together two or three people who will teach us to gather in the name of Jesus?

2. A SPACE CREATED BY JESUS

The first generations of Christians apparently weren't very worried about numbers. At the end of the first century there were only about twenty thousand of them, lost in the midst of the Roman Empire. But it didn't matter how many there were. They were the Church of Jesus, and what mattered was living by his Spirit. Paul constantly invited the members of his small communities to «live in Christ». The fourth gospel exhorted its readers to «abide in him».

Matthew's Jesus says, «Where two or three are gathered in my name, I am there among them». In Jesus' Church people don't come together out of habit, inertia, or fear. His followers are to «gather in his name», be converted to him, feed on his gospel. That is also our first task, even if there are only two or three of us.

To gather in Jesus' name is to create a space for living our whole existence around him, within his horizon. A spiritual space not defined by doctrines, customs or practices but by the Spirit of Jesus, who helps us to live in his way.

The telling of the gospel is at the center of this «Jesus space». That is the essential experience of every Christian community: we do it «in memory of Jesus», recalling his words, accepting them with faith and living them with joy. The art of accepting the gospel in the context of our lives brings us into contact with Jesus, and gives us the experience of growing as his disciples and followers.

In this space created in his name, we walk —with all our weaknesses and sin— toward the truth of the gospel. On the way we discover together the essential nucleus of our faith, and recover our Christian identity even in the midst of a Church weakened by routine and paralyzed by fear.

This space, dominated by Jesus, is the first thing we need to protect, consolidate, and deepen in our communities and parishes. Let us be clear about this. The renewal of the Church always begins in the heart of two or three believers, gathering in the name of Jesus.

3. A CHURCH GATHERED IN THE NAME OF JESUS

People who live apart from religion, or who are discouraged by the behavior of believers, may start to think of the Church only as a large organization. A kind of «multinational corporation» mainly concerned with defending and promoting its own interests. These people generally know the Church only from outside. They talk about the Vatican, criticize the pronouncements of the hierarchy, get annoyed at things the pope does. The Church seems to them like an anachronistic institution, far removed from their lives.

People who see themselves as members of a believing community have a different experience. For them the face of the Church is almost always their own parish. They are a group of friends who meet every Sunday to celebrate the eucharist. This is the community where they baptize their children, or say farewell to their loved ones until they meet again in the other life.

For those to whom the Church is the community of Jesus, it is almost always a source of both joy and suffering. On the one hand it enlivens us to experience the memory of Jesus there, to listen to his message, feel his spirit, nourish our faith in the living God. On the other, we grieve over incoherence and fixed routine in the Church, the great distance between what the Church preaches and what it lives, its lack of evangelical vitality, the many ways it is forgetting the way of Jesus.

This is the great tragedy of the Church. We do not love or worship Jesus as the first communities did. We do not know or understand his uniqueness. Many of us can't even imagine the saving experience that the first followers lived with him. We have built a Church where many Christians think that by accepting certain doctrines and fulfilling certain religious practices, they are following Christ as the first disciples did.

And yet this is the essential nucleus of the Church. It is a lived adherence to Christ in community, re-living the experience of those who saw in him the nearness, the love and the forgiveness of God. For this reason, perhaps the most fundamental insight of ecclesiology is in these words of Jesus in the gospel of Matthew: «Where two or three are gathered in my name, I am there among them».

The first task of the Church is to learn to «gather in the name of Jesus». To nourish his memory, live in his presence, renew its faith in God, open new paths for his Spirit. If we're not doing that, all our efforts may be defeated by our mediocrity.

4. WHAT CAN I DO FOR A CHURCH MORE FAITHFUL TO JESUS? «Where two or three are gathered in my name, I am there among them». The best way to make Christ present in his Church is to work together «in his name», moved by his Spirit. The Church doesn't need our professions of love, or our criticism, as much as it needs our real commitment. This raises a lot of questions.

How can I help to create a climate of collective conversion in this Church, which is always in need of renewal and transformation? What would the Church be like, if everyone lived their loyalty to Christ the way I do? Would it become more or less faithful?

What am I contributing to the spirit, truth, and authenticity of this Church, which is so much in need of radical evangelicalism in order to offer a credible witness to Jesus in the midst of an indifferent, unbelieving society?

How am I helping to build a Church close to the men and women of our time, a Church that can not only teach, preach, and exhort, but above all accept, listen to, and walk with people who have never known love or friendship?

What am I contributing to a Samaritan Church, big-hearted and compassionate, that can forget its own self-interest and devote its life to the great problems of humankind?

What am I doing to free the Church of the fears and enslavements that paralyze it and tie it down to the past, so that it can be penetrated and enlivened by the freshness and creativity that comes from the gospel of Jesus?

What am I doing right now to help the Church learn to «live as a minority», without great social pretensions, but in humility —like «yeast» hidden in the dough, «salt» that transforms, a «seed» that is prepared to die in order to give life?

What am I doing to build a more joyful and hopeful Church, freer and more understanding, more transparent and loving, more believing and believable, belonging more to God and less to the world, closer to Jesus and less tied to our own self-interest and ambitions? The Church changes when we change; it is converted when we are converted.

Weary from everyday experience, we sometimes feel dark, disturbing questions rising within us. Can we be much better than we are? Can we make real changes in our lives? Can we transform our misguided attitudes and adopt new behaviors? Often what we see, what we hear, what we breathe in the air around us doesn't help us to be better people; it doesn't raise our spirits and help us become more human.

Perhaps we have lost the ability to get inside our own conscience, discern our own sinfulness and renew our way of living. We have set aside the traditional «examination of conscience», which used to shed some light on our lives, as something old-fashioned and useless. We don't want to rock the boat. We would rather not listen to any calls, pay attention to our responsibilities. Determined to protect what happiness we have in the usual selfish ways, we ignore anything that might challenge our lives.

How can we start listening to the call for change? How can we shake off our laziness? How can we recover our old feelings of kindness, generosity, commitment?

Today more than ever, we believers need to hear Jesus' call to change our ways and help one another to become better. Jesus invites us to take action patiently and unhurriedly, going to the one who needs correction in a personal, friendly way. «If another member of the church sins, go and point out the fault when the two of you are alone. If the member listens to you, you have regained that one».

That kind of friendly, loyal criticism, that timely intervention, that sincere support at a time of disorientation, can be helpful to us all. Everyone is capable of turning away from sin and returning to reason and kindness. But people often need to hear from someone who truly loves them, who invites them to think about what they are doing, who passes on to them a new desire for truth and generosity.

Perhaps what causes most people to change is not a great idea or a beautiful thought, but an encounter with someone who has gone to them in friendship and helped them to become new.

28

Forgiving Seventy-Seven Times

Then Peter came to him and said, «Lord, if another member of the church sins against me, how often should I forgive? As many as seven times?» Jesus said to him, «Not seven times, but, I tell you, seventy-seven times».

«For this reason the kingdom of heaven may be compared to a king who wished to settle accounts with his slaves. When he began the reckoning, one who owed him ten thousand talents was brought to him; and, as he could not pay, his lord ordered him to be sold, together with his wife and children and all his possessions, and payment to be made. So the slave fell on his knees before him, saying, "Have patience with me, and I will pay you everything". And out of pity for him, the lord of that slave released him and forgave him the debt. But that same slave, as he went out, came upon one of his fellow slaves who owed him a hundred denarii, and seizing him by the throat, he said, "Pay what you owe". Then his fellow slave fell down and pleaded with him, "Have patience with me, and I will pay you". But he refused; then he went and threw him into prison until he would pay the debt. When his fellow slaves saw what had happened, they were greatly distressed, and they went and reported to their lord all that had taken place. Then his lord summoned him and said to him, "You wicked slave! I forgave you all that debt because you pleaded with me. Should you not have had mercy on your fellow slave, as I had mercy on you?" And in anger his lord handed him over to be tortured until he would pay his entire debt. So my heavenly Father will also do to every one of you, if you do not forgive your brother or sister from your heart» (Matthew 18:21-35).

1. ALWAYS FORGIVING

Matthew is clearly concerned with setting right the conflicts, disputes, and confrontations that come up in the community of Jesus' followers. He is probably writing at a time when, as he says in the gospel, the love of many has grown cold (Matthew 24:12).

So he gives detailed instructions on how to deal with the problem within the community: by always showing respect for persons, correcting one another «when the two of you are alone», bringing «witnesses» into the dialogue, seeking the intervention of «the church», isolating those who can bring harm to Jesus' followers.

This may all be necessary, but what should be the specific behavior of the person who is offended? What is required of the disciple who wants to follow in Jesus' footsteps, to collaborate with him in opening ways to the reign of God, the reign of mercy and justice for all?

Matthew was remembering a saying of Jesus from «Q». The saying was hard to understand, but it reflected what was in Jesus' heart. Twenty centuries later, his followers still have to take it very seriously.

As he has done before, Peter brings the group's question to Jesus: «If another member of the church sins against me, how often should I forgive? As many as seven times?» It's not a self-serving question, but a generous one. He has listened to Jesus' parables about God's mercy. He knows about Jesus' understanding, his lenience, his willingness to forgive. Peter too is willing to forgive many times, but isn't there a limit?

Jesus answers firmly: «Not seven times, but seventy-seven times». You have to keep forgiving, every time, unconditionally. Through the centuries people have found many ways to get around his meaning: it can be harmful to forgive time after time; it encourages the offender; repentance has to come before forgiveness. This all seems very reasonable, but it conceals and distorts the way Jesus thought and lived.

We have to come back to Jesus. His Church needs men and women who can forgive as he did, who can show us how free and how great Jesus' forgiveness really is. That is the best way to let the face of Christ shine in the Church.

2. WHERE WOULD WE BE WITHOUT FORGIVENESS?

It has been called «the parable of the merciless slave». A man whose king has forgiven him a debt so large he can never repay it, is unable in turn to forgive a fellow slave who owes him a small amount. The story seems clear and simple. But biblical scholars are still debating its original meaning, because the way Matthew tells it, it doesn't fit well with Jesus' call to «forgive seventy-seven times».

The parable begins so hopefully, with the king's forgiveness, but it ends in tragedy. The king's forgiveness does not lead to more compassionate behavior among his servants. The forgiven slave has no mercy for his fellow slave. The other slaves can't forgive him, and ask the king to give him what he deserves. The indignant king withdraws his forgiveness, and hands the slave over to torturers.

For a moment a new age of understanding and mutual forgiveness seemed to have begun. But no. In the end no one shows compassion. No one hears the call to forgiveness: not the slave, not his fellow slaves, not even the king. The king has made a good start, but even he can't forgive «seventy-seven times».

What is Jesus trying to tell us? Sometimes we naively think that the world would be more human if everything were done by the rule of order, strict justice, and punishment for bad behavior. But wouldn't that be a world of darkness? What would society be like without forgiveness? What would become of us without God's forgiveness?

To refuse forgiveness sometimes seems like a normal, even a fair reaction to injury, humiliation, or injustice. But that is not the way to humanize the world. A marriage without mutual understanding is destroyed; a family without forgiveness becomes a hell; a society without compassion becomes inhuman.

Jesus' parable is a kind of «trap». We all think the slave who was forgiven by the king ought to forgive his fellow slave. It was the least he could do. But then, isn't forgiveness the least we can expect of those who live by God's forgiveness and mercy? We think of forgiveness as an admirable, heroic act. Jesus thought of it as normal.

3. AN APOLOGY FOR FORGIVENESS

Almost every time I write about forgiveness, I get letters —usually anonymous— accusing me of forgetting the suffering of the victims of terrorism, of not understanding the humiliation of a betrayed spouse, of not being «realistic».

I can understand why people are reluctant to forgive. How can I not feel the anger, powerlessness, and pain of those who have suffered violence, disrespect, or betrayal? Precisely because of the resentment and aggressiveness they express, I can see even more clearly what the world would be like without forgiveness.

Psychologists have described a defense mechanism, a «mysterious mimesis», that leads the victims of aggression to imitate their aggressor in some way. It is an unconscious, almost instinctive, individual or collective reaction that can even be passed on from generation to generation.

Unless the cycle is broken at some point, evil becomes self-perpetuating. When victims cannot or will not forgive, they are left with an «unhealed wound» that goes on harming them, by repeating the harm of the past. The same thing happens in society, preventing it from finding ways to live together, and eventually blocking all efforts to resolve its conflicts.

The desire for revenge is surely the most instinctive reaction to an offense. People need to defend themselves against the injury they have received, but as the well-known expert Jacques Pohier points out, we can't heal our wounds by inflicting pain on the aggressor. Someone else's suffering cannot cure the humiliation or aggression that was inflicted on us. It may give us a momentary satisfaction, but we need something more in order to return to a healthy way of living. Henri Lacordaire said long ago: «Do you want to be happy right now? Take revenge. Do you want to go on being happy? Forgive».

Sometimes we forget that forgiveness does the most good to the forgivers; it releases them from the hurt, increases their dignity and nobility, gives them the strength to rebuild their lives, and lets them start over again. When Jesus says we should forgive «seventy-seven times», he is showing us the healthiest, most effective way to uproot evil from our lives. His words are even more true for people who believe in God as the ultimate source of forgiveness: «Forgive, and you will be forgiven».

4. THE SOCIAL VALUE OF FORGIVENESS

It is not easy to hear Jesus' call to forgive, or to fully understand that people are more human when they forgive than when they take revenge.

We need to understand Jesus' thinking. Forgiving does not mean ignoring injustice, or accepting it passively or indifferently. On the contrary, we forgive precisely in order to destroy the spiral of evil and to rehabilitate the other, enabling him or her to act differently in the future.

The dynamic of forgiveness includes an effort to overcome evil with good. An act of forgiveness qualitatively changes the relationship between the people involved, and seeks to establish a new and different kind of life together. For that reason forgiveness is not only an individual act, but also has social implications.

Society must not abandon anyone, not even the guilty. Everyone has a right to be loved. We cannot accept a jail sentence that only «returns evil for evil», binding prisoners to their crime, degrading their existence and cutting off the possibility of true rehabilitation.

The great jurist G. Radbruch says that punishment, as the imposition of evil for evil, must be gradually replaced by efforts «to bring good out of evil; that is the only way to bring about justice in the world that does not make the world worse, but transforms it into a better world».

There is no justification for humiliating or unfair treatment of either common or political prisoners. We will never move toward a more human society until we give up reprisals, hatred and vengeance.

That is why it is also wrong to incite people to revenge. We can understand the cry, «the people will never forgive», but it is not the right way to build a more human future.

As believers we can never support the call to reject forgiveness, because it is a rejection of the community beloved by the One who forgives us all.

5. FORGIVING IS GOOD FOR US

The great schools of psychology have barely begun to study the healing power of forgiveness. Psychologists have only recently begun to recognize its role in the development of a healthy personality. They thought wrongly—and some still do—that forgiveness is a purely religious attitude.

For its part, the Christian message has often been reduced to telling people to forgive generously, based on God's forgiveness, without helping people find ways of forgiving from the heart. So it is not surprising that some people have little understanding of the process of forgiveness.

Yet we need forgiveness in order to build a healthy life together: in our families, where day-to-day relationships often produce tension and conflict; in friendship and love, where we must learn to respond to humiliation, deception, and sometimes unfaithfulness; and in many other life situations where we have to respond to aggression, injustice, and abuse. Those who cannot forgive may have to live with these hurts forever.

One thing needs to be made clear from the beginning. Many people think they cannot forgive, because they confuse anger with revenge. Anger is a healthy reaction to an offense, aggression, or injustice: we rebel almost instinctively in order to defend our life and dignity. Hatred, resentment, and vengeance go beyond that first reaction; the vengeful person seeks to harm, humiliate, and even destroy the one who has hurt him or her.

Forgiving does not necessarily mean repressing anger. On the contrary, it can be harmful to repress those initial feelings; they may build up into an inner rage that lashes out later at other people, or at the one who harbors it. It is healthy to acknowledge and accept our anger, perhaps by sharing it with someone who can understand.

That makes it easier to calm down, and decide not to go on feeding the resentment and fantasies of revenge that only increase the harm to us. Faith in a forgiving God can be an invaluable source of energy and strength. Those who live by God's unconditional love will find it easier to forgive others.

29

God is Good to Everyone

Jesus told his disciples this parable:

«For the kingdom of heaven is like a landowner who went out early in the morning to hire laborers for his vineyard. After agreeing with the laborers for the usual daily wage, he sent them into his vineyard. When he went out about nine o'clock, he saw others standing idle in the marketplace; and he said to them, "You also go into the vineyard, and I will pay you whatever is right". So they went. When he went out again about noon and about three o'clock, he did the same. And about five o'clock he went out and found others standing around; and he said to them, "Why are you standing here idle all day?" They said to him, "Because no one has hired us". He said to them, You also go into the vineyard. When evening came, the owner of the vineyard said to his manager, "Call the laborers and give them their pay, beginning with the last and then going to the first". When those hired about five o'clock came, each of them received the usual daily wage. Now when the first came, they thought they would receive more; but each of them also received the usual daily wage. And when they received it, they grumbled against the landowner, saying, "These last worked only one hour, and you have made them equal to us who have borne the burden of the day and the scorching heat". But he replied to one of them, "Friend, I am doing you no wrong; did you not agree with me for the usual daily wage? Take what belongs to you and go; I choose to give to this last the same as I give to you. Am I not allowed to do what I choose with what belongs to me? Or are you envious because I am generous? So the last will be first, and the first will be last"» (Matthew 20:1-16).

1. THE SCANDALOUS GOODNESS OF GOD

It was probably autumn, and the Galilean villages were intensely engaged in the grape harvest. Jesus watched in the town square, as the workers who didn't have land of their own waited for a chance to earn a day's wage. How could he help these poor workers understand God's mysterious goodness to everyone?

He told them a surprising parable. He talked about a landowner who hired as many day workers as he could. He went personally to the town square again and again, at different times. At the end of the day, although they had not all done the same amount of work, he gave each one a denarius, the amount they needed to live on for a day's work.

The first group protests. Not because they have been paid too little, but because the landowner has paid the others the same amount. The landowner's answer to their spokesman is admirable: «are you envious because I am generous?»

The parable is so revolutionary that even after twenty centuries we don't dare take it seriously. Can it be that God is good even to those who haven't earned it by their merit and works? Can it be that in the Father's heart there are no special privileges according to the work we do in his vineyard?

All our expectations crumble when the free and unfathomable love of God comes into the picture. That is why we are scandalized that Jesus seems to have forgotten about the «pious ones», with all their good works, and gone instead to the people who have no right to a reward from God: sinners who do not comply with the Covenant, and prostitutes who aren't allowed into the temple.

Sometimes we get wrapped up in our calculations, and don't allow God to be good to everyone. We can't tolerate his infinite goodness to everyone; some people just don't deserve it. We think God should give everyone what they deserve, and nothing more. Fortunately God isn't like us. His heart of a Father knows how to give his saving love to the people we don't know how to love.

2. GOD IS GOOD TO ALL

This is certainly one of Jesus' most surprising and provocative parables. We used to call it «the parable of the employer in the vineyard», but the real protagonist is the owner of the vineyard. Some scholars today call it «the parable of the boss who wanted work and bread for everyone».

This man goes personally into the town square to hire different groups of workers. The first go out at six in the morning, others at nine, others at noon and three in the afternoon. He hires the rest at five o'clock, when there is only an hour left in the workday.

This is strange behavior. He apparently isn't just in a hurry to finish the grape harvest. What he wants is for no one to go without work. He even goes out at the last hour, to hire those who were not called. At the end of the day he gives everyone what they need in order to eat that night, even if they haven't earned it. When the first group protests, he replies: «Are you envious because I am good?»

What is Jesus saying? That God's criteria of justice and equality are different from ours? Can it be that instead of counting people's merits, God is responding to their needs?

It is not easy to believe in the unfathomable goodness of God that Jesus is describing. Many people are scandalized to think that God is good to everyone, regardless of whether they deserve it, whether they are believers or agnostics, whether they call on his name or turn their backs on him. But that's how God is. It would be better to let God be God, rather than shrink him to fit our ideas and expectations.

The image of God that many Christians hold is a mixture of heterogeneous and even contradictory elements. Some aspects come from Jesus, others from the judgmental God of the Old Testament, others from our own fears and fantasies. Thus God's goodness to all his creatures gets lost or distorted.

One of the most important tasks of a Christian community is always to look more deeply into Jesus' lived experience of God. Only by witnessing to that God can we fill the world with a different kind of hope.

3. TRUSTING THE GOODNESS OF GOD

I am increasingly convinced that many people who call themselves atheists are not rejecting God, but a «mental idol» of God that they constructed as children. The idea of God that they've lived with for years has gotten too small for them. Eventually that God became so strange, uncomfortable, and bothersome to them that they gave up on him.

I find it easy to understand these people. Talking with some of them, I am often reminded of the true words of the patriarch Maximus IV during the Council: «I also don't believe in the god that the atheists don't believe in». The god that some people have put out of their lives is a false caricature that they have made of God. If they have taken that false god out of their soul, could it be to make room for the true God to come in some day?

But where can people find God today? If they come to us who call ourselves believers they may well find us praying, not to the true God but to a small idol on whom we have projected our own self-interest, fears, and obsessions. A God we want to own and use for our own benefit, forgetting his immense, incomprehensible goodness to everyone.

Jesus breaks down all our expectations when he shows us, in the parable of the «owner of the vineyard», a God who gives everyone their daily wage whether they've earned it or not, and who says to the complainers, «Are you envious because I am generous?»

God is good to everyone, whether or not they deserve it, whether they are believers or atheists. His mysterious goodness is greater than the faith of the believers, and greater than the unbelief of the atheists.

We have to forget our expectations, be still and listen deeply to the life that pulsates within us—and wait, trust, open our being to him. God does not hide forever from those who seek him with a sincere heart.

4. GOD IS NOT WHAT WE THINK

In the last years of his life, the great German theologian Karl Rahner often used a well-worn expression to describe God. Instead of naming God directly, he called him «the Mystery we ordinarily call God». This was his way of pointing out that «we should not put just anything under the name of God: a bearded old man, a tyrannical moralist who keeps watch on our live, or anything of that sort».

We are right to think of God as «an unfathomable mystery», but we have to admit that believers, especially the clergy, often speak of him as if we had seen him and completely understood his way of seeing things, feeling, and acting.

Worse yet, when we close God up in our narrow viewpoints and make him fit our expectations, we almost always end up shrinking him to our size. Sometimes we end up with a God as inhuman as we are, sometimes less human.

Many people, for example, believe in a God whose main job is to write down the merits and demerits of human beings, in order to pay each one according to his or her works. Can we imagine anything less human than a being whose whole existence is devoted to that task?

That would be a God without a heart. A God as small and threatening as we are. We would have to be always «in good standing» with him, scrupulously complying with all our religious duties and building up credit in order to ensure our eternal salvation.

The parable of «the owner of the vineyard» revolutionizes our way of conceiving of God. According to Jesus, God's goodness is unfathomable and does not fit any calculations that we can do.

God is not unfair to anyone. But just as the lord of the vineyard does what he wants with his money—and no one has the right to protest—God too can give his life, even to those who don't deserve it according to our calculations.

We have to learn over and over, not to confuse God with our religious and moral expectations. We have to let God be greater than we are. We have to let God simply be God.

We run the risk of thinking of ourselves as Christians when we have never assimilated the message Jesus offers, about a God whose infinite goodness mysteriously reaches all his sons and daughters.

Probably many Christians today would be scandalized to hear talk of a God who does not impose canon law, who can give away grace without going through any of the seven sacraments, and who can save —even outside the Church— men and women we think of as lost.

5. LETTING GOD BE GOD

Sometimes we talk a lot about the importance of believing, or not believing, in God. We forget that the important thing is knowing what God we believe in. There is a difference between believing in a God who is good to everyone, who «makes his sun rise on the evil and on the good», and believing in a God of law and order, for whom we have to calculate everything we do.

To believe in God as an unconditional Friend can be the most liberating, joyful experience we can imagine, the most invigorating force for living and dying. In contrast, believing in a judgmental, threatening God can become a dangerous neurosis, destroying our humanity.

The image of God that we have inherited is inevitably an amalgam of ideas and conceptions from the past, some of them shining with truth, others full of dangerous ambiguity. How can we free our understanding of God from the misconceptions that may be accumulating in the depth of our consciousness?

First we have to let God be God. We must not shrink him to our size, box him in to our expectations, or reduce him to our calculations. We must let God be greater and more human than the greatest and most human aspects of ourselves. We cannot relate to God through our own mediocrity and resentment; rather we must seek God's true face by following Jesus, although the image of God that he shows us is sometimes surprising and «scandalizing».

I shall never forget how surprised I was, many years ago, to discover that it was not Jesus' power or radicality that led people to hate and reject him, but his proclamation of a «scandalously good» God.

The parable of the «owner of the vineyard» is especially meaningful. Its message is so revolutionary that we are still afraid to accept it. But Jesus' message is clear: just as the owner of the vineyard gives every worker his «denarius» whether or not they have earned it, simply because he has a great heart, in the same way

God is not being unfair when he offers salvation even to those who have not earned it by our calculations.

God is good to everyone, whether or not they deserve it, whether they are believers or atheists. His mysterious goodness overflows all our calculations, and goes beyond both the faith of believers and the atheism of unbelievers. The only thing we can do with this God is to give him joyful thanks and absolute trust in his goodness.

30

The Prostitutes are Going before You

Jesus said to the chief priests and elders of the people:

«What do you think? A man had two sons; he went to the first and said, "Son, go and work in the vineyard today". He answered, "I will not"; but later he changed his mind and went. The father went to the second and said the same; and he answered, "I go, sir"; but he did not go. Which of the two did the will of his father?» They said, «The first». Jesus said to them, «Truly I tell you, the tax collectors and the prostitutes are going into the kingdom of God ahead of you. For John came to you in the way of righteousness and you did not believe him, but the tax collectors and the prostitutes believed him; and even after you saw it, you did not change your minds and believe him» (Matthew 21:28-32).

1. THEY ARE AHEAD OF YOU

It's such a simple parable that it hardly seems worthy of a great prophet like Jesus. But it isn't addressed to the children running around him; it is for «the chief priests and the elders of the people» who have been hounding him since he came into the temple.

In this story, a father asks two of his sons to work in the vineyard. The first says brusquely, «I won't go», but he remembers his father's request and ends up working in the vineyard. The second replies dutifully, «Yes, sir, of course, sir», but it's all words. No one is going to see him working in the vineyard.

The message of the parable is clear. Even the religious leaders agree with Jesus. The important thing in God's eyes is not to «talk the talk» but to «walk the walk». Words, promises and prayers will not fulfill God's will; what counts is action and everyday living.

What is surprising is how Jesus uses it. His words are indeed harsh. Only Matthew tells this story, but there is no doubt that the words come from Jesus. Only he would have dared tell the religious leaders, «The tax collectors and the prostitutes are going into the kingdom of God ahead of you».

Jesus is talking from his own experience. The religious leaders have said «yes» to God. They are the first to talk about God, God's law, and God's temple. But when Jesus calls on them to «strive for the kingdom of God and his righteousness», they close the door to his message and refuse to go that way. They are saying «no» to God through their resistance to Jesus.

The tax collectors and prostitutes have said «no» to God. They live outside the law; they are excluded from the temple. But when Jesus offers them God's friendship, they hear his call and take steps toward conversion. For Jesus there is no question about it: Zacchaeus the publican, the prostitute who washed his feet with her tears, and so many others—they are leading the way to the reign of God.

The way is led, not by the people who make solemn professions of faith, but by those who open themselves up to Jesus by taking real steps toward conversion to the Father's project.

2. THINGS ARE NOT ALWAYS WHAT THEY SEEM

This is one of Jesus' clearest, simplest parables. A father asks his two sons to work in the vineyard. The first says «no», but later he thinks better of it and goes. The second is ostentatiously polite: «I go, sir», but it's all words; he doesn't go.

The message is also clear, beyond debate. What God wants is not talk but action; not promises or confessions, but obedience to his will. There's nothing new in Jesus' words.

The scribes are constantly talking about the law; the name of God is always on their lips. The temple priests are tireless in their praise of God; their mouth is full of psalms. No one would doubt that they are doing the Father's will. But things are not always as they seem. The tax collectors and prostitutes don't talk about God to anyone. They've forgotten God's will a long time ago. Yet according to Jesus, they will enter the reign of God ahead of the chief priests and scribes.

What did Jesus see in those men and women, despised by everyone? Perhaps he saw their humiliation. A heart more open to God, more in need of forgiveness. Maybe it was their greater understanding of and nearness to the last and the least in society. Or because they were less proud and arrogant than the scribes and chief priests.

We Christians have filled our 2,000-year history with beautiful words. We have constructed impressive systems that express Christian doctrine with deep concepts. Yet today as always, the people who really do the Father's will are those who express the gospel of Jesus in their actions, and those who open themselves to his forgiveness with simplicity and trust.

3. FOR JESUS, THE LAST COME FIRST

Jesus lived in a society divided by walls of separation and complex rules of exclusion. There were Jews who could enter the temple, and pagans were who excluded from worship; «pure» people whom one could talk to, and the «impure» who had to be avoided; the «neighbor» whom one must love, and the «stranger» who could be ignored; «pious men» who observed the law, and «the wicked» who did not know or obey its prescriptions; «healthy» people who were blessed by God, and «the sick» who were not allowed to enter the temple; «the righteous», and «sinners».

Jesus' activity in that divided society is so surprising that even today we have a hard time accepting it. He does not adopt the position of the Pharisees, who avoid all contact with the impure and with sinners. He does not follow the elitist attitude of Qumran, which has official lists of the people to be excluded from the community.

Jesus goes precisely to the most discriminated people. He sits down to eat with publicans. He lets a sinner kiss his feet. He touches lepers with his hand. He seeks to save «the lost». People call him «a friend of sinners». He keeps saying provocatively that «the last will be first», and that the publicans and prostitutes will go ahead of the scribes and priests on the way to the reign of God.

Does anyone today really think that alcoholics, vagrants, beggars, and the other dregs of society are the first in God's eyes? Who would dare suggest that prostitutes, heroin addicts, or people with AIDS are going ahead of all those irreproachable men in clerical collars?

Most people won't tell you this, you undesirables and reprobates, but the God revealed in Jesus Christ is still truly your friend. You understand and accept God's forgiveness more readily than all the Christians who feel no need to repent for anything.

When we turn away from you, God comes near to you. When we humiliate you, God defends you. When we push you aside, God accepts you. Even in your darkest nights, you are not alone. In your deepest humiliation, you are not abandoned. There is no room for you in our society or in our hearts; that is exactly why you have a privileged place in God's heart.

4. CRITIQUE OF THE RELIGIOUS PROFESSIONALS

Jesus' parable is short and clear. A father sends his sons to work in the vineyard. The first son says «no», but then he repents and goes. The second says «I go, sir!» but then doesn't go. Jesus asks, «Which of the two did the will of his father?»

Addressed to the priests and religious leaders of Israel, the parable is a sharp critique of the religious «professionals» who have God's name continually on their lips, but who are so concerned with religion that they end up ignoring the will of the heavenly Father.

Jesus says that the only thing God wants is a life of dignity and happiness for his sons and daughters, starting now. That is always the criterion for doing God's will. When we help people to live, when we treat everyone with respect and understanding, when we spread trust and contribute to a more human life, we are doing the Father's will.

Jesus often warns the scribes, priests, and religious leaders about one of the dangers that threaten religious professionals: they talk a lot about God, they think they know a lot about God, they preach in the name of law, order and morality. They are zealous and diligent, but they end up making people's life harder and more painful than it already is.

They are not acting out of ill will, but some ways of understanding religion do not contribute to a fuller, more human life. Some «religious» people accuse, threaten, and even condemn others in God's name, but never awaken in anyone the desire for a better life. In this way of understanding religion, everything seems to be in order, everything is perfect, everything is according to the law, but at the same time everything is cold and hard, nothing invites us to live.

At the end of the parable Jesus adds these terrifying words: «The tax collectors and the prostitutes are going into the kingdom of God ahead of you». The ones who seem furthest away from God are often closer than the theologians and priests, because they can see and accept God's understanding and goodness to everyone.

5. THE RISK OF SETTLING DOWN IN RELIGION

Many Christians end up settling down comfortably in their faith, although it seldom affects their life directly. We might say their faith is an add-on, not a central motivation for their everyday life.

So often our life as Christians seems to be cut in two parts. We organize and live our everyday life the way everyone else does; on Sundays we set aside some time to worship a God whom we never see during the rest of the week.

These Christians seem to change personalities, between praying to God and carrying out their day-to-day activities. God plays no part in their family life, their work, their social relationships, their projects and interests. Faith becomes a habit, a reflex, what Jean Onimus calls a «weekly relaxation», and in any case, a prudent safety measure for whatever future might await us after death.

We all need to ask ourselves sincerely, what God means to us in everyday life. Often the opposite of faith is not unbelief, but a lack of coherence.

What difference does it make to recite a creed, if our lives show no effort to follow Jesus sincerely? What difference does it make to say we're going to work in the vineyard, Jesus asks in the parable, if we don't go? As beautiful as our words are, they're still just words.

Aren't we reducing our faith to words, ideas, or sentiment? Haven't we forgotten that a true faith gives new meaning and direction to people's way of living? Let us be aware that what we believe is not what we say with our lips, but what we express with our whole lives.

31

The Danger of Defrauding God

Jesus said to the chief priests and elders of the people:

«Listen to another parable. There was a landowner who planted a vineyard, put a fence around it, dug a wine press in it, and built a watchtower. Then he leased it to tenants and went to another country. When the harvest time had come, he sent his slaves to the tenants to collect his produce. But the tenants seized his slaves and beat one, killed another, and stoned another. Again he sent other slaves, more than the first; and they treated them in the same way. Finally he sent his son to them, saying, "They will respect my son". But when the tenants saw the son, they said to themselves, "This is the heir; come, let us kill him and get his inheritance". So they seized him, threw him out of the vineyard, and killed him. Now when the owner of the vineyard comes, what will he do to those tenants?» They said to him, «He will put those wretches to a miserable death, and lease the vineyard to other tenants who will give him the produce at the harvest time».

Jesus said to them, «Have you never read in the scriptures»:

«The stone that the builders rejected
has become the cornerstone;
this was the Lord's doing,
and it is amazing in our eyes?»

«Therefore I tell you, the kingdom of God will be taken away from you and given to a people that produces the fruits of the kingdom» (Matthew 21:33-43).

1. THE DANGER OF DEFRAUDING GOD

The parable of the «murderous tenants», addressed by Jesus to the religious leaders of his time, is so harsh that many Christians have a hard time seeing what it has to do with us.

It tells about workers hired by a landowner to cultivate his vineyard. When harvest time comes, something unexpected happens. The workers refuse to hand over the crop. The landowner will not get the fruits he was waiting for.

Their audacity is incredible. One by one, they kill the servants the landowner has sent to collect the fruit. Worse yet: when he sends his own son, they throw him out of the vineyard and kill him, planning to take everything for themselves.

What can the landowner do with these workers? The religious leaders listen nervously and come to a fearful conclusion: he will kill them and bring in other workers «who will give him the produce at the harvest time».

There is no place in God's «vineyard» for those who don't produce the fruits. In the reign of God that Jesus is proclaiming and promoting, there is no role for unworthy «workers» who do not recognize the authority of his Son because they consider themselves the sole proprietors, lords and masters of the people of God. Their place will be taken by others who will «produce the fruits».

Sometimes we think this threatening parable is addressed to people in the Old Testament—not to us, the people of the New Covenant who have Christ's promise to be with us always.

That would be a mistake. The parable is addressed to us too. God does not bless a sterile Christianity that does not bring in the expected fruits. God does not identify with our incoherence, our deviations, our disloyalty. Now too, God is planning to replace the unworthy workers in the vineyard with a people who will produce fruits worthy of the reign of God.

2. HARSH CRITICISM FOR RELIGIOUS LEADERS

The parable of the «murderous tenants» is surely the harshest of Jesus' critiques against the religious leaders of his people. We do not have the story exactly as he told it, but it was probably close to the one we can read today in the gospel tradition.

Certainly the main protagonists are the workers in the vineyard. Their behavior is evil. They aren't at all like the owner, who gives the land the attention and love it needs.

The workers don't accept him as the owner. They want to be the sole proprietors. One after another they kill off the servants whom he sends to them so patiently. They don't even respect his son. When the son comes, they throw him out of the vineyard and kill him. They are obsessed with «getting his inheritance».

What can the owner do? He will get rid of these workers and give the vineyard to others who will produce the fruits. Jesus' conclusion is tragic: «The kingdom of God will be taken away from you and given to a people that produces the fruits of the kingdom».

After the destruction of Jerusalem in 70 A.D., the parable was read as a confirmation that the Church had taken over the responsibility for Israel—but it was never taken to mean that the «new Israel» would always be faithful to the lord of the vineyard.

The kingdom of God does not belong to the Church. It does not belong to the hierarchy. It is not the property of this or that theological current. The Father is the only owner. No one should claim ownership of God's truth or God's spirit. The reign of God is in «the people who produce the fruits» of justice, compassion, and the defense of the last and the least.

The most tragic thing that could happen to Christianity today would be to kill the voice of the prophets, to let the chief priests consider themselves the owners of the Lord's vineyard, or for all of us together to «throw the Son out» by suppressing his Spirit. If the Church does not respond to the hopes that the Lord has placed in it, God will open new ways of salvation among peoples who produce fruit.

3. THE DANGER OF SUPPRESSING THE VOICE OF THE PROPHETS

When the Roman troops destroyed Jerusalem in 70 A.D., and the Jewish people disappeared as a nation, Christians read a terrible meaning into that tragic event. Israel, so beloved by God, has not responded to his calls. Their religious leaders have killed his prophets, and then crucified his own Son. Now God has abandoned them and allowed their destruction; Israel's place will be taken by the Christian Church.

That is how the first Christians read the parable of the «murderous tenants», addressed by Jesus to the chief priests of Israel. The workers charged with caring for the Lord's vineyard kill the servants he has sent to collect the fruit. Finally they kill the owner's son, in order to keep the vineyard for themselves. The landowner has no choice but to kill them and hand over the vineyard to more faithful workers.

The gospel writers did not retell the story in order to feed the pride of the Church, the new Israel, against the Jewish people, defeated by Rome and dispersed around the world. They were asking, could the same thing happen to the Christian Church that happened to the old Israel? Can the Church fail to live up to God's expectations? If the Church does not produce the expected fruit, what will God do to carry out his plan for salvation?

The danger is always the same. Israel was very sure of itself: it had the Holy Scriptures; it had the temple; it scrupulously celebrated the ritual of worship; it preached the Law; it defended the religious institutions. It saw no need for anything new. It was satisfied with keeping everything in order. That is the most dangerous thing that can happen to a religion: the voice of the prophets is suppressed and the priests, seeing themselves as the owners of «the Lord's vineyard», expect to administer it as their own property.

That is our danger too. We like to think the Church's loyalty is guaranteed because it belongs to the New Covenant. We feel secure because we hold the title to Christ. But God doesn't belong to anyone. God's vineyard belongs to God alone. And if the Church doesn't produce the expected fruit, God will go on opening new ways to salvation.

4. IS KILLING GOD THE SAME AS KILLING HUMAN BEINGS?

We are naturally horrified by the cries of the madman in Nietzsche's *The Gay Science*: «Where has God gone? I shall tell you. We have killed him, you and I. We are his murderers. But how have we done this?... What did we do when we unchained the earth from its sun? Whither is it moving now? Whither are we moving now?»

According to Nietzsche, the greatest event of modern times is the «death of God». God does not exist. He has never existed. In any case, human beings are left alone to construct our own future.

This is the underlying conviction of many modern liberation projects, whether they are grounded in scientism, Marxism, or Freudian psychology. Religions are now considered an archaic, ineffective, or inadequate response to the need for human liberation, a response growing out of an immature stage of human history.

The time has come, they say, to emancipate ourselves from all religious tutelage. God is an obstacle to human autonomy and growth. We have to kill God so that true humanity can be born. This too is like the attitude of the workers in the parable: «Come, let us kill him and get his inheritance».

In recent years we have seen that it is not so easy to get the inheritance of a «dead God». After the solemn declaration of the death of God, many people began to see the death of humanity coming. Some have asked, with André Malraux, whether «God's torturer» can outlive his victim.

Socialist revolutions have not achieved the freedom that human beings so deeply wish for. The free exercise of our instinctive impulses has not opened up the way to a healthier and more mature human being, as Sigmund Freud expected;

rather it has produced new neuroses, frustrations, and a profound inability to love. «Scientific development, deprived of direction and meaning, is turning the world into an enormous factory» (Herbert Marcuse); it is not only producing machines that look like men, but «men that look more and more like machines» (Ignazio Silone).

Frustrated in their most authentic needs; stricken by «the most radical neurosis», the lack of meaning for existence; terrified by the real possibility of total self-destruction, modern human beings are surely more than ever in need of God. But will they find that God—one who can make humanity more responsible, more free, and more human—among believing Christians?

5. THE FRUITS OF TODAY'S SOCIETY

It is not an oversimplification to say that «private property, profit and power» have become the pillars of Western industrial society. If we analyze the framework on which our social behavior is based, we can almost always see its roots in an unlimited desire for acquisition, enrichment, and domination. The bitter fruits of this behavior are evident in our time.

Eagerness to possess is gradually shaping a new and self-serving way of life, almost exclusively concerned with material goods, indifferent to the common good of society. We speak of «private property» precisely because the owner has the power to «deprive» everyone else of its use or enjoyment. The result is a society structured around the interests of the powerful, not at the service of the people most in need and most «deprived» of well-being.

The unrestrained desire to acquire, conserve, and increase our own goods is creating human beings who struggle for themselves and organize their lives to defend against everyone else. Thus a society is emerging which separates individuals and turns them against each other, pushing them toward rivalry and competition, not toward solidarity and mutual service.

Finally, the desire for power promotes a society based on aggressiveness and violence, where often the only law is the law of strength and power.

Let us not forget that society can only reap the fruits it has planted in our families, our schools, political institutions, social structures, and religious communities.

Erich Fromm rightly wondered: «Is the Western world Christian?» Judging by its fruits, we would generally have to say no. Our Western society seldom produces the «fruits of the reign of God»: solidarity, brotherhood, mutual service, justice for the least favored, forgiveness.

Today we hear again Jesus' warning cry: «the kingdom of God will be given to a people that produces the fruits of the kingdom». This is not an empty warning. The creation of a new society is only possible if the incentives of enrichment, power and domination are replaced by those of solidarity and brotherhood.

32

An Invitation from God

Once more Jesus spoke to them in parables, saying: «The kingdom of heaven may be compared to a king who gave a wedding banquet for his son. He sent his slaves to call those who had been invited to the wedding banquet, but they would not come. Again he sent other slaves, saying, "Tell those who have been invited: Look, I have prepared my dinner, my oxen and my fat calves have been slaughtered, and everything is ready; come to the wedding banquet". But they made light of it and went away, one to his farm, another to his business, while the rest seized his slaves, mistreated them, and killed them. The king was enraged. He sent his troops, destroyed those murderers, and burned their city. Then he said to his slaves, "The wedding is ready, but those invited were not worthy. Go therefore into the main streets, and invite everyone you find to the wedding banquet". Those slaves went out into the streets and gathered all whom they found, both good and bad; so the wedding hall was filled with guests».

«But when the king came in to see the guests, he noticed a man there who was not wearing a wedding robe, and he said to him, "Friend, how did you get in here without a wedding robe?" And he was speechless. Then the king said to the attendants, "Bind him hand and foot, and throw him into the outer darkness, where there will be weeping and gnashing of teeth". For many are called, but few are chosen» (Matthew 22:1-14).

1. AN INVITATION FROM GOD

The parable of the banquet was apparently very popular in the first Christian generations; it is retold in Luke, Matthew, and the apocryphal Gospel of Thomas. However their versions, and the lessons they draw from the story, are so different that we cannot recover exactly the essential elements of the original story.

God is preparing a final banquet for all his children; he wants to see them all sitting around the table with him, enjoying abundant life forever. This was certainly one of Jesus' favorite ways of symbolizing the ultimate end of human life. It wasn't enough for him to tell about it in words. He sat at the table with everyone, eating even with sinners and undesirables, because he wanted everyone to get a picture of what God was doing.

Jesus understood his life as a great invitation from God. He wasn't pressuring, he wasn't forcing anything on anyone. He was proclaiming the good news of God, awakening their trust in the Father, taking away their fears, infusing them with joy and a desire for God. Everyone should receive his invitation, especially the people most in need of hope.

Jesus was a realist. He knew that the invitation might be refused. Matthew's version tells of different reactions. Some people rejected the invitation consciously: «They would not come». Others responded with indifference: «They made light of it». They cared more about their lands and businesses. Some reacted with hostility toward the servants.

Today many people no longer hear any call from God. They would rather be responsible only to themselves. Without being fully aware of it they live a solitary existence, talking to themselves in a perpetual monologue. The danger is always the same: becoming more and more deaf to any call that might transform their life at its roots.

Perhaps one of the most important tasks facing the Church today is to create spaces and facilitate experiences in which people can listen simply, transparently, and joyfully to God's invitation as it is proclaimed in the gospel of Jesus.

2. GOING INTO THE MAIN STREETS

Jesus knew the hard, monotonous life of the peasant farmers. He knew how eagerly they awaited the sabbath, which brought «freedom» from their work. He saw how they enjoyed their feasts and weddings. What could give these people greater joy than being invited to a banquet, where they would sit at the table with their neighbors to share a wedding feast?

Moved by his experience of God, Jesus began to talk in a surprising way. Life is not only about work and worry, troubles and sorrows. God is preparing a final feast for all his sons and daughters. He wants to see them all sitting with him, around a table, enjoying a life forever full of happiness.

What is this invitation about? Who is bringing it? Who can hear it? Where can we find out about this feast? We are so satisfied with our own well-being, so deaf to everything but our own interests, that we don't feel a need for God. Are we gradually getting used to living without a need for any ultimate hope?

In Matthew's parable, when the people with lands and businesses refuse his invitation, the king tells his servants: «Go therefore into the main streets, and invite everyone you find to the wedding banquet». It is an unheard-of order, but it reflects what Jesus is feeling. In spite of all the rejection and disrespect, there is going to be a feast. God hasn't changed. The invitation is still there.

But now the best thing to do is to go into the main streets where people without lands or businesses go by, people who have never been invited to a feast. They will understand the invitation better than anyone else. They can remind us of our ultimate need for God. They can teach us to hope.

3. EVEN TODAY WE CAN HEAR GOD

All the studies say the same thing. Religion is in crisis in the developed societies of the Western world. Fewer and fewer people are interested in religious beliefs. Hardly anyone listens to the formulas of the theologians. Young people are turning away from religious practices. Society is sliding into a growing indifference.

But we believers need to remember: God is not in crisis. The supreme Reality, to which all the different religions are pointing, is still alive and active. God is also in direct contact with every human being. The religious crisis cannot stop God from offering himself to us all, in the mysterious depth of our consciousness.

From this perspective we should not be so quick to «demonize» the current religious crisis, as if it were an impossible situation for God's saving action. It isn't impossible. Every socio-cultural context is more or less favorable for the development of a particular religion, but human beings still have the possibility of opening themselves to the ultimate Mystery of life which calls to them in the intimacy of their consciousness.

The parable of the banquet is an eloquent reminder of that fact. God doesn't exclude anyone. God's only wish is for a joyful feast at the end of human history. God's only desire is to see the great banquet hall filled with guests. Everything is ready. No one can stop God's invitation from reaching everybody.

It is true that many people have refused the call of religion, but God's invitation keeps coming. Everyone can hear it, «good people and evil», those who live in «the city» and those who are lost on the highways. Everyone who hears the call of goodness, love, and justice is accepting God.

I'm thinking about many people who know almost nothing of God. They have only seen a caricature of religion. They cannot imagine «the joy of believing». I am certain that God is alive and active in their most intimate being. I am convinced that many of them are accepting God's invitation in ways that I cannot discern.

4. THE DANGER OF TURNING A DEAF EAR TO GOD

Jesus' parable is a story for our time. The invitation to the feast of love and brotherhood can still be heard in every human heart, but people aren't paying attention. They are busy with their lands, their businesses.

Where do people today look for happiness? What doors do they knock on in search of salvation? For most people, happiness lies in owning more, buying more, having more things and more security. «Accumulate, accumulate: this is the law and the prophets» (Karl Marx). Others find immediate, individual joy in sex, drugs, entertainment, weekend dinner parties. We have to get away from our problems, take refuge in today's pleasures. Some work at caring for the body: the important thing is staying in shape, staying young, never growing old.

Our society has many ways of offering salvation. But they are partial, reductionist options; they do not give us everything that human beings are searching for. Men and women are still unsatisfied. Yet God's invitation keeps coming. We need to hear the invitation, not at the margins but in the midst of the dissatisfactions, joys, struggles, and uncertainties of our life. «Even when we see people accepting something partial, we can discern God trying to get through to humanity» (José María Mardones).

It is good to keep looking for well-being, but what fullness can there be in that eagerness to have ever larger-screen TV sets, faster cars, more sophisticated household appliances? Don't some people have too much to be happy? After so much searching for things, are they losing their freedom, their ability to love, their tenderness, even the simple enjoyment of life?

It is normal for new generations to look eagerly for different kinds of salvation. But what fullness can there be when they have tried every kind of sex, when they have returned from their «drug trips», when they have utterly stopped caring about anything?

The search for meaning, happiness, fullness, truth, and love, will always be a part of human nature. We will always, in some way, be looking for the Absolute. In the midst of our disoriented, superficial life, in the midst of our vain search for total happiness, are we turning a deaf ear to an invitation that is bringing joy to simple men and women «on the main streets» of this crazy world?

5. LOSING OUR EAR FOR RELIGION

More and more people are calling themselves unbelievers. But if we look closely, perhaps we can see that their unbelief is not so much a serious, well-considered decision as the result of an alienated life, deprived of interiority.

Many people in our time are not in a position to make a serious, responsible choice between faith and unbelief. Their way of living leaves them with no need to give ultimate meaning to their existence. In the words of one atheist, «we have to give meaning to our own life, by living it» (F. Jeanson).

But when people are only looking for more and more material well-being, only interested in making money and buying «status symbols», trying to «be something» rather than to «be someone», they lose the ability to hear the deepest calls that come to them.

Such people have lost their ear for any sound that comes from outside the world of their self-interest. They have no eyes to see other dimensions beyond material well-being, possessions, and social status. In the words of Max Weber, they have «lost their ear for religion».

Jesus' parable reminds us again that at the deepest level of life there is an invitation to seek other paths to freedom and fullness. Our greatest mistake would be to make light of God's call, and go off by ourselves to our lands and businesses.

We can keep on running away from ourselves, losing ourselves in a thousand kinds of escape, trying to forget God, and scrupulously refusing to take life seriously. But the invitation keeps coming. When we call ourselves unbelievers, are we not trying to hide our fear of the changes that would come in our life if we took God seriously?

The prayer of St. John of the Cross conveys a great truth: «Lord, my God, you are not a stranger to people who are not strangers to you. Why do they say that you are absent?»

33
To God the Things that are God's

Then the Pharisees went and plotted to entrap him in what he said. So they sent their disciples to him, along with the Herodians, saying, «Teacher, we know that you are sincere, and teach the way of God in accordance with truth, and show deference to no one; for you do not regard people with partiality. Tell us, then, what you think. Is it lawful to pay taxes to the emperor, or not?» But Jesus, aware of their malice, said, «Why are you putting me to the test, you hypocrites? Show me the coin used for the tax». And they brought him a denarius. Then he said to them, «Whose head is this, and whose title?» They answered, «The emperor's». Then he said to them, «Give therefore to the emperor the things that are the emperor's, and to God the things that are God's» (Matthew 22:15-21).

1. TO GOD THE THINGS THAT ARE GOD'S

They have laid a clever trap for Jesus: «Is it lawful to pay taxes to the emperor, or not?» If he says no, they can accuse him of rebelling against Rome. If he agrees with the tax, he will be discredited in the eyes of his followers who are wrung dry by taxation, the people he loves and defends.

Jesus asks them to show him «the coin used for the tax». He doesn't have one; he lives like a vagrant with no land or fixed address; he doesn't have any problems with tax collectors. Then he asks about the image that appears on the silver denarius. It is the face of Tiberius, and the legend says: «*Tiberius Caesar, Divi Augusti Filius Augustus*». On the back it says: «*Pontifex Maximus*».

Jesus' request and his question are telling. His adversaries are slaves of the system; by using that coin, engraved with political and religious symbols, they are recognizing the sovereignty of the emperor. Not Jesus; he lives poor but free, devoted to the poorest and most excluded people in the Empire.

Then he answers a question that no one has asked. They ask him about Caesar's rights, and his answer reminds them of God's rights: «Give to the emperor the things that are the emperor's, and to God the things that are God's». The coin bears the image of the emperor, but a human being—as the Book of Genesis tells us—is «the image of God». So human beings should never be subjected to any emperor. Jesus has said that many times. The poor belong to God; the poor are God's favorite children; the reign of God belongs to them. No one should abuse them.

Jesus doesn't say that one half of life, the material and economic side, belongs to Caesar; or that the other half, the spiritual and religious, belongs to God. His message is different. If we enter the kingdom, we must never allow any Caesar to sacrifice what only belongs to God: the world's hungry people, the boat people who come to Europe from Africa, the «illegal aliens» in our cities. The emperor can't count on our support.

2. THE POOR BELONG ONLY TO GOD

«To the emperor the things that belong to the emperor, and to God the things that belong to God». Few of Jesus' sayings are quoted as often as this one. And probably none are as often distorted by interests so different from those of this Prophet —who lived in total commitment, not to the Roman emperor, but to the people most forgotten, impoverished, and excluded by the Empire.

The moment is charged with tension. The Pharisees have pulled back to plan a decisive attack against Jesus. They don't come to him themselves but send «their disciples»; they are avoiding direct contact with Jesus. They are the defenders of the prevailing order, and they don't want to lose their privileged status in this society that Jesus is challenging. But the disciples are accompanied by «the Herodians», people from the court of Herod Antipas. Perhaps there are also some landowners and tax collectors with them, whose task it is to store the grain produced by Galilean farmers and collect their tribute to the emperor.

Praise for Jesus sounds strange on their lips: «We know that you are sincere, and teach the way of God in accordance with truth». It's a trick, but they don't know how true it is. Jesus is totally committed to preparing «the way of God» so that a more just society can be born.

He is not at the service of the Roman emperor; he has entered into the dynamic of God's reign. He does not live for the development of the Empire, but to make God's justice possible among God's sons and daughters. When they ask him «if it is lawful to pay taxes to the emperor, or not», he answers firmly: «Give to the emperor the things that are the emperor's, and to God the things that are God's».

Jesus isn't thinking of God and Caesar as two powers, each of whom can demand certain rights from his subjects. As a faithful Jew he knows that «the earth is the Lord's and all that is in it, the world and those who live in it» (Psalm 24). What can belong to Caesar and not to God? Only his unrighteous wealth.

If anyone is tangled up in Caesar's system, let them fulfill their obligations; but if they enter into the dynamic of the reign of God, they must know that the poor belong only to God; the poor are his favorite children. Let no one abuse them. That is what Jesus teaches «in accordance with truth».

As his followers we have to protect everyone, near us or far away, from being sacrificed to any political, economic, religious or ecclesiastical power. The people humiliated by the powerful belong to God, and to no one else.

3. LIFE BELONGS ONLY TO GOD

Modern biblical exegesis is very clear about this: for Jesus the most important thing was life, not religion. The whole pattern of his life points in that direction. He is always concerned with awakening and developing a life of health and dignity in the society around him.

We see it in his activity among the sick: Jesus brings fuller life to everyone whose life is diminished or threatened. We see it in his approach to sinners: Jesus offers the forgiveness that helps them live with dignity, rescued from humiliation and disrespect. We see it in the demon-possessed, who have no control over their own existence; Jesus liberates them from a life alienated and driven mad by evil.

As Jon Sobrino points out, life is a heavy burden for the poor who do not have even a minimal level of dignity. Their poverty goes against the original plan of the Creator of life. When human beings cannot live with dignity, we see God's creation vitiated and destroyed in their lives.

This is why Jesus is so concerned with the life of the Galilean peasants in particular. The first thing they need is to live, and to live with dignity. It is not the only thing they need, but for now it is the most urgent. Jesus invites them to trust in the ultimate salvation of the Father, but he does it by saving people from sickness and alleviating their pain and suffering. He proclaims definitive happiness in the arms of God, but he does it by bringing dignity, peace, and happiness into this world.

Sometimes we Christians teach the faith in such a tangle of concepts and words that when we are done, most people still don't know exactly what Jesus meant by the reign of God. It really isn't all that complicated. This is the only thing God wants: a more human life for everyone, starting now and moving toward the fullness of eternal life. Therefore we must never give to any emperor what belongs to God: the life and dignity of God's sons and daughters.

4. WE BELONG ONLY TO GOD

«Give to the emperor the things that are the emperor's, and to God the things that are God's». Jesus' words are often used to draw a sharp line between politics and religion, which protects the absolute autonomy of the State against any challenge from the faith.

In this interpretation, Jesus separates our civic and political obligations from the requirements of our faith—making people responsible to the political power for social and political matters, and to God for religious matters.

That is not what Jesus intended. His emphasis is on the second part. He has been asked a devious question about the problem of taxation, and he starts by answering that question: If you use Caesar's money, you must accept the consequences. But then he introduces a new idea, which was not implied in his adversaries' question.

Suddenly he brings God into the equation. The image on the coin is the emperor's, but people must not forget that they are made in God's image; they belong only to God. That is what the biblical tradition says. Here we see what Jesus is thinking: «Give to the emperor the things that are the emperor's, but don't forget that you belong to God».

For Jesus, Caesar and God are not two parallel authorities, dividing human loyalty between them. God is above any emperor, and the emperor must never demand what belongs to God.

At a time when the power of the State is growing, and it is getting harder for citizens to defend their freedom in a society where almost everything is ordered and controlled, we believers must resist any power that tries to rob us of our conscience and our freedom.

We must loyally comply with our civic obligations, but we must not be shaped or directed by any power that would bring us into conflict with the fundamental requirements of the reign of God.

5. RELIGION AND POLITICS

Relationships between faith and politics have never been easy. The same is true of the Church and the politicians. Sometimes politicians try to use religion for their own purposes. Other times the Church tries to use the politicians to serve its own interests. Too often we fail to evaluate the legitimate task of politicians and to discern the role that faith can play in that task.

We might begin by recalling two facts that are widely accepted by biblical scholars. First, the project of the reign of God, which Jesus set in motion, is to promote a profound transformation in human social life. For political life in its broadest sense, this means promoting the common good in society.

But second, Jesus never uses political power to promote the project; for that reason he does not engage in «politics» in its modern sense, which is the technical use of power to structure social life. The reign of God is not to be imposed by power, by force, or by coercion; rather it penetrates into society by planting and promoting values like justice, solidarity, or the defense of the weak.

The conversation about taxes to Caesar is enlightening. Jesus says: «Give to the emperor the things that are the emperor's, and to God the things that are God's». It is anachronistic and misleading to see in these words a «separation of politics and religion», as if one had to do with earthly problems and the other only with spiritual problems. Jesus' meaning is very different. They have asked him about the rights of Caesar, and he has answered by reminding them of the rights of God —which no one was asking about. The imperial coin bears Caesar's image, but human beings are «the image of God», and their dignity as children of God must never be handed over to any Caesar.

Christian politicians must never use God to legitimize their partisan political positions. The Christian faith is never identified with any partisan option, because different technical means can be used to implement evangelical values. But this does not mean that faith must be relegated to the private arena. The gospel offers Christian politicians an inspiration, a vision of personhood, and a set of values that can redirect and motivate their activity. The great challenge for the Christian politician is to bring into public life the values that defend human beings from dehumanization, and make those values politically effective.

Loving God and Our Neighbor

When the Pharisees heard that he had silenced the Sadducees, they gathered together, and one of them, a lawyer, asked him a question to test him. «Teacher, which commandment in the law is the greatest?» He said to him, «"You shall love the Lord your God with all your heart, and with all your soul, and with all your mind". This is the greatest and first commandment. And a second is like it: "You shall love your neighbor as yourself". On these two commandments hang all the law and the prophets» (Matthew 22:34-40).

1. DON'T FORGET THE MOST IMPORTANT PART

It was not easy for the people of Jesus' time to see what was most important in their religion. The simple people felt lost. The scribes talked about 613 commandments in the law. How could people find their way in such a complex web of precepts and prohibitions? At some point Jesus was asked: what is the most important part? Which is the principal commandment, the one that gives meaning to the others?

Jesus didn't have to think twice. He answered with the words that Jewish men repeated at the beginning and end of every day: «Hear, O Israel: The Lord is our God, the Lord alone. You shall love the Lord your God with all your heart, and with all your soul, and with all your might». He had recited those words that morning. They helped him center his life on God. This was the most important thing for him.

Then he added something that no one had asked him. «A second is like it: "You shall love your neighbor as yourself"». There is nothing more important than these two commandments. For Jesus they cannot be separated. One cannot love God and turn away from one's neighbor.

We can think of lots of questions. What does it mean to love God? How can we love someone we can't even see? When the Hebrews spoke of loving God, they weren't talking about feelings that spring up in our heart. Faith in God is not an emotional state. Loving God simply means centering our life on him, living to do God's will.

That is why Jesus adds the second commandment. One cannot love God and neglect the people who suffer, whom God loves so much. There is no «sacred space» where we can «commune» alone with God, away from other people. Any love of God that leaves out God's sons and daughters is a great lie.

The Christian religion seems complicated and hard to understand for many people today. The Church probably needs a way to filter out the less important things that have been added along the way, and concentrate on the essentials: to love God with all my being, and to love others as much as I love myself.

2. PASSION FOR GOD AND COMPASSION FOR HUMAN BEINGS

When religions lose track of the important things, they easily wander into paths of pious mediocrity or moral casuistry, which not only interfere with a healthy relationship with God, but can also do great damage to their people. No religion is immune to this danger.

The gospels present this story in a religious environment in which the priests and teachers of the divine Law divided its hundreds of commandments into «easy» and «hard», «serious» and «light», «small» and «large». It was almost impossible to find one's way through such a maze.

This question to Jesus seeks to recover the most important part, to find the «lost spirit». Which is the most important commandment? What is essential? Where is the nucleus of everything? Jesus answers as Rabbi Hillel and other Jewish teachers did, by summarizing the basic faith of Israel: «You shall love the Lord your God with all your heart, and with all your soul, and with all your mind». «You shall love your neighbor as yourself».

No one should think that loving God is a matter of feeling certain emotions or sentiments toward an imaginary Being, a matter of prayer and devotions. «To love God with all your heart» means humbly acknowledging the ultimate Mystery of life; living trustingly in accordance with God's will; loving God as a good Father who wants the best for us.

All this gives shape to our life, because it means affirming life at its very roots, living life with thankfulness, always choosing the good and the beautiful; living with a heart of flesh and blood and not of stone; resisting everything that betrays God's will by denying the life and dignity of God's sons and daughters.

This is why loving God is inseparable from loving our neighbor. That is why Jesus adds: «You shall love your neighbor as yourself». We cannot truly love God and not listen to the suffering of God's sons and daughters. What kind of religion would it be, if the hunger of some and the excess of others didn't raise questions or discomfort for its believers? Some people have rightly summarized the religion of Jesus as «passion for God and compassion for human beings».

3. LOVE IS EVERYTHING

The Jews could count 613 commandments that had to be observed in order to be in full compliance with the Law. So it is not surprising that the question came up in rabbinical circles about which one was most important: Which commandment is the greatest?

Jesus' answer is clear and precise: «The first is, "You shall love the Lord your God with all your heart, and with all your soul, and with all your mind". The second is, "You shall love your neighbor as yourself"». What do these words mean for us today?

They make one thing clear: love is everything. Love is the one thing that is asked of us in life. That is the key. Later we can draw all sorts of implications from it, but the important thing is to live before God and others in an attitude of love. If we always did that, everything would be fine. There is nothing more important than this, not even a specific set of religious practices.

But why is love the power that gives meaning, truth, and fullness to life? According to the Christian faith, the centrality of love is based on one reality: God, the creator of all life, is love. This is the bold and unsurpassable definition of Christian faith: «God is love» (1 John 4:8). In other words, God consists of loving; God doesn't know, doesn't want, and cannot do anything else but love. We may doubt everything else, but the one thing we must never doubt is God's love.

For this reason, to love God is to discover our own well-being. What truly glorifies God is not our suffering, but our life and fullness. Those who love God and have felt his infinite love for us are able to see ourselves, value ourselves, and care for ourselves with true love. This unique way of understanding ourselves gives us strength and vitality. Our fears and anxieties gradually disappear. Our life is changed when we learn to say, «Your will be done, Lord, because your will leads to my well-being».

Then we begin to understand the second commandment in all its depth: «You shall love your neighbor as yourself». Those who love God know that they cannot remain indifferent, unconcerned, or forgetful toward other people. Then we cannot relate to the people around us with any other attitude besides love.

This does not mean we relate to everyone at the same intimate level: a spouse, a client, the people one meets on the street by chance. What it requires in each case is to seek that person's good in the same way that we seek our own good. At a time when everything seems to be thrown into doubt, it is good to remember that one thing is beyond doubt: we are more human when we have learned to live in love for God and our neighbor.

4. THE ONLY TASK

We do many things in life. Many things move us and worry us. But what is truly important? What does it mean to do the right thing in life?

Jesus summarizes everything as love, bringing together two precepts that the Jewish people knew very well: «You shall love the Lord your God with all your heart, and with all your soul, and with all your mind»; and «You shall love your neighbor as yourself».

Everything is reduced to love of God and love of the neighbor. According to Jesus, everything else grows out of that. To many people this may seem too familiar, trite and inefficient. Yet we need to remember it today more than ever. Knowing how to love is the only thing that matters.

Why do so many people seem to be unhappy? Why do all our possessions leave us so empty and unsatisfied when all is said and done? Why are we unable to build a better society, without resorting to extortion, lies or violence? What is missing is love.

Little by little, our lack of love makes us solitary beings, always busy, never satisfied. The lack of love dehumanizes our efforts and our struggles toward political and social goals. We don't have love. And if we don't have love, we don't have anything. We have lost our roots. We have cut ourselves off from the most important source of life and happiness.

Jesus is not confusing the love of God with love for the neighbor. The «greatest and first commandment» is to love God, seek his will, listen for his call. But we cannot love God as a Father «with all our heart», unless we love our neighbors with all our might.

We often hear about the renewal of society, about the reform of social structures. Most people are not concerned with increasing their ability to love. Yet all the social improvements we make will do little to change things if we are cut off from love, from caring for the weak, from freely serving others, from unselfish generosity and sharing with people in need.

5. IN THE FACE OF MODERN INDIVIDUALISM

The characteristic symptoms of modern individualism are easy to see in our society. The goal of life is to «feel good»; everything else is secondary. The important thing is to improve our quality of life, protect against anything that bothers us, and do whatever we need to in order to ensure our own material, psychological, and emotional well-being.

In this view, the way to do that is to organize our individual life as we want it. We don't have to worry about other people's problems; what they do is their business. It's not good to interfere with other people's life. We have enough to do, taking care of ourselves.

Modern individualism is changing many people's way of life. A «morality without commandments» is gradually taking over. Anything that doesn't harm me is good. The important thing is to be smart and clever. Naturally we have to respect everyone and not hurt anyone, but that is all.

Our way of living the faith is also changing. We all know «what we like» and «what we don't like». The important thing is that religion should help everyone feel good. Religion always does something good for us. We just need to «manage» our religious life properly.

As a result our society is settled down in its own well-being, made up of respectable individuals who behave properly in every way—but who are turned in on themselves, separated from their own soul, from God, and from their neighbors.

There is a simple way to see how much «Christianity» is left in this modern individualistic culture; that is to see if we still care about the people who suffer. Jesus identified the important thing very clearly: «You shall love the Lord your God with all your heart», and «you shall love your neighbor as yourself». Being Christian doesn't mean either feeling good or feeling bad, but feeling with other people, thinking about those who suffer, and responding to their powerlessness without escaping into our own well-being.

We should not take for granted that we are Christians, because it may not be true. It's not enough to ask ourselves whether we believe in God, or whether we love him. We need to ask whether we love our suffering neighbors as much as we love ourselves.

Practice what you teach

Then Jesus said to the crowds and to his disciples: «The scribes and the Pharisees sit on Moses' seat; therefore, do whatever they teach you and follow it; but do not do as they do, for they do not practice what they teach. They tie up heavy burdens, hard to bear, and lay them on the shoulders of others; but they themselves are unwilling to lift a finger to move them. They do all their deeds to be seen by others; for they make their phylacteries broad and their fringes long. They love to have the place of honor at banquets and the best seats in the synagogues, and to be greeted with respect in the marketplaces, and to have people call them rabbi. But you are not to be called rabbi, for you have one teacher, and you are all students. And call no one your father on earth, for you have one Father—the one in heaven. Nor are you to be called instructors, for you have one instructor, the Messiah. The greatest among you will be your servant. All who exalt themselves will be humbled, and all who humble themselves will be exalted» (Matthew 23:1-12).

1. NO TEACHERS, NO FATHERS

Matthew has passed on to us these sharp, antihierarchical words, in which Jesus asks his followers to resist the temptation to turn their movement into a group led by wise teachers, authoritarian fathers, or leaders ranked above everyone else.

Matthew has probably worked these words into a critique of the aspirations to greatness and power that were already evident in the second generation of Christians, but there is no doubt that the words reflect Jesus' own thinking.

«You are not to be called rabbi, for you have one teacher, and you are all students». In Jesus' community, no one has a copyright on his or her teaching. Nor are they to submit to one another's doctrine. They are all brothers and sisters, helping one another to live the experience of a Father God—who deliberately reveals himself to the little ones.

«And call no one your father on earth, for you have one Father—the one in heaven». There are no «fathers» in Jesus' movement, except for the one in heaven, and no one must take his place. No one must be over anyone else. Any title that implies superiority over other people works against brotherhood.

Few of the gospel teachings have been so directly ignored or disobeyed over the centuries as this one has. Even today the Church stands in flagrant opposition to the gospel. It has so many titles, prerogatives, honors, and ranks that we have a hard time living the experience of true community.

Jesus was thinking about a Church without an «upstairs» and a «downstairs», a Church of equality and solidarity among brothers and sisters. It doesn't help to disguise the reality with pious talk about «servants», or by calling ourselves «brothers and sisters» in the liturgy. It's not a matter of words, but of a new spirit of mutual, friendly and brotherly service to one another.

Will we ever live up to this call? When will we meet followers of Jesus who don't allow others to call them Teacher, Father, or anything else of that sort? Is it impossible to create a simpler, friendlier environment in the Church? What is stopping us?

2. THEY DON'T PRACTICE WHAT THEY TEACH

Jesus always denounced the lies he encountered in daily life, but never more forcefully than in his confrontations with the leaders of society. He could not tolerate the behavior of those who «sit on Moses' seat» in the midst of the people, and demand of others what they themselves will not do. Jesus condemned their shameless incoherence: «They do not practice what they teach». There is a chasm between what they teach and what they practice, between what they expect of others and of themselves.

Jesus' words are still true. People listen to leaders who don't practice what they teach; to defenders of order whose own life is disordered; to people who proclaim justice but do not live justly; to teachers whose behavior undermines their teaching; to reformers who cannot reform their own lives; to revolutionaries who have no interest in a radical transformation of their own existence; to socialists who have never even begun to «socialize» their lives.

But Jesus' invective was specifically addressed to the religious leaders. In the Church too, there are people obsessed with a rigorous application of the law in other people's lives, who do not follow Jesus with the same radical zeal. Even today we have teachers who detect «hidden heresies» and threats to orthodoxy, without helping people live faithfully their commitment to Jesus Christ. Even today, people in high places rigorously condemn the sins of the small and weak, but scandalously overlook the injustice of the powerful.

Our society doesn't need preachers of beautiful words, but leaders who encourage social transformation with their own behavior. Our Church has less need of sharp-eyed moralists and orthodox theologians than of true believers whose life shines with evangelical light. We need «teachers of life», believers whose existence leads us to believe. «By returning to the essentials of the gospel, with their friendliness and sincerity, they can "detoxify" the atmosphere in the Church» (Ladislao Boros).

3. CHRISTIAN RABBINICALISM

One of Jesus' harshest criticisms of the rabbis in his time is that they imposed a moral mosaic on the people, but did not help them live a more human life. He said it this way: «They tie up heavy burdens, hard to bear, and lay them on the shoulders of others; but they themselves are unwilling to lift a finger to move them».

Jesus was warning the Church about the danger of a «Christian rabbinicalism» that can always spring up in the ecclesial community.

The Church must boldly and clearly proclaim the message of Christ, and the moral requirements it entails. It betrays its mission if it does not defend the principles of morality, by reminding people of their responsibility before God and their own human dignity. But as Jesus warned, the Church must also help people to live that morality in human ways.

Therefore an insistence on doctrinal purity is not enough, let alone a narrow condemnation or bitter indignation against the immorality of the modern world. People need more than condemnation; they need the strength to change. We also need to show in practice, in our lives, that Christian morality is not just a collection of rules arbitrarily imposed by God to «bother» us; it is a healthier and more effective way to live.

In addition, at a time when people find it harder and harder to believe in God, believers need to be able to share with others the joyful, radiant, and liberating experience of the Mystery of Love that we call God. If people have not even begun to experience the God who frees us from loneliness, despair, and fear, how will they come to understand «God's commandments»? How can they grasp what Christian faith means when it speaks of sin as an offense against God?

Thus it is important not only to speak the moral word of the Church boldly and clearly, but to speak it in a way that does not create a false image of a mean, judgmental God. Christian words and testimony should leave no doubt about the goodness and mercy of God.

We have to thank John Paul II for reminding us in his encyclical *Veritatis splendor*, after outlining the basic elements of Christian morality, that «in the word proclaimed by the Church» we must also hear «the voice of God who "alone is good", who "alone is Love"».

4. CONTRIBUTING TO THE CONVERSION OF THE CHURCH

Many people have turned away from the faith, scandalized or disillusioned by the behavior of a Church that in their view is not faithful to the gospel nor acting coherently with what it preaches. Jesus also forcefully criticized the religious leaders who «do not practice what they teach». But Jesus didn't stop there. He went on seeking and calling everyone to a life of dignity and responsibility before God.

Through the years I too have seen, sometimes close at hand, behaviors in the Church that do not fit with the gospel. Sometimes I was scandalized, sometimes I was harmed by them; they almost always fill me with sorrow. Yet today I understand more clearly than ever that mediocrity in the Church does not justify the mediocrity of my faith.

The Church needs to change a great deal, but what matters is for each of us to renew our faith, to learn to believe in a different way, to stop running away from God, to listen honestly to the voice of our conscience, to change our way of looking at life, to discover the heart of the gospel and live it joyfully.

The Church will have to overcome its inertia and fears in order to incarnate the gospel in modern society, but each of us needs to discover that today we can follow Christ more faithfully than ever before, without false social support and without religious routines. Each of us must learn to live more evangelically at work and in celebration, in activity and silence, without letting society shape us, and without losing our Christian identity in the midst of modern frivolity.

The Church will have to examine in depth its faithfulness to Christ, but each of us must also assess the quality of our belonging to him. We all have to give careful attention to our faith in the God revealed in Jesus. The sin and the failings of the ecclesial institution do not relieve me of any of my responsibilities. Only I can decide to open myself up to God or turn away from him.

The Church will have to build up its self-confidence and free itself from the cowardice and fears that keep it from spreading hope in today's world, but each of us is responsible for our own inner joy. Each of us must nourish our hope by going to its true source.

For many years we have had a large, active clergy. On the one hand this has been a rich, valuable resource for our Church; it has also led to passiveness and a lack of initiative in the rest of the community of believers.

We have gotten used to thinking of the priests as the only players, responsible for the life and functioning of the Church; we expect them to think, plan, and do everything else for us.

We tend to see the Church as a great pyramid, in which all the responsibility resides at the top with the pope, the bishops, and the priests. At the bottom of the pyramid are the faithful, waiting to listen, learn, and receive what they are told. But this shape does not reflect Jesus' original hope; nor does it reflect the mystery of the Church, which is called to be a community, the living Body of Christ.

Jesus was thinking of a Church where no one would be called «father» or «teacher» or «boss». A Church made up of brothers and sisters, where everyone finds a place and a task of service to others.

No one in the Christian community should expect to carry all the responsibility, or do all the work. Neither should any consider themselves superfluous or remain passive. We are all called to participate actively; we are all responsible for the Church and its mission, even when our responsibilities are different.

This requires a change and a conversion on everyone's part. Lay people must accept their own responsibility, collaborating with eagerness and generosity, not pulling back from the tasks that belong to them.

We priests must learn to work not only for the faithful, but with them. We need to be priests in a Church of shared responsibility, to value the role of the laity, to promote their active participation and entrust more responsibility to them. It is the priests' responsibility to help everyone take responsibility.

This is one of our great tasks in the Church: to help each one to find his or her true place in the Christian community, collaborating and sharing responsibility in the life and mission of the whole Church.

36
Keep Awake

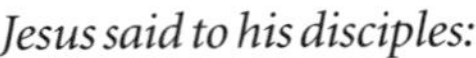

Jesus said to his disciples:

«For as the days of Noah were, so will be the coming of the Son of Man. For as in those days before the flood they were eating and drinking, marrying and giving in marriage, until the day Noah entered the ark, and they knew nothing until the flood came and swept them all away, so too will be the coming of the Son of Man. Then two will be in the field; one will be taken and one will be left. Two women will be grinding meal together; one will be taken and one will be left. Keep awake therefore, for you do not know on what day your Lord is coming. But understand this: if the owner of the house had known in what part of the night the thief was coming, he would have stayed awake and would not have let his house be broken into. Therefore you also must be ready, for the Son of Man is coming at an unexpected hour» (Matthew 24:37-44).

1. ARE WE STILL AWAKE?

One day the exciting history of humankind will end, just as each of our lives inevitably ends. The gospels attribute to Jesus this teaching about the last days, and they all emphasize this admonition: «keep awake», «be alert», «be vigilant». The first generations of Christians gave great importance to that vigilance. The end of the world was not coming as quickly as some people expected. They could see the danger of gradually forgetting Jesus, and they did not want him to return one day and find them «asleep».

Many centuries have passed since then. How do Christians live today? Are we still awake, or are we gradually falling asleep? Are we being drawn in by Jesus, or distracted by all kinds of secondary issues? Are we following him, or have we learned to live as everyone else does?

To keep awake means, above all, to come out of unconsciousness. To listen to the cries of the suffering. To feel God's love for life. To be more attentive to God's mysterious presence among us. Without that attentiveness it is very hard to follow in Jesus' footsteps.

Sometimes we become immune to the call of the gospel. We have a heart, but it has grown hard; we have ears, but we don't hear what Jesus heard; we have eyes, but we don't see life as he did, or look at people the way he looked at them. What he feared might happen to his followers, may be happening to us: we become like «the blind leading the blind».

Unless we wake up, the same thing may happen to us as to the people in the parable who were still asking, at the end of time, «Lord, when did we see you hungry, or thirsty, or a stranger, or naked, or sick, or in prison, and did not take care of you?»

2. HOW SHALL WE WAKE UP?

Jesus said again and again: «Keep awake». He was afraid the fire would go out and his followers would fall asleep. That is the great risk for Christians: getting comfortably settled in our beliefs, getting used to the gospel, drifting off to sleep while we practice a religion that has flickered out. How shall we wake up?

The first thing is to return to Jesus and become attuned to the experience that started it all off. It is not enough to settle down «correctly» in the tradition. We have to put down roots in Jesus, to be reborn in his spirit. That is the most important thing in the Church. Only Jesus can lead us back to the important things.

We also need to renew our experience of God. The essential parts of the gospel cannot be learned from outside. We discover the Good News of God within us. We have to teach and learn ways to come to God. Lectures on religion and debates on «sexual morality» will do no one any good, unless we are able to awaken in others a taste for God as a friend, as the source of an abundant and happy life.

One thing more. The key by which Jesus lived God and looked at all of life was not sin, morality, or the law, but the suffering of people. Jesus not only loved the unfortunate; he loved them more than anything else. We are not truly following the steps of Jesus if we are more concerned about religion than about human suffering. Nothing will wake the Church out of its routine, its paralysis, and its mediocrity, until we learn compassion for the hunger, humiliation, and suffering of people.

The important thing for Jesus is always the dignity and happiness of human life. Therefore if our «Christianity» does not help people to live and grow, it is not doing the essential things, no matter how many pious and venerable names we give it. Each of us must shake off the indifference, the routine, and the passivity that are putting us to sleep.

3. RESISTANCE

The articles I have seen about today's world say a lot about the contradictions of today's society, the gravity of the socio-culture and economic crisis, and the decadence of our time.

Sometimes they also give glimpses of goodness and beauty, acts of nobleness and generosity, but those things seem to be hidden behind the power of evil, the decline of human life, and injustice. In the end they are all «prophecies of doom».

One enormously hopeful fact is usually forgotten. A sense of indignation is growing in many people, in the face of so much injustice, degradation and humiliation. Many men and women are no longer resigned to living in such an inhuman society. A firm «no» to inhumanity is rising from their heart.

This resistance to evil is coming from both Christians and agnostics. The Dutch theologian E. Schillebeeckx describes it as «a common front of believers and nonbelievers, turning their faces toward a better, more human world».

Behind this reaction is a search for something different, a remnant of hope, a yearning for something that has gone unfulfilled in this society. It is the feeling that we could be more human, happier, better people, in a more just society —as limited and precarious as it may be.

Jesus' call becomes especially timely in this context: «Keep awake». These words invite us to wake up and live more alertly, not to be passively dragged along or molded by whatever society imposes on us.

Perhaps this is the most important thing: To react, to keep resistance and rebellion awake. To dare to be different. Not to act as everyone else does. Not to identify with the inhuman side of this society. To live in contradiction to so much mediocrity and senselessness. To start a reaction.

We should be inspired by two convictions. First, that human beings have not lost the ability to be more human, to build more dignity into society. Second, that God's Spirit is still acting in history and in the heart of each person.

We can turn this society in a new direction. What is needed is a growing number of wide-awake people who dare to bring common sense into the midst of so much madness, morality into such ethical emptiness, human warmth and solidarity into such heartless pragmatism.

4. IT IS NEVER TOO LATE

Ever since Sigmund Freud developed the thesis that a whole society can become sick, people have been diagnosing the possible neuroses and ailments of our society.

There has been talk recently about a «pathology of abundance» in our society, with diverse symptoms. A certain kind of easily achieved well-being can lead to personal atrophy, spiritual lethargy, and a loss of vitality.

But perhaps one of its most serious and widespread symptoms is frivolity. The glib way we talk about life's most serious problems. The superficiality that invades all our discourse. Cultivating frivolity has led to a readily visible incoherence in our lives.

The teaching of ethics is neglected in education, the fundamentals of morality are eliminated, and then we're surprised at the spread of corruption in public life.

Money-making schemes are promoted, gambling is encouraged, and then we complain about the rise of frauds and scams. Children are taught to look out for themselves and protect their own selfish interests, and we're surprised when they neglect their aging parents.

We're appalled by all kinds of sexual violation and harassment, but we continue to encourage sexual impulsiveness in many ways. We exalt free love and make light of adultery, but we are also troubled by the inevitable failure of marriages.

Everyone does his or her own thing, ignoring those who don't fit into their plans, and then we wonder why we feel so terribly alone. We are troubled by the modern plague of chronic depression and stress, but we go on promoting an agitated, superficial, and empty way of life.

The only cure for frivolity is to wake up, react vigorously, and learn to live more lucidly. That is the cry of the gospel: Wake up. Shake off your drowsiness. Become alert. It is never too late to hear Jesus' call to «keep awake», to pull ourselves out of frivolity and begin living more responsibly.

5. REORIENTING OUR LIFE

It is hard to put a name on the deep and persistent discomfort we sometimes feel. That is what I hear from people who are looking for «something different», a new approach, perhaps an experience that puts their daily life in a new light.

We might call it «inner emptiness», dissatisfaction, an inability to find something solid that makes us want to live life to the fullest. Perhaps we should call it «boredom»; weariness with the sameness of life; a feeling that we're missing something important, but we don't know what.

Sometimes the crisis takes on religious overtones. Should we call it a «loss of faith»? We no longer know what to believe in, we cannot find an inner light; we have left our childhood religion behind, but haven't found anything better to replace it. Sometimes we get a strange feeling that we can't find a landmark by which to orient our life. What should we do?

The first thing is not to shrivel up or give in to sadness: everything is calling us to live. There is something very healthy about that bad feeling: our desire for something more positive, less synthetic, more worth while, less artificial. What we need is to reorient our life. Not to correct a particular aspect of our personality; perhaps that will come later. What we need now is to dig down, find a source of life and salvation.

Can we stop and listen to Jesus calling us to wake up? Don't we need to hear him say «be vigilant», «pay attention to the signs of the times», «it's time to get up»? We all need to ask what we are neglecting in our life, what needs to be changed, where we should focus more time and attention.

Jesus' words are addressed to us all: «Keep awake». We have to react. If we do, we will experience one of those rare moments when we feel awake from the deepest level of our being.

37

With Lighted Lamps

Jesus told his disciples this parable:

«Then the kingdom of heaven will be like this. Ten bridesmaids took their lamps and went to meet the bridegroom. Five of them were foolish, and five were wise. When the foolish took their lamps, they took no oil with them, but the wise took flasks of oil with their lamps. As the bridegroom was delayed, all of them became drowsy and slept. But at midnight there was a shout, "Look! Here is the bridegroom! Come out to meet him". Then all those bridesmaids got up and trimmed their lamps. The foolish said to the wise, "Give us some of your oil, for our lamps are going out". But the wise replied, "No! there will not be enough for you and for us; you had better go to the dealers and buy some for yourselves"».

«And while they went to buy it, the bridegroom came, and those who were ready went with him into the wedding banquet; and the door was shut. Later the other bridesmaids came also, saying, "Lord, lord, open to us". But he replied, «Truly I tell you, I do not know you». Keep awake therefore, for you know neither the day nor the hour» (Matthew 25:1-13).

1. BEFORE IT'S TOO LATE

Matthew wrote his gospel at a critical time for Jesus' followers. The return of Christ had been delayed. The faith of many people had become relaxed. They needed a parable of Jesus to reawaken their first conversion.

The story is about a wedding feast. A group of young women had come out joyfully «to meet the bridegroom». They were not all well prepared. Some had brought oil to light their lamps; the others hadn't even thought about that. They thought it was enough to have a lamp in their hands.

It is irresponsible to call ourselves Christians and live our religion without really trying to be like him. It is a mistake to live a self-satisfied life in the Church, without being truly converted to evangelical values. Only the unconscious can think of themselves as followers of Jesus unless they «join in» with the project that he was setting in motion.

Today it is so easy to relax, to fall into skepticism, and to «go along» with the usual ways, that there is only one way to be the Church: through conversion to Jesus Christ.

2. WAITING FOR JESUS WITH OUR LAMPS LIT

Among the first Christians there were certainly «good» disciples and «bad» disciples. But when Matthew wrote his gospel, he was mainly thinking about the «wise» disciples in the Christian community who were acting responsibly, and the «foolish» disciples who were acting frivolously and carelessly. What does that mean?

Matthew is combining two of Jesus' parables. The first one is very clear: Some people hear Jesus' words and put them in practice. They take the gospel seriously and live by it. They are like the «wise man» who built his house on rock. They are the responsible ones, who build their lives and the Church's life on the truth of Jesus.

But there are others who hear Jesus' words and do not put them in practice. They are as «foolish» as the man who built his house on sand. Their life has no meaning. If it were up to them, Christianity would be a mere façade, with no real foundation in Jesus.

That parable helps us understand the message behind this story, in which a group of young women come out joyfully to meet the bridegroom and accompany him to the wedding feast. We are told at the beginning that some of them are «wise», and some are «foolish».

The wise ones bring oil to keep their lamps lit; the foolish ones aren't even thinking about that. The bridegroom is delayed, but he arrives around midnight. The wise ones bring out their lamps to light the way, meet the bridegroom, and «go with him into the wedding banquet». The foolish ones don't know what to do; «our lamps are going out». They can't go with the bridegroom that way. When they finally arrive, it's too late; the door is shut.

The message is clear and urgent. It is foolish to go on hearing the gospel without putting it in practice; that is like building Christianity on the sand. And it is foolish to confess Jesus Christ with a burnt-out life, empty of his spirit and his truth; that is like waiting for Jesus with burnt-out lamps. Jesus may be delayed, but our conversion cannot wait any longer.

3. FOOLISH BELIEVERS

Many of Jesus' parables convey the same message in different ways. The best thing you have is hope. Don't waste it. Keep it alive. Don't let your eagerness for eternal life fade out. Wait for it with a burning heart. Be alert. There is nothing sadder than a «burnt-out» person who has lost all hope in God.

Jesus isn't using moral language. For him, letting hope die out is not a sin, but foolishness. The young women in the story, whose lamps go out before the bridegroom arrives, are «foolish» because they did not keep their hope alive. They are not doing the most important thing a human being can do: wait for God until the end.

It is not easy to hear this message today. We have lost the ability to live anything with intensity, over time. Everything fades away with time. People today only care about the new, the up to date, the here and now. We are unable to hold on to it, to keep it alive, to keep it from burning out.

We have found a reasonable, sensible way of looking at the future. We have mastered the art of making calculations and planning ahead to avoid future risks. We are concerned with protecting our health and guaranteeing our standard of living; we plan for retirement and a peaceful old age. That is all well and good, but we are foolish if we do not see the obvious: all our carefully planned security is itself insecure.

The gospel warning is not irrational or absurd. Jesus simply invites us to live within the horizon of eternal life, not to be deceived by the disintegration and narrowness of life as we know it. How are you preparing for life beyond this visible and perishable one? Where will you find security when all your securities crumble?

To keep hope alive means not settling for just anything, not giving up on humanity, not losing the yearning for «eternal life» for all, never ceasing to search, to believe, and to trust. People who live this way are waiting for the coming of God, even if they don't realize that they are.

4. COMPLETE HUMAN BEINGS

It is surprising how insistently Jesus talks about staying awake. Many of his parables invite us to keep a wakeful attitude toward life. Our greatest foolishness is to live «without horizons». To plunge into the present, without a broader perspective. To drown our sense of the infinite in the vulgarity of a superficial, satisfied life.

Christian hope is not unrealistic. On the one hand it can free us from naïve optimism, from thinking that we can always find what we're looking for. On the other, it can wake us up out of passivity, resignation, or self-satisfaction.

Human beings do not only have «needs» that disappear when they are satisfied. We also have «wants» that are never satisfied, because they are open to the infinite and universal. To be human is to want love, truth, fullness, total happiness. «For humans, nothing is ever complete» (L. Aragón). We are never completely satisfied.

Our greatest mistake is to get bogged down in the mere satisfaction of some of our needs. Haven't we seen «complete» men and women, with nothing left to overcome, settled down in a boring, satisfied life? Haven't we seen people who don't want anything to change? Individuals turned in on themselves, insensitive to other people's pain, people whose lamps of free and generous love have burned out long ago?

The gospel invites us to keep awake. Christian hope does not settle down into sleep. It is restless; it keeps our sense of responsibility and creativity alert; it won't let us sleep. People who keep their lamps of hope burning are eternally unsatisfied people, never completely happy with themselves or with the world they live in. That is precisely why they get involved wherever others are struggling for a better, freer world.

These are the «wise» believers that our society so badly needs. People of tireless hope. Men and women who know that a rising standard of living is not the final salvation that can satisfy human needs. Believers who struggle for a more human world, knowing that it will never just develop out of our own efforts, but comes as a gift from the One in whom we will one day find our fullness.

5. WHEN HOPE DIES OUT

Sometimes we think that the opposite of hope is despair. That's not always true. At a time of crisis like ours, the loss of hope is expressed in an attitude of hopelessness that penetrates everything. We can easily see this «exhaustion» of hope in people today.

Sometimes the most obvious symptom is a negative attitude toward life. People without hope start to see everything through dark glasses. They cannot see the goodness, the beauty in life. They cannot see the positive side of things, other people, or events. Everything is going wrong, everything is useless. This hopelessness begins to exhaust their best energies.

Sometimes hopelessness is evident in lowered expectations. People no longer expect much from life, from society, from other people. Above all, they don't expect much from themselves. They begin to lower their aspirations. This makes them inwardly uncomfortable, but they don't know how to react. They can't find the energy to live. They fall easily into passivity and skepticism.

Other times, hopelessness is accompanied by sadness. Their joy in life fades away. Outwardly they may laugh and have fun, but something within them has died. Bad moods, pessimism, and bitterness are increasingly present. Nothing is worth it. There is no «what for» in living. They just let life drag them along.

Sometimes hopelessness feels like simple weariness. Life becomes a heavy burden, hard to bear. They lack energy and enthusiasm. They are tired of everything. It's not like being tired after a day at work or a particular task. This is an existential weariness, a deep sense of boredom that comes up from inside and saps the life out of them.

This sense of crumbling hope has many possible causes, but it often begins with people's loss of an «inner life». Often their problem is not that they «have problems», but that they don't have the inner power to face the problems.

I remember the words of Rafael Argullol, an agnostic philosopher who doesn't usually play around with spiritual ideas: «I think there is a real weakness underlying our apparent material and technical strength. Man's spiritual silhouette is getting thin». According to this Catalonian writer, getting thin spiritually has contributed to the fear, insecurity, and inconsistency of contemporary human life.

This is a time to recall Jesus' parable and its warning. It is foolishness to let the oil in our lamps burn out. People with a spiritual emptiness and inner poverty cannot walk toward real progress, or orient their lives toward definitive salvation.

38

No To Conservatism

Jesus told his disciples this parable:

«For it is as if a man, going on a journey, summoned his slaves and entrusted his property to them; to one he gave five talents, to another two, to another one, to each according to his ability. Then he went away. The one who had received the five talents went off at once and traded with them, and made five more talents. In the same way, the one who had the two talents made two more talents. But the one who had received the one talent went off and dug a hole in the ground and hid his master's money. After a long time the master of those slaves came and settled accounts with them. Then the one who had received the five talents came forward, bringing five more talents, saying, "Master, you handed over to me five talents; see, I have made five more talents". His master said to him, "Well done, good and trustworthy slave; you have been trustworthy in a few things, I will put you in charge of many things; enter into the joy of your master". And the one with the two talents also came forward, saying, "Master, you handed over to me two talents; see, I have made two more talents". His master said to him, "Well done, good and trustworthy slave; you have been trustworthy in a few things, I will put you in charge of many things; enter into the joy of your master". Then the one who had received the one talent also came forward, saying, "Master, I knew that you were a harsh man, reaping where you did not sow, and gathering where you did not scatter seed; so I was afraid, and I went and hid your talent in the ground. Here you have what is yours". But his master replied, "You wicked and lazy slave! You knew, did you, that I reap where I did not sow, and gather where I did not scatter? Then you ought to have invested my money with the bankers, and on my return I would have received what was my own with interest. So take the talent from him, and give it to the one with the ten talents. For to all those who have, more will be given, and they will have an abundance; but from those who have nothing, even what they have will be taken away. As for this worthless slave, throw him into the outer darkness, where there will be weeping and gnashing of teeth"» (Matthew 25:14-30).

1. DON'T BURY LIFE

The parable of the talents is surely one of the best known. Before he goes on a trip, a man entrusts his goods to three of his employees. The first two immediately go to work. When the owner returns, they bring him the results: each one has doubled the talents he was given. Their efforts are generously rewarded, because they were responsive to their master's expectations.

The third employee does a strange thing. The only thing that occurs to him is to bury the talent he was given, and keep it safely until the end. When the master returns, he gives it back and thinks he has faithfully done what the master wanted: «Here you have what is yours». Instead the master condemns him as a «wicked and lazy slave» who didn't understand anything; he was only thinking of his own security.

Jesus' message is clear: No to conservatism, Yes to creativity. No to a sterile life, Yes to an active response to God. No to an obsession with security, Yes to a risky effort to change the world. No to a faith buried in conformity, Yes to a committed following of Jesus.

We are always tempted to avoid problems and disturbances: to protect our modest well-being, not to do anything that might complicate our life. That is the best way to live a sterile, petty life, a life without horizons.

The same thing is true of the Christian life. If we go outside the usual boundaries we may go too far and fall into wild exaggerations, but an even greater danger is staying safe, letting our faith cool, closing out the freshness of the gospel. We have to ask ourselves what we are planting in society, where we are spreading hope and alleviating sorrow.

It would be a mistake to come to God with the attitude of the third servant: «Here you have what is yours». Here is your gospel, your project of the reign of God, your message of love for those who suffer. We have kept it faithfully. We haven't used it to transform our life or to introduce your kingdom in the world. We didn't want to take chances. But here it is, undamaged.

2. AWAKENING RESPONSIBILITY

The parable of the talents is an open-ended story; we can read it in different ways. Scholars and preachers have often given it allegorical meanings that point in different directions. It is important to focus on the third servant, because he gets most of the attention and space in the parable.

His behavior is odd. While the other servants are trying to make their share of the master's goods bear fruit, the third can't think of anything better than to hide his talent in the ground. On his return the master calls him a «wicked and lazy servant» who hasn't understood anything. Why did he act so oddly?

This servant doesn't identify himself with his master or his master's interests. He is not acting out of love. He doesn't love the master; he is afraid of him. It is fear that leads him to do the safe thing. He explains: «I was afraid, and I went and hid your talent in the ground».

This servant doesn't understand his responsibility. He thinks he is fulfilling the master's expectations by keeping his talent safe, even if not productive. He doesn't understand what active, creative faithfulness is. He doesn't feel engaged in his master's projects. When the master returns, he says that clearly: «Here you have what is yours».

For many people today, Christianity seems to have reached the point where the main goal is to «conserve», not to courageously seek out new ways to accept, live, and proclaim Christ's project of the reign of God; now more than ever we need to listen carefully to this parable.

If we never feel called to follow Christ beyond what we have always been taught and instructed to do; if we don't take any risks to make the Church more faithful to Jesus; if we avoid any changes that might complicate our life; if we don't take responsibility for the reign of God as Jesus did, by putting «new wine in new wineskins», then we need to learn the active, creative, and risky faithfulness that the parable shows us.

3. AFRAID TO RUN RISKS

Religion is often seen as a system of beliefs and practices that protect us from God, but don't help us to live creatively. That kind of religion leads to a sad, sterile life devoted to safeguarding our relationship with God —a life without joy or vitality.

There's no easy way to say this: that kind of religion is a religion of fear. People protect themselves against God because they are afraid of him. They don't love God, don't trust him, don't feel his mercy. They are afraid, and they look to religion to overcome their fears and their nightmares.

Having met Jesus, we have no excuse for seeing our religion that way. God is not a tyrant, who seeks his own interest by intimidating human beings; God is a Father who entrusts the great gift of life to each of us. Jesus did not think of his followers as «pious observers» of a religion, but as bold believers, prepared to take risks and overcome problems in order to «create» a life of dignity and happiness for everyone. Jesus does not call his disciples to bury their lives.

The third servant is condemned, not for doing something bad, but because he was so paralyzed by fear that he buried the talents that were entrusted to him. The message is clear. We cannot hand our life back to God and say, «Here you have what is yours. I didn't use it for anything». It is a mistake to live a «religiously correct» life, without taking the risk of living love, audaciously and creatively.

When we only care about saving our life, protecting and defending it, we lose it. If we are so afraid of failure that we don't follow the noble aspirations of our heart, we have already failed. If we don't take the initiative because we might be wrong, we are already wrong. If we are only concerned with conserving our virtue and our faith, we run the risk of burying our life. In the end we will not have made any big mistakes, but we will not have lived.

Jesus is our invitation to live with intensity. The only thing we have to fear is the fear of taking risks, the fear of not being «right», the fear of living without the audacity to change, without the courage to make the gospel real, without the imagination to invent Christian love.

4. JESUS' CRITIQUE OF CONSERVATISM

No one in our day would dare to criticize Christian conservatism as boldly as Jesus did in this parable of the talents. We must not forget that he condemns the third servant in the parable, not for committing any sin, but for conserving what was entrusted to him without making it fruitful.

What Jesus criticizes is not just a «sin of omission», but the act of reducing the faith to mere self-preservation, preventing it from growing and spreading.

We shouldn't look around at other people. The fear of risk and the temptation of conservatism is a problem for all of us. But it is not a Christian fear, and it can mask our lack of faith in the power of the gospel.

It is understandable that today's ecclesiastical leaders are concerned with protecting orthodoxy and keeping order within the Church, but is that the way to bring new life to the spirit of today's believers?

It may be easier for theologians to «recite» the theology we have inherited, ignoring the questions, intuitions and values of modern men and women, but by doing so, aren't we sterilizing Christianity and making it look like a relic of past history?

It may be easier and more gratifying for pastors to «restore» the traditional forms of religion and offer them to the people who still come to church, but is that the most evangelical way to pass on the saving power of Jesus Christ to future generations?

It may seem easier and more prudent to defend the faith in a kind of ghetto and wait for better times, but wouldn't it be more faithful to live in the midst of today's society and try to build a better, more human world?

The conservative attitude is even more dangerous when we don't call it that, but justify it by invoking orthodoxy, the sense of the Church, or the defense of Christian values. But isn't that just another way of freezing out the gospel?

The Church doesn't lose its power and evangelical vitality because of attacks from outside, but because we on the inside have lost our radical trust in the Spirit, and are unable to respond audaciously to the challenges of our time.

What is worse, like the third servant in the parable, we think of our conservative attitude as a faithful response to God —when in reality we are not living up to God's expectations.

5. PRESERVING THE PAST IS NOT OUR JOB

The task of the Church is not to keep the past safe. No one doubts the Church's need to be nourished by the foundational experience of Christ, and to keep renewing what the Spirit of Jesus has done for us through the centuries, but the Church must not become a monument to what once was. It does no good to be faithful to the past, when the past has very little relationship to the questions and challenges of the present.

Nor is it the Church's job to survive. That would mean neglecting its most important mission in every moment of history, which is to proclaim the Good News of God the Father as the motivation, horizon and hope for human beings. It does no good to restore the past if we are unable to pass on something meaningful to men and women today.

For this reason the virtues we need to develop in today's Church are not «prudence», «conformity», «resignation», «faithfulness to the past». The virtues we need are «courage», «the ability to risk», «creative searching», «listening to the Spirit» who makes everything new. Taking risks is not easy an easy path for any institution, including the Church, to follow. But it is the only path to follow if we want to pass on the Christian experience in a world that has changed radically.

When we live by the creative Spirit of God, the Church's two-thousand year history is not an excuse to avoid risks. Something is wrong in the Church if its own security is more important to us than a creative and risky search for new ways to communicate the gospel and Christian hope to today's men and women.

The greatest mistake of the third servant in the parable is not that he buried his talent without making it produce anything, but that he thought he was responding faithfully to God by keeping it safe from risks. We are not being faithful to God by leaving everything unchanged. That kind of faithfulness masks things like rigidity, cowardice, paralysis, comfort, and a lack of faith in the creativity of the Spirit. True faithfulness is not lived in passivity and inertia, but in the vitality and courage of those who try to hear God's call in our own time.

39
An Unexpected Judgment

Jesus told his disciples this parable:

«When the Son of Man comes in his glory, and all the angels with him, then he will sit on the throne of his glory. All the nations will be gathered before him, and he will separate people one from another as a shepherd separates the sheep from the goats, and he will put the sheep at his right hand and the goats at the left. Then the king will say to those at his right hand, "Come, you that are blessed by my Father, inherit the kingdom prepared for you from the foundation of the world; for I was hungry and you gave me food, I was thirsty and you gave me something to drink, I was a stranger and you welcomed me, I was naked and you gave me clothing, I was sick and you took care of me, I was in prison and you visited me". Then the righteous will answer him, "Lord, when was it that we saw you hungry and gave you food, or thirsty and gave you something to drink? And when was it that we saw you a stranger and welcomed you, or naked and gave you clothing? And when was it that we saw you sick or in prison and visited you?" And the king will answer them, "Truly I tell you, just as you did it to one of the least of these who are members of my family, you did it to me". Then he will say to those at his left hand, "You that are accursed, depart from me into the eternal fire prepared for the devil and his angels; for I was hungry and you gave me no food, I was thirsty and you gave me nothing to drink, I was a stranger and you did not welcome me, naked and you did not give me clothing, sick and in prison and you did not visit me". Then they also will answer, "Lord, when was it that we saw you hungry or thirsty or a stranger or naked or sick or in prison, and did not take care of you?" Then he will answer them, "Truly I tell you, just as you did not do it to one of the least of these, you did not do it to me". And these will go away into eternal punishment, but the righteous into eternal life» (Matthew 25:31-46).

1. A STRANGE JUDGMENT

The gospel writers leave no room for doubt. Jesus is entirely devoted to the people who need help. He cannot pass them by. No one's suffering is foreign to him. He identifies with the smallest and most helpless, and does whatever he can for them. Compassion is the most important thing for him. That is the only way to be like God: «Be compassionate, as your Father is compassionate».

We should not be surprised that when he speaks of the final Judgment, Jesus presents compassion as the ultimate and decisive criterion by which our lives and our identification with him will be judged. Why should it surprise us that he shows his identification with all the poor and unfortunate in history?

In Matthew's story, «all the nations» appear before the Son of Man, that is, before the compassionate Jesus. He doesn't distinguish between «the chosen people» and «the pagan peoples». He says nothing about different religions and cults. He talks about something very human, that everyone understands: What have we done for the people who are suffering around us?

The gospel writer does not dwell on the details of the judgment scene. He highlights a two-part dialogue which sheds great light on our present situation, and opens our eyes to the two ways of responding to those who suffer: either we help them, or we turn away and leave them behind.

The speaker is a judge who identifies with all who live in poverty and in need: «Just as you did it to one of the least of these who are members of my family, you did it to me». Those who held out a hand to a person in need were holding out a hand to him. They will be with him in the reign of God: «Come, you that are blessed by my Father».

Then he addresses those who lived their lives without compassion: «Just as you did not do it to one of the least of these, you did not do it to me». Those who have turned their backs on the suffering have turned away from Jesus. Naturally he says to them: «Depart from me». Stay on the path you have chosen.

Our life is at stake right now. We don't need to wait for the judgment. Right now we are coming near or turning away from those who suffer. Right now we are coming near or turning away from Christ. We are making the decision for our lives.

2. RELIGION IS NOT THE IMPORTANT THING

The parable of the «last judgment» is really an elaborate description of the final verdict on human history. It is hard to reconstruct the story as Jesus told it, but the scene helps us to grasp the «revolution» that he was introducing in the world.

People from every race and nation, from every culture and religion, are gathered there. They have come to hear the final word that will make everything clear. Two groups are emerging in their midst. Some are called to receive God's benediction: they are the ones who have held out a compassionate hand to those in need. The others are invited to depart: they have remained indifferent to other people's suffering.

What will decide our final destiny is not the religion we belong to or the faith we confess during our life. The important thing is whether we live with compassion, helping those who suffer and need our help. What we do for those who are hungry, defenseless immigrants, people crippled by sickness, and prisoners forgotten by everyone, we are doing to God incarnate in Jesus. The religion that pleases God most is help for people who suffer.

This gospel story doesn't use big words like «justice», «solidarity», or «democracy». Words do no good without real help for the suffering. Jesus talks about food, clothes, something to drink, a place to stay.

There is no talk of «love» either. That language is too abstract for Jesus. He almost never uses it. This story is about specific things like «feeding», «clothing», «welcoming», «visiting», «taking care». At the end of life we will not be asked about love; we will be asked what we have done for the people who need our help.

This is Jesus' call to all humanity: go to the people who suffer, care for the little ones. The only way to build life as Jesus wants it is by liberating people from suffering. No religion will be blessed by God unless it moves people to compassion for the last and the least.

3. THE FINAL SURPRISE

Christians have been talking about love for two thousand years. We keep repeating that love is the ultimate standard of attitudes and behavior. We say that all persons, structures, and human activity will be judged on the basis of love. But we may be using the beautiful language of love to conceal Jesus' authentic message, which is much more direct, simple, and specific.

It is surprising how seldom Jesus uses the word «love» in the gospels. Not even in this parable, which describes the final destiny of human beings. In the end we will not be judged on the basis of love in general, but on something much more specific: what have we done when we met someone who needed us? How have we responded to the problems and suffering of the specific people we met along our way?

The important thing in life is not what we say or think, what we believe or write. Beautiful feelings and sterile protestations will get us nowhere. The important thing is helping those who need us.

Most Christians feel satisfied and secure because we have never done anything particularly bad to anyone. We forget Jesus' warning that we are setting ourselves up for failure whenever we close our eyes to other people's needs, whenever we avoid any responsibility that does not serve our own interests, whenever we criticize without doing something to help other people.

Jesus' parable forces us to ask very specific questions: Am I doing something to help someone? Whom can I help? What am I doing to bring a little justice, solidarity and friendship to the people I know? What more could I be doing?

This is Jesus' last and most decisive teaching: the reign of God belongs and always will belong to those who love the poor and help them in their need. This is the most essential and definitive teaching. One day we will open our eyes to the surprising discovery that love is the only truth, and that God reigns wherever men and women are able to love and care for others.

4. MORE THAN CHARITY

It is good to remember this definitive test of our existence, even though Jesus' teaching makes us uncomfortable. Our fate will be decided by our practical response to the suffering of the poor, the hungry, the sick, the imprisoned. The question will be: What have you done for the brother or sister that you saw suffering on your way through life?

We sometimes try to resolve the problem simply by giving money, putting something in the alms box, contributing to a collection. But it isn't that simple. «The demands of love are not satisfied by the sacrament of money, because the very way we get the money increases the poverty we are trying to alleviate» (Johann Baptist Metz).

Love for people in need cannot be reduced to «giving money», among other things because it doesn't make sense to express our solidarity and compassion with money that we may have gotten by not showing solidarity or compassion to others.

Almsgiving in biblical times had a profound meaning that it does not have today. The Hebrew word for charity was *tsedaqah*, which means «justice». We might say that «giving charity» means «doing justice» in God's name, for those who have not received justice from human beings.

Our love for people in need requires much more than providing assistance, although that is also indispensable in emergency situations. We need to discern the injustice that is hidden in our lives, by gradually learning to see ourselves and our possessions through the eyes of poor individuals and peoples.

Today as always we are asked to give a cup of water to those who thirst, but we are also asked to transform our society into one that serves the poor and dispossessed.

Christians cannot claim neutrality in the face of injustice in our society, by saying that we don't want to «get involved in politics». In one way or another, through our actions or our inaction, every individual and institution is «involved in politics».

So it is not a matter of choosing to do politics or not, but rather of deciding for whose benefit we will do politics. A believer who listens to Jesus' words, regardless of his or her party membership, can only do one kind of politics: the kind that benefits the people in greatest need.

5. I AM IN PRISON AND YOU HAVE NOT VISITED ME

Jails do not rehabilitate criminals; everyone knows that. Criminologists talk about punishment contributing to the socialization of offenders, by «restoring» or «reintegrating» them into society. It doesn't happen that way. On the contrary, prison often further degrades and destroys their personality, and may even push them permanently into a life of crime.

The criminologists' critique of the existing penal system is persuasive. For one thing it doesn't make sense to remove people from society into a harsh prison environment, and then try to reinsert them. For another, we cannot expect a purely external intervention to produce fundamental changes in the prisoner's personality, values, or attitude toward life.

Meanwhile, the general attitude of society is forgetfulness and indifference. People don't care about the prisoners. There aren't many of them, and politicians don't win votes by defending their cause. People are annoyed by the groups that speak out on their behalf. The prevailing view is based on two simple principles: protect the public order by «locking them up and throwing away the key», and enforce strict justice by making sure that «if you do the crime, you do the time».

In our supposedly progressive society, most people don't want to hear that many prisoners need help —they too have suffered marginalization, drug addiction, poor physical or mental health, a lack of love— and that unless they receive the help they need, they are doomed to an even more hopeless future.

There have been increased efforts to provide better medical and psychological treatment for them, to arrange for home leave or psychological treatment, and to ensure their rights of due process. That is not enough. Prisons do not contribute to the human and social rehabilitation of prisoners. Society needs a better understanding of the suffering and destruction to which these people are subjected. Criminologists need to initiate a broader social debate. Political leaders need to search for more effective alternatives. Meanwhile the call of Christ should echo in the conscience of all believers: «I am in prison and you have not visited me».

40
On the Cross

Those who passed by derided him, shaking their heads and saying, «You who would destroy the temple and build it in three days, save yourself! If you are the Son of God, come down from the cross». In the same way the chief priests also, along with the scribes and elders, were mocking him, saying, «He saved others; he cannot save himself. He is the King of Israel; let him come down from the cross now, and we will believe in him. He trusts in God; let God deliver him now, if he wants to; for he said, "I am God's Son"». The bandits who were crucified with him also taunted him in the same way.

From noon on, darkness came over the whole land until three in the afternoon. And about three o'clock Jesus cried with a loud voice, «Eli, Eli, lema sabachthani?» that is, «My God, my God, why have you forsaken me?» When some of the bystanders heard it, they said, «This man is calling for Elijah». At once one of them ran and got a sponge, filled it with sour wine, put it on a stick, and gave it to him to drink. But the others said, «Wait, let us see whether Elijah will come to save him». Then Jesus cried again with a loud voice and breathed his last (Matthew 27:39-50).

1. DON'T COME DOWN FROM THE CROSS

In the gospel narrative, the people who passed by the crucified Jesus mocked him, laughed at his suffering, and gave him two sarcastic suggestions: If you are the Son of God, «save yourself» and «come down from the cross».

We react in the same way to suffering: trying to save ourselves, thinking only of our own well-being. So we go through life trying to filter out anything that might make us suffer. Is God like us? Someone who thinks only of himself and his own happiness?

Jesus doesn't react to the provocation of the people who are mocking him. He doesn't say a word. He doesn't try to explain. His response is silence. In that silence there is respect for those who disrespect him, and above all, compassion and love.

Jesus only breaks his silence to appeal to God with a horrifying cry: «My God, my God, why have you forsaken me?» He doesn't ask God to save him by bringing him down from the cross. He only asks God not to stay hidden, not to abandon him in this moment of death and anguish. And God, his Father, remains silent.

Only by listening deeply to God's silence can we begin to understand his mystery. God is not a powerful and triumphal being, impassive and happy, detached from human suffering. Rather, God is silent, powerless and humiliated, suffering our pain, darkness, and even death along with us.

So when we look on the Crucified One, our response can never be mocking or disrespectful, but rather prayerful, trusting, and thankful: «Don't come down from the cross. Don't leave us alone in our affliction. How can God help us without feeling our suffering? Who can understand us?»

Who else can give hope to the torture victims in so many secret prisons? In whom can defenseless women, humiliated and violated, place their hope? What can the chronically sick and dying cling to? Who can comfort the victims of war, terrorism, hunger and misery? No. Don't come down from the cross, because if we don't feel you crucified with us, we will be even more lost.

2. CRUCIFIED WITH US

Suffering leads many people to cry out to God. We don't all do it in the same way. Some of us look for theoretical explanations: «How can God let this happen?» We think of God as a kind of blind, unfeeling power who doesn't care about anyone. This usually happens when we're looking at suffering from a distance. That is not usually what we ask when we ourselves are in pain. Then our cries are more desperate: «My God, where are you? Why are you hiding from me? Can't you feel my pain and sorrow?»

There is a history of passion at the heart of the Christian faith. It is the story of Jesus persecuted, abandoned, tortured, and crucified. No other religion is based on a martyred hero. But what is even more scandalizing is that this passion story is about abandonment by God. After three hours of silence, nailed to the cross, Jesus cries out in despair: «My God, my God, why have you forsaken me?»

It is not only death that causes Jesus anguish. It is the fear that he has been «forsaken» after placing all his trust in the Father. What will become of the reign of God, the happiness that Jesus has promised to the poor and unfortunate men and women of the world? It is God's horrifying silence that makes him cry out. And that is the same cry that so many tormented people are raising today, for it expresses what they are feeling: «My God, my God, why have you forsaken me?»

But has Jesus really been forsaken? If he was left to die alone and forsaken on the cross, then God is not only unfeeling, but cruel. The first community of Christians vehemently disagrees. «In Christ God was reconciling the world to himself» (2 Corinthians 5:19). When Christ suffers on the cross, the Father is suffering the death of his beloved Son. They both suffer, in different ways. Christ suffers death in his human flesh; God suffers the death of his Son in his heart of a Father. The passion of Christ is the suffering of God, the passion of God.

That changes everything. If God is suffering in Christ, then Christ is bringing God's communion to those who are humiliated and crucified as he is. The cross of Christ, standing beside our crosses, is the sign that God suffers in all human suffering. God hurts with the hunger of the children in Ethiopia, the humiliation of the women in Iraq, in the anguish of everyone who is tormented by abuse and injustice.

This God «crucified with us» is our hope. We don't know why God allows evil to happen. It wouldn't help us much if we did know. We know that God suffers with us. That is the important thing, because with God, the cross ends in resurrection; suffering ends in eternal happiness.

3. THE WAY TO SALVATION FOR HUMAN BEINGS

For Christians, the cross is not just another event in the forgotten past. It is the decisive event in which God saves humankind. Thus Jesus' life of commitment, up to and including death, shows us the way to liberation and salvation for human beings.

The cross shows us, in the first place, the importance of «bearing the burden of sin». Of course evil and injustice must be eliminated; we have to struggle against them in every possible way. But we have to be ready to bear that burden as long as necessary. Jesus redeems by suffering. Only when people are directly involved, even suffering evil in their own flesh, can the world be humanized.

The cross shows us that love redeems the world from cruelty. Many people say that the important thing is to defend democracy and its values; what good does love do? But we need love simply in order to become human. In the Age of Enlightenment, democracy was based on «liberty, equality, and fraternity». We talk a lot these days about liberty; not so much about equality, and almost never about fraternity. Christ redeems by loving to the end. Democracy without brotherly love will not lead to a more human society.

The cross shows that truth redeems the world from falsehood. We think that the only good way to combat evil is to have an effective strategy. That's not true. Without a will to truth, whenever lies are spread or reality is hidden, the way to reconciliation is closed off. Christ redeems by witnessing to the truth up to the end. Only when people seek truth beyond their own self-interest, can the world be humanized.

Our society is still urgently in need of love and truth. Of course we need to identify the specific demands of love and truth in our time. Making them specific does not mean reducing them, manipulating them, or eliminating them. Those who «bear the sin» of all, and who struggle to the end for love and truth among human beings, generate hope. The German theologian Jürgen Moltmann says it this way: «Not every life is a source of hope, but the life of Jesus is, because for the sake of love he takes the cross and death on himself».

4. BEARING THE CROSS

What makes us Christian is following Jesus. That is all. Following Jesus is not something theoretical or abstract. It means following his steps, committing ourselves as he did to «humanizing life», and in that way gradually turning into reality his project of a world where God and his justice reign.

This means that the followers of Jesus are called to bring truth wherever falsehood prevails, to introduce justice wherever there is abuse and cruelty to the weak, to call for compassion wherever there is indifference to those who suffer. It means building communities that live the project of Jesus, with his spirit and his attitudes.

Following Jesus in this way leads to conflicts, problems, and suffering. We have to be ready to bear the reaction and resistance of those who for one reason or another are not seeking a more human world, according to the will of God incarnate in Jesus. They are looking for something different.

The gospels have transmitted to us Jesus' realistic call to his followers. The image is so scandalous that it could only have come from him: «If any want to become my followers, let them deny themselves and take up their cross and follow me» (Matthew 16:24). Jesus makes no false promises. If they are really following him, they will have to share his fate. They will end up as he does. That is the best proof that they are following him faithfully.

Following Jesus leads to a life of passion. We cannot imagine a more worthy, noble life. But it is costly. Following Jesus is partly about what we «do»: we are making the world more just and more human, making the Church more faithful to Jesus. But what we «suffer» is at least equally important: we will suffer for a more just world, suffer for a more evangelical Church.

Karl Rahner wrote near the end of his life: «I believe that being Christian is the simplest task there is; at the same time it is the heavy "light burden" that the gospel talks about. When one carries the burden one is carried by it, and the longer one lives, the heavier and at the same time lighter the burden becomes. At the end there is only mystery. But it is the mystery of Jesus».

5. FOLLOWING JESUS LEADS TO THE CROSS

We are so familiar with the cross of Calvary that it no longer makes an impression on us. Familiarity tames it and «cheapens» it. So it is good to recall some of the forgotten aspects of the Crucified One.

To begin with, Jesus did not die a natural death. His death was not the predictable extinction of his biological life. He was killed violently. Neither did he die in an unfortunate accident, but as a criminal tried and convicted by the most influential religious and civil authorities in his society.

His death was caused by a reaction to his free, brotherly, and solidary action on behalf of the poorest and most abandoned people in his society.

This means that we cannot live the gospel with impunity. We cannot build the reign of God, which is the reign of brotherhood, liberty and justice, without provoking rejection and persecution from those who do not want anything to change. There can be no solidarity with the powerless, without suffering the reaction of the powerful.

Jesus' commitment to creating a more just and human society was so real and so serious that his life itself was at stake. Yet Jesus was neither a guerrilla fighter, nor a political leader, nor a religious fanatic. He was a man in whom the unfathomable love of God for humanity was incarnated and made real.

We know now what forces are provoked when real love comes into a society, and how violently those forces react by trying to suppress the people who are working for a more brotherly, just, and free society.

The gospel will always be persecuted by those who give precedence to security and order over brotherhood and justice (the Pharisees). The reign of God will always be opposed by the political forces that see themselves as the absolute power (Pilate). The message of love will be radically rejected by any religion in which God is not the Father of those who suffer (the temple priests).

Following Jesus always leads to the cross; it means being ready to suffer conflict, polemics, persecution, and even death. But his resurrection shows that a crucified life, lived to the end with Jesus' spirit, always leads to resurrection.

41

Raised by God

After the sabbath, as the first day of the week was dawning, Mary Magdalene and the other Mary went to see the tomb. And suddenly there was a great earthquake; for an angel of the Lord, descending from heaven, came and rolled back the stone and sat on it. His appearance was like lightning, and his clothing white as snow. For fear of him the guards shook and became like dead men. But the angel said to the women, «Do not be afraid; I know that you are looking for Jesus who was crucified. He is not here; for he has been raised, as he said. Come, see the place where he lay. Then go quickly and tell his disciples, "He has been raised from the dead, and indeed he is going ahead of you to Galilee; there you will see him". This is my message for you». So they left the tomb quickly with fear and great joy, and ran to tell his disciples. Suddenly Jesus met them and said, «Greetings!» And they came to him, took hold of his feet, and worshiped him. Then Jesus said to them, «Do not be afraid; go and tell my brothers to go to Galilee; there they will see me» (Matthew 28:1-10).

1. CHRIST IS ALIVE

Easter Sunday is not the celebration of an event that is fading away with every passing year. Believers celebrate the Risen One who lives today, filling human history with life.

Believing in the risen Christ does not just mean believing in something that happened to the dead Jesus. It means hearing these words from the depth of our being: «Do not be afraid; I am the first and the last, and the living one. I was dead, and see, I am alive forever and ever» (Revelation 1:17-18).

The risen Christ lives today, infusing us with his vital energy. In a hidden but very real way, he is drawing our lives toward the final fullness. He is the «secret law» who leads the procession of the whole world toward Life. He is «the heart of the world», in the beautiful words of Karl Rahner.

For that reason, celebrating Easter means understanding life in a different way. It means joyfully sensing that the Risen One is there, in the midst of our poor things, forever upholding the moments of goodness and beauty that flower within us as a foretaste of the infinite, even if the moments pass without reaching their fullness.

He is there in our tears and sorrows, as a mysterious, everlasting comfort. He is there in our failures and helplessness, defending us with his enduring power. He is there in our times of depression, silently accompanying our loneliness and sadness.

He is there in our sins, as the mercy that sustains us with infinite patience, understanding and accepting us to the end. He is even there in our death, as life that triumphs when it seems to be extinguished.

No human being is alone. No one is forgotten. None of our laments fall into the void. None of our cries go unheard. The Risen One is with us and in us forever.

Thus Easter is the feast of those who feel alone and lost. The feast of those who are ashamed of their meanness and sin. The feast of those who feel dead inside. The feast of those who wail in anguish over the weight of life and the mediocrity of their heart. The feast of all of us who know we are mortal, but have discovered the hope of eternal life in the risen Christ.

Blessed are they who let the words of Christ penetrate their hearts: «I have said this to you, so that in me you may have peace. In the world you face persecution. But take courage; I have conquered the world!» (John 16:33).

2. RECOVERING THE RISEN ONE

For some Christians, Jesus' resurrection is just an event from the past. Something that happened to the dead Jesus, after his execution outside Jerusalem two thousand years ago. An event that is gradually fading into the distance, losing its power to influence the present.

For others, the resurrection of Christ is a dogma that they have to believe and confess. A truth that is in the creed along with other truths of faith, but the source of its effectiveness is not clear. These Christians have faith, but they have not witnessed «the power of faith»; they do not know from experience what it means to live with our roots in the Risen One.

This can have serious consequences. If they lose their living contact with the Risen One, these Christians are left without his «life-giving Spirit». The Church can go through a process of aging, sameness, and decay. It may grow sociologically, but become inwardly weak; its body may be large and powerful, but its power to transform becomes small and weak.

Unless we are in vital contact with Christ as someone alive and life-giving, Jesus becomes just another historical personality whom we may admire, but who does not make our hearts burn within us; his gospel becomes a «dead letter», trite and worn out, that no longer gives life. The empty space where the risen Christ was, begins to fill up with doctrine, theology, rites, or pastoral activities. But none of that gives life if the Risen One is not at its roots.

Few things are more damaging to Christian life than letting an institution, theology, or organization take the place of a faith that can only come from the life-giving power of the Risen One. For that reason we urgently need to recover in our own lives the foundational experience of the early Christians. The first disciples feel the hidden power of the resurrection of Christ; they are living «something» that transforms their lives. In the words of St. Paul, they know «the power of his resurrection» (Philippians 3:10). The Swiss biblical scholar R. Pesch says that in that first experience, «the disciples let themselves be caught, fascinated, and transformed by the Risen One».

3. BELIEVING IN THE RISEN ONE

We Christians must never forget that faith in the risen Jesus Christ is much more than reciting a creedal formula. It is even more than affirming that something extraordinary happened to the dead Jesus about two thousand years ago.

Believing in the Risen One means believing that Christ is alive now, full of power and creativity, drawing life toward its ultimate destiny, and liberating humanity from its gradual slide into permanent chaos.

Believing in the Risen One means believing that Jesus is present in the midst of the believers. It means taking an active part in the meetings and tasks of the Christian community, joyfully affirming that where two or three are gathered in his name, he is there bringing hope into our lives.

Believing in the Risen One means discovering that our prayer to Christ is not an empty monologue with nobody listening, but a dialogue with someone who is alive with us, at the heart of life itself.

Believing in the Risen One means letting his living word challenge us, and discovering in practice that his words are «spirit and life» for our nourishment.

Believing in the Risen One means knowing from personal experience that Jesus has the power to change our lives, to raise up the good in us and gradually free us from what kills our freedom.

Believing in the Risen One means being able to see him in the last and the least of our brothers and sisters, calling us to compassion and solidarity.

Believing in the Risen One means believing that he is «the firstborn of the dead», the beginning of our resurrection, and the one who has already opened up for us the possibility of eternal life.

Believing in the Risen one means believing that neither suffering, nor injustice, nor cancer, nor heart attack, nor automatic rifles, nor oppression, nor death have the last word. The Risen One is the only Lord of life and death.

4. GOD HAS THE LAST WORD

The resurrection of Jesus is more than a liturgical celebration. It is the manifestation of God's powerful love, which saves us from death and from sin. Can we experience that life-giving power today?

First we need to become aware that life is inhabited by an all-embracing Mystery whom Jesus calls «Father». With so much suffering in the world, life may seem chaotic and absurd to us. It is not. Although it is not always easy to feel it, our existence is sustained and oriented by God toward a final fullness.

To feel it we need to begin living from within ourselves: I am loved by God, and an endless fullness is waiting for me. There are so many frustrations in our life, and sometimes we love ourselves so little, that the joy of living dies within us. Jesus' resurrection reminds us that God exists and saves. God will show us the fullness of life that we have not experienced here.

Celebrating Jesus' resurrection means opening ourselves to the life-giving energy of God. The true enemy of life is not suffering, but sadness. We lose our passion for life and compassion for those who suffer. And we overflow with the apathy and cheap hedonism that deprives us of the best part of existence: love. The resurrection can be a source and motivation for new life.

5. WHAT GOOD DOES IT DO TO BELIEVE IN THE RISEN ONE?

Once after I gave a talk on the resurrection of Christ, someone raised a hand and told me something like this: «After the resurrection of Christ, human history went on as it was before. Nothing changed. What good does it do to believe that Christ has risen? How does that change my life?

I know it is not easy to convey one's own experience of faith to someone else. What words can we use to describe the inner light, the hope, the dynamism that comes from living with our roots in the risen Christ? But it is good for Christians to describe it from our own life context.

The first thing is to experience a great trust in our existence. We are not alone. We are not wandering lost and aimless. In spite of our sin and meanness, human beings are accepted by God. We can never get enough of Jesus' greeting: «Peace be with you». Even after he was crucified by humanity, God goes on offering us friendship.

We can also live freely, not letting ourselves be enslaved by the desire for possessions and pleasures. We do not need to «stop the clock», as if time were running out. We do not need to hoard life, or squeeze out whatever we can before it ends. We can live more sensibly. Life is much more than this life. We have only begun to live.

We can live generously, in radical commitment to others. To live in unselfish love does not mean losing our life, but gaining it forever. The resurrection of Christ shows us that love is stronger than death. To live by doing good is the best way to grasp the mystery of the beyond.

We can also enjoy the beauty and goodness of life, joyfully accepting all the experiences it gives us of peace, loving communion, or solidarity. Although they may be momentary experiences, they make God's salvation manifest in this life.

One day, everything that in this life could not be, or became halfway real, or was ruined by sickness, failure, or lack of love, will find its fullness in God.

We know that our time to die will come one day. There are many ways to approach this decisive moment. Believers do not die into darkness, emptiness, nothingness. They give themselves up to the mystery of death with humble faith, entrusting themselves to the unfathomable love of God.

Manuel Fraijó has written: «Faith in the resurrection is hard to share, but it is not hard to admire. It represents a noble effort to go on affirming life, even where life is defeated by death». This is the faith that sustains the followers of Jesus.

42

I am with You

Now the eleven disciples went to Galilee, to the mountain to which Jesus had directed them. When they saw him, they worshiped him; but some doubted. And Jesus came and said to them, «All authority in heaven and on earth has been given to me. Go therefore and make disciples of all nations, baptizing them in the name of the Father and of the Son and of the Holy Spirit, and teaching them to obey everything that I have commanded you. And remember, I am with you always, to the end of the age» (Matthew 28:16-20).

1. JESUS IS WITH US

Matthew does not want his gospel to end with the Ascension story, as Luke's does. Matthew is writing in a difficult situation for the community of believers; his gospel needs a different ending.

The Ascension could have been understood in a naïve and mistaken way, which might give those communities the impression that at his departure, Jesus had abandoned them as orphans. So Matthew ends with an unforgettable phrase from the risen Jesus: «Remember, I am with you always, to the end of the age».

This is the faith that has always animated the Christian communities. We are not alone, lost in the midst of history, left to our own strength and our sinfulness. Christ is with us. At times like the ones we are now living, it is easy to give in to lamentation, discouragement, and defeatism. We are in danger of forgetting what we urgently need to remember: He is with us.

The bishops, meeting at the Second Vatican Council, saw the need for a true theology of the presence of Christ in his Church. Our concern for defending and describing the presence of the Body and Blood of Christ in the eucharist may have unconsciously led us to forget the living presence of the risen Lord in the heart of the whole Christian community.

For the first believers Jesus was not a personality from the past, a dead leader whom they worshiped and venerated, but someone alive who animated, energized, and inspired the believing community.

When two or three believers are gathered in his name, he is there in the midst of them. A gathering of believers is not an assembly of orphans who try to encourage each other. The Risen one is in their midst, with his encouragement and life-giving power. To forget that is to risk cutting off our hope at its roots.

That is not all. When we meet a person in need, disrespected or abandoned, we are meeting the one who radically identifies with them. There is no better way to show Christ's presence, than with our help and solidarity for those in need. «Just as you did it to one of the least of these who are members of my family, you did it to me».

The risen Lord is in the eucharist, feeding our faith. He is in the Christian community, filling us with his Spirit and motivating us for mission. He is in the poor, moving our hearts to compassion. He is there every day, until the end of the age.

2. MAKE DISCIPLES FOR JESUS

Matthew describes Jesus' leave-taking by marking the path that he wants the disciples to take, the characteristics his Church will need in order to carry out their mission faithfully.

Their point of departure is Galilee. Jesus calls them there. The resurrection must not lead them to forget what they lived with him in Galilee. There they heard him telling inspiring parables about God. There they saw him alleviating suffering, offering God's forgiveness, and embracing the forgotten ones. Those are the things he wants them to pass on to others.

Among the disciples around Jesus, there are «believers» and «doubters». The narrator is realistic. The disciples «worship him». They certainly want to believe, but some of them are feeling doubt and indecision. Perhaps they are frightened, unable to grasp the meaning of it all. Matthew knows how fragile the Christian communities are. If they can't count on Jesus, it will all fade away.

Jesus «comes to them», makes contact with them. He has the strength and the power they need. The Risen One has received from his Father the authority of the Son of God: «All authority in heaven and on earth has been given to me». If they feel supported by him, they will not doubt.

Jesus tells them precisely what their mission will be. Their mission is not to «teach doctrine», or to «proclaim the Risen One». They must certainly attend to those aspects —witnessing to the Risen One, proclaiming the gospel, planting communities— but in the end everything revolves around one goal: «making disciples» for Jesus.

That is our mission: to make «followers» of Jesus who know his message, are attuned to his project, learn to live like him, and reproduce his presence in today's world. They will learn to be his disciples through such activities as baptizing and obeying his commandments. Jesus promises them his constant presence and help. They will not be alone and abandoned, even if there are few of them. Not even if there are only two or three.

The Christian community is like that. It is upheld by the power of the Risen One, through his Spirit. Everything is focused on learning and teaching others to live like Jesus, from their knowledge of Jesus. He is alive in their communities. He is with us and among us, healing, forgiving, accepting; in other words, saving.

3. IN THE NAME OF THE FATHER AND OF THE SON AND OF THE HOLY SPIRIT

How did Jesus communicate with God? What feelings were in his heart? How did he experience God day by day? The gospel stories lead us to a double conclusion: Jesus felt God as a Father, and lived his whole life in the energy of God's Spirit.

Jesus knows he is God's «beloved Son». He always calls God «Father», never anything else. For him God is not only the «Holy One» that everyone else talks about; he is the «Compassionate One». He does not live in the temple, accepting only those with clean hearts and hands. Jesus knows him as a Father who excludes no one from his compassionate love. Every morning he rejoices because God makes the sun rise on the evil and on the good.

The Father has a great project in his heart: to make the earth a good place to live. Jesus has no doubt about that: God will not rest until his sons and daughters are gathered around him in the final banquet. No one can stop that, not even the cruelty of death or the injustice of humankind. Just as no one can stop the spring from coming and filling everything with life.

Faithful to the Father and moved by his Spirit, Jesus is devoted to just one thing: making a more human world. Everyone must hear the Good News, especially the people who least expect it: the sinners and the despised. God doesn't give anyone up for lost. He seeks out everyone, calls everyone. He doesn't keep a balance sheet on his sons and daughters, but opens up ways toward a more human life for all of them. Everyone can hear him by listening to their own heart.

The Spirit keeps drawing Jesus toward the people who suffer most. That is not surprising, because he can see the names of the loneliest, most unfortunate people engraved in God's heart. The ones who mean nothing to us, are God's favorites. Jesus knows that the great people don't know God; the little ones do. Those who seek God discover his love, because they have no one else to wipe away their tears.

The best way to believe in the triune God is not by trying to understand the theologians' explanations, but by following in the steps of Jesus —who lived as the beloved Son of a Father God, and who was moved by his Spirit to make the world friendlier for everyone.

4. THE ESSENTIALS OF THE CREED

Over the centuries, Christian theologians have written profound studies on the Trinity. Yet many Christians in our time cannot see what these impressive doctrines have to do with their lives.

Apparently what we need today is to hear God described in humble, simple language that can touch our poor, confused and discouraged hearts and bring comfort to our vacillating faith. Perhaps we need to recover the essentials of our Creed in order to live it more joyfully.

«I believe in God the Father, creator of heaven and earth». We are not alone with our problems and conflicts. We have not been forgotten. God is our beloved Father. That is what Jesus called him, and it is what we call him. God is the origin and the goal of our life. He has created us all, out of love alone, and he is waiting for us all with his heart of a Father at the end of our journey through this world.

Today God's name is forgotten and denied by many people. The younger generations are turning away from him, and we believers don't know how to reach them with our faith, but God keeps looking at us all with love. Although we are full of doubts, we must not lose faith in this God, the Creator and Father, because that would mean losing our last hope.

«I believe in Jesus Christ, his only Son, our Lord». Christ is God's great gift to the world. He has told us what the Father is like. For us, Jesus will never be just a man. When we look at him we see the Father; in his acts we see the Father's tenderness and understanding. In Jesus we feel God as human, close to us, a friend.

This Jesus, the beloved Son of God, has called us to build a happier, more brotherly life for everyone. That is what the Father wants most. He has also showed us the way to follow: «Be compassionate, as your Father is compassionate». If we forget Jesus, who will take his place? Who can offer his light and his hope?

«I believe in the Holy Spirit, the Lord and giver of life». This divine mystery is not beyond us. It is inwardly present in each of us. We can understand it as the Spirit that nourishes our lives, the Love that brings us near to those who suffer. This Spirit is the most valuable thing we have within us.

Grace enables us to go through life, baptized in the name of the Father and the Son and the Holy Spirit. Let us never forget it.

5. IS IT NECESSARY TO BELIEVE IN THE TRINITY?

Do we have to believe in the Trinity? Can we believe in the Trinity? What does it do for us? Isn't it an unnecessary intellectual construct? Does something change in our faith if we don't believe in a trinitarian God? The famous philosopher Immanuel Kant wrote these words two hundred years ago: «From a practical viewpoint, the doctrine of the Trinity is perfectly useless».

Nothing could be further from the truth. Faith in the Trinity changes not only our understanding of God, but our understanding of life. To confess the divine Trinity means believing that God is a mystery of communion and love. God is not a closed and impenetrable being, immovable and indifferent. God's mysterious intimacy is love and communication. This means that Love alone is at the deepest level of reality, giving meaning and existence to everything. Everything that exists comes from Love.

The Father is original Love, the source of all love. God is the beginning of love. «God alone sets selfless love in motion; what is more, from the beginning it was God who started love» (Eberhard Jüngel). The Father loves from the beginning and forever, without being obligated or moved by any outside force. He is the «eternal Lover». He loves and will go on loving forever. He never withdraws his love and faithfulness from us. Nothing comes from him but love. This means, because we are created in God's image, that we are made to love. We exist only by loving.

The being of the Son consists of receiving the love of the Father. He is the «eternally Beloved», from before the creation of the world. The Son is the acceptance of Love, the eternal response to the Father's love. Thus the mystery of God consists of giving and also receiving love. In God, being loved is no less important than loving. Receiving love is also divine! This means, because we are created in God's image, that we are made not only to love but to be loved.

The Holy Spirit is the communion of the Father and the Son. The Spirit is eternal Love between the loving Father and the beloved Son, the one who shows us that God's love is neither a jealous possession of the Father nor a selfish entitlement of the Son. True love is always an opening, a gift, an overflowing communication. Thus the Love of God is not self-contained, but is communicated and shared with God's creatures. «God's love has been poured into our hearts through the Holy Spirit that has been given to us» (Romans 5:5). This means, because we are created in God's image, that we are made to love one another, without grasping and without limiting ourselves to fictitious, selfish kinds of love.

A GUIDE FOR READING MATTHEW THROUGHOUT LITURGICAL YEAR A

Advent

1st Sunday. Keep Awake (24:37-44)
2nd Sunday. Prepare the Way of the Lord (3:1-12)
3rd Sunday. Liberating Life (11:2-11)
4th Sunday. The Name of Jesus (1:18-24)

Christmas

Epiphany. The Adoration of the Wise Men (2:1-12)
Baptism of Our Lord. The Baptism of Jesus (3:13-17)

Lent

1st Sunday. The Temptations of Jesus (4:1-11)
2nd Sunday. The Transfiguration of Jesus (17:1-9)
Palm Sunday. On the Cross (27:39-50)

Easter

Easter Day. Raised by God (28:1-10)
Ascension. I Am With You (28:16-20)

Ordinary Time

Rethinking the crisis in ordained ministry

It is exceedingly possible that the Church might be reaching what has been called «the time of the laity», and yet it is also possible that we might pass through this time in a sterile way, not because of not having known of its arrival, or what it was about, but because of not having understood the specificity of the ordained ministry and that of other ministries within Christian communities.

José Ignacio González Faus was born in Valencia, Spain, in 1935. He has a PhD in Theology from Innsbruck and is currently Professor of Theology and Director of the Centro de Estudios (Cristianismo y Justicia) in Barcelona. He is dedicated to the promotion and defense of freedom and justice within the framework of an integral vision of the human person. His numerous published works include *La humanidad nueva: Ensayode cristología* (1974), *Acceso a Jesús* (1979), *El proyecto hermano: Visión creyente del hombre* (1989), *Ningún obispo impuesto* (1992) and *Where the Spirit Breathes: Prophetic Dissent in the Church* (1989).

BUY IT AT:

www.conviviumpress.com

Builders of Community: Rethinking Ecclesiastical Ministry
José Ignacio González Faus
ISBN: 978-1-934996-25-6
Series Ministeria

The Way Opened Up by Jesus:
a Commentary on the Gospel of Matthew

This book was printed on *thin opaque smooth white Bible paper*, using the *Minion* and *Type Embellishments One* font families.
This edition was printed in D'VINNI, S.A., in Bogotá, Colombia, during the last weeks of the sixth month of year two thousand twelve.

Ad publicam lucem datus mense junii Sacri Cordis Iesus